Taking Your iPod touch to the Max

to the Max

Michael Grothaus

Apress®

Taking Your iPod touch to the Max

ISBN-13 (pbk): 978-1-4302-3732-7

ISBN-13 (electronic): 978-1-4302-3733-4

Trademarked names, logos, and images may appear in this book. Rather than use a trademark symbol with every occurrence of a trademarked name, logo, or image we use the names, logos, and images only in an editorial fashion and to the benefit of the trademark owner, with no intention of infringement of the trademark.

The use in this publication of trade names, trademarks, service marks, and similar terms, even if they are not identified as such, is not to be taken as an expression of opinion as to whether or not they are subject to proprietary rights.

President and Publisher: Paul Manning
Lead Editors: Michelle Lowman
Technical Reviewer: Steve Sande
Editorial Board: Steve Anglin, Mark Beckner, Ewan Buckingham, Gary Cornell, Morgan Ertel, Jonathan Gennick, Jonathan Hassell, Robert Hutchinson, Michelle Lowman, James Markham, Matthew Moodie, Jeff Olson, Jeffrey Pepper, Douglas Pundick, Ben Renow-Clarke, Dominic Shakeshaft, Gwenan Spearing, Matt Wade, Tom Welsh
Coordinating Editor: Kelly Moritz
Copy Editors: Kim Wimpsett
Compositor: MacPS, LLC
Indexer: SPi Global
Artist: SPi Global
Cover Designer: Anna Ishchenko

Distributed to the book trade worldwide by Springer Science+Business Media, LLC., 233 Spring Street, 6th Floor, New York, NY 10013. Phone 1-800-SPRINGER, fax (201) 348-4505, e-mail orders-ny@springer-sbm.com, or visit www.springeronline.com.

For information on translations, please e-mail rights@apress.com, or visit www.apress.com.

Apress and friends of ED books may be purchased in bulk for academic, corporate, or promotional use. eBook versions and licenses are also available for most titles. For more information, reference our Special Bulk Sales–eBook Licensing web page at www.apress.com/bulk-sales.

To Rosa Marks, the coolest girl I know.
—Michael

Contents at a Glance

Contents

About the Author

 **Michael Grothaus** is an American novelist and journalist living in London. He was first introduced to Apple computers in film school and went on to use them for years to create award-winning films. However, after discovering many of Hollywood's dirty little secrets while working for 20th Century Fox, he left and spent five years with Apple as a consultant. He's since moved to London and earned his master's degree in creative writing. His first novel, *Epiphany Jones*, is a story about trafficking and America's addiction to celebrity. Currently, Michael is a staff writer at AOL's popular tech news site The Unofficial Apple Weblog (TUAW.com), where he writes about all things Mac. Additionally, Michael has written several other books for Apress, including *Taking Your iPad to the Max*, *Taking Your OS X Lion to the Max*, and *Taking Your iPhoto '11 to the Max*. When not writing, Michael spends his time traveling Europe, Northern Africa, and Asia. You can reach him at www.michaelgrothaus.com and www.twitter.com/michaelgrothaus.

About the Technical Reviewer

 **Steve Sande** has been a loyal fan of Apple technology since buying his first Mac in 1984. Originally trained as a civil engineer, Steve's career as an IT professional blossomed in the 1990s. A longtime blogger, Steve is the features editor at AOL's The Unofficial Apple Weblog (TUAW.com), the author of three books about Apple's iWeb application, and a collaborator on *Taking Your iPad 2 to the Max* and *Taking Your iPhone 4 to the Max*. You can join Steve every Wednesday for the popular TUAW TV Live show and follow his exploits at www.twitter.com/stevensande. He lives with Barb, his wife of 32 years, in Highlands Ranch, Colorado.

Acknowledgments

Thanks to the great team at Apress, including Kelly and Michelle. Also thanks to Apple for making the best iPod touch yet. And of course thanks to you, the reader, for buying this book. I hope you enjoy reading it as much as I enjoyed writing it.

—Michael

Preface

It's been just over ten years since Apple first introduced the iPod to the world. In that short time, technology—and the iPod itself—has progressed in leaps and bounds. The first iPod had a black-and-white screen and a mechanical scrollwheel interface. This latest iPod, the fifth generation of the iPod touch, has a Retna Display that allows you to view videos in high definition and has a Multi-Touch screen that lets you interact with your device like never before. The first iPod was solely for music. This iPod touch is for…well, everything, it seems.

Apple's latest iteration of its wonder gadget leapfrogs even last year's model. But it's not because of any hardware enhancements. Indeed, this year Apple only altered the iPod touch by adding a new color option: white. What makes this iPod touch (and any iPod touch from the last three years) so impressive is its operating system: iOS 5.

This is the third edition of *Taking Your iPod touch to the Max*. It's been completely revised and updated with entirely new content, images, and tips. We talk you through the iPod touch's new operating system, iOS 5, and all of its new features including the Notification Center, iMessages, Newsstand, Reminders, photo editing, and more. We also explore all the other features of the iPod touch including multitasking, HD video recording, creating folders, and of course FaceTime—the revolutionary way for you to communicate with your friends and family. You'll learn the guesture-based, Multi-Touch vocabulary that allows you to manipulate the iPod and its hundreds of thousands of apps. We'll show you how to connect to the Internet, browse the Web, touch your music and videos, and find and download apps from the App Store. You'll discover how to buy and navigate books using Apple's incredible iBooks app, view slideshows and photos, send e-mail, create notes and calendars, and even stream video from your iPod to your TV.

This book is written for anyone with an iPod touch or who is thinking of getting one (you won't be sorry!). It doesn't matter whether you're a Mac or PC user or, in fact, even if you've never used a computer at all. This book's thorough coverage and step-by-step discussions allow all iPod touch owners to learn about their device and come away with both the skills and the knowledge they need to use it to its fullest.

How you read the book is up to you. If you are totally new to the iPod touch (or computers in general), I suggest you read the book cover to cover, but feel free to jump around from chapter to chapter if that works better for you. For readers who have owned iPod touches before, you may benefit the most from checking out the chapters on the major new features first. However, there are so many new, subtle changes to almost every aspect of the iPod touch and its iOS 5 operating system that even experienced users will benefit from reading the entire book.

Have fun while you're learning everything that the iPod touch can do. It's the future in the palm of your hands, and it's a blast. Thanks for letting me show it to you.

Chapter 1

Bringing Home the iPod touch

Since 2001, the iPod has changed the way we listen to our music. It has allowed us to carry virtually our entire music collection around with us in a beautiful little package, and thanks to its unique scroll wheel, it has made that beautiful little package easy to navigate. Each year the iPod has evolved, getting physically smaller while its storage capacity and popularity have grown. Then came the iPod touch, and Apple reinvented what the MP3 player was capable of. The iPod touch, like its predecessor, quickly became the most popular MP3 player on the market, but it was so much more than *just* an MP3 player. It added Internet capabilities, a Multi-Touch display, and hundreds of thousands of apps for almost anything you could imagine. Now Apple's iPod touch offers amazing features such as front and rear cameras with FaceTime video calling, a high-resolution Retina display, and Apple's incredibly fast A4 processor.

You're about to read how to select and purchase your iPod touch and how to get started using it. This chapter covers the first steps you'll need to take and the decisions you'll need to make.

Buying Your iPod touch

If you don't already have an iPod touch, your first two decisions are which model to buy and where to buy it. The following sections cover some things to consider in the decision-making process.

Picking Your iPod touch

In the world of the touch, the choices aren't wide. As with other iPods, usually only a couple of models are available at a particular time. In the iPod touch's case, there are six different models. That sounds like a lot, but that's only because there are white and black models to choose from. When you take the color choice out of the equation, there are actually only three different iPod touch models to choose from and their only difference is the size of their storage capacity.

So, how do you choose the model that is right for you? It all comes down to the storage capacity. Do you want to pay more for a few more gigabytes of storage? It's not as if those extra gigabytes offer an inexhaustible resource. With enough videos and movies, you can easily run out of storage on a 160GB iPod classic, let alone the flash-memory-based iPod touch. Here are some questions you need to ask yourself:

How big is your music library? If it's large, the extra space on some iPod models helps store additional music and podcasts. Remember that you don't need to bring your entire media collection with you—and with the iTunes Music Store, you can buy music and movies on the go.

How many videos do you want to carry around? A single two-hour movie can occupy more than a gigabyte of storage. If you travel a lot, especially on airplanes, you may want to pay more to store additional movies and TV shows with those extra gigabytes. A few extra gigabytes can make a big difference in deciding whether you have the space to rent or buy a video on the go.

Do you plan to carry a lot of pictures? Although pictures are pretty small, if you carry a few thousand of them around, they do add up to some serious storage consumption. Did you laugh at the idea of carrying that many pictures around on your iPod? Apple's built-in iPhoto support makes it simple to put years of photo archives onto your touch with a single synchronization option.

Do you plan to take a lot of pictures or record a lot of video? The iPod touch can both take and record still photos and HD video. Recording a lot of HD video takes up space. The larger the storage capacity of the iPod touch, the more video you can record.

Are you going to download a lot of apps? There are hundreds of thousands apps available on Apple's App Store. Some apps are very small, taking up less than 1MB of disk space. Other apps—notably games—can take up hundreds of megabytes, even gigabytes, of space. What's more, apps can consume additional space by saving documents, downloading data, and so on. It's not just about the initial download.

The more apps you have on your iPod, the more space you take up.

Do you need to carry a lot of data? You might not think of your iPod as a data storage device, but there are ways to use it to bring data along with you on the road. If you think you might need to do this, those extra gigabytes could be put to good use. Of course, if you are going to use Apple's online iCloud storage, you might not need as much physical storage space on yoruu iPod as you think. We'll talk about iCloud in Chapter 2.

How long do you plan to use this iPod? If you're an early adopter who plans to trade up at the earliest possible opportunity whenever Apple offers a new unit, you may want to save your pennies now and trade space for the fiscal liquidity to support your little habit. But if you want to get the most use out of the iPod for the longest period of time, paying more up front means you won't outgrow the memory quite as fast.

Considering System Requirements

In order to effectively use your iPod touch, you must have a computer with an Internet connection, a Universal Serial Bus (USB) 2.0 port, and iTunes 10.5 or newer. While iPods no longer need to be connected to your computer to sync, they still need to be charged via a USB cable. Your computer's USB port will act as a charging station when the iPod is connected. You need iTunes for loading media onto your iPod and synchronizing it to your computer-based calendar and bookmarks. At the time this book was written, you'll also need to be running a Mac with 10.5.8 or newer or a PC with Windows Vista, Windows 7, Windows XP Home, or Professional (SP3) or newer.

> **NOTE:** If you haven't yet put iTunes on your computer, grab your free copy from `www.apple.com/itunes`. Versions are available for both OS X and Windows systems, and installing iTunes is quick and easy.

Deciding Where to Buy Your iPod

After deciding which model you want, you're probably ready to pull out your credit card and get that iPod (see Figure 1–1). Where should you go? To an Apple Store? To another retailer like Target? Or should you buy online? Here are some points to consider.

- *Availability:* Non-Apple retailers may or may not have the most up-to-date Apple units. Apple retail stores and Apple's online store always do. Third-party retailers often have a better repository of cheaper out-of-date units, though. And it's not that Target/Costco doesn't carry new iPods; it's that there's usually a few weeks or month delay in stocking new stuff.

- *Price:* As far as the online/offline question goes, price-wise it's mostly a wash. At a store or online, you'll pay the same amount for your iPod. The taxes are the same, and shipping is free. Non-Apple retailers rarely offer price breaks on Apple products, although they sometimes offer deals, such as included gift cards, that provide extra value for your money.

Figure 1–1. *The iPod touch in its acrylic packaging. You can purchase your touch online at* http://store.apple.com, *at a brick-and-mortar Apple Store, or at third-party retailers.*

- *Refurbs*: If you want to buy a refurbished iPod touch, select retailers sell refurbished models. Refurbished models usually debut a few months after product rollout. Refurbs also usually have a full one-year warranty. Not a bad deal!

- *Wait time*: Buying at a store means you don't need to wait—the iPod is in your hands immediately. Buying online means your product must be shipped, and you'll need to pay extra if you want expedited service.

- *Engraving*: If you want your iPod engraved, you can do so at the online Apple Store. Apple offers free laser engraving with your iPod purchase. This allows you to add a personal message or identifying information, such as an e-mail address or phone number, that will help your iPod make its way back to you if lost.

- *Hands-on testing*: Whether you make your purchase online or at a retail location, you can always walk into an Apple retail store and test an iPod in person before you buy one. Of course, once you're there, it's pretty easy to hand over a credit card and walk out of the store with a new iPod touch right there and then.

■ ***The personal touch:*** Unless you need an online-only feature (such as engraving), we recommend buying in person at a store. You can ask questions. You can make human connections. If something goes wrong with your purchase, a person is there to help you work through it. This is not to say that calling Apple's support line is insufficient, but being face-to-face with a real person makes solutions happen more readily.

> **NOTE:** A significant, although small, percentage of iPod purchases do not go smoothly. Some people end up with a screen flaw, such as dead screen pixels, which appear as small, black dots on your display. If such a problem is found soon after purchase, it may involve a trade for a new unit. The chances of resolving issues increase significantly when you talk to someone in person. The chances increase further when you deal with certain retailers with superior consumer-protection policies. Apple or (even better) Costco policies generally produce more satisfactory results than Target or Best Buy policies.

Understanding Return and Exchange Policies

When your touch is purchased from Apple, standard iPod return and exchange policies are in effect. These policies are distinct from the ones that apply to iPod touch's cousin, the iPhone. The touch policies are, instead, in line with other iPods:

■ You have 14 days from the time of purchase to return or exchange your unit.

■ A 10 percent open box fee will be assessed on any opened hardware or accessory.

■ You cannot return the iPod if it has been engraved.

In addition to these policies, Apple will usually swap out, without penalty, any unit that's clearly defective because of manufacturing issues.

Bringing Your iPod Home

Once you buy your iPod touch, it's time to take it home and get it set up. This involves several steps. The following sections walk you through this process.

Unpacking Your iPod touch

iPod packaging (see Figure 1–1) is a small work of art. The touch ships in an acrylic package that contains the player, a USB connector cable, those famous white earbuds, and a packet of documentation. Each of these items is important and helps you in the day-to-day use of your iPod.

Here's a rundown of what's in the box (Figure 1–2):

- **Cable:** The USB cable attaches your iPod to your computer.

- **Stereo headset (earbuds):** It wouldn't be an iPod without those iconic white earbuds. Seriously, you can do better both in terms of audio quality and protecting your ears, but people do love those white earbuds. They tell the world that you're listening to an iPod.

- **Documentation:** A quick start guide that tells you how to get your iPod up and running.

Figure 1–2. *The iPod touch package combines compactness with beauty. It contains your new iPod as well documentation, earbuds, and more.*

Reviewing the iPod touch Features

After unpacking your iPod, take a few minutes to discover more about your new purchase. Figure 1–3 identifies the basic features on your touch.

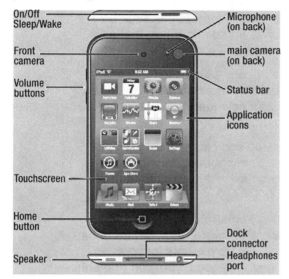

On/Off Sleep/Wake

Front camera

Volume buttons

Touchscreen

Home button

Speaker

Microphone (on back)

main camera (on back)

Status bar

Application icons

Dock connector

Headphones port

Figure 1–3. *Some important iPod touch features include the Sleep/Wake button, which allows you to conserve energy by sleeping the screen; the Home button, which takes you to your iPod's home screen from any application; and the dock connector at the bottom, which allows you to connect your iPod to your personal computer.*

The bottom of the iPod houses a jack (or, as Apple calls it, the "headphones port"), into which you can plug your earbuds; a dock connector port for connecting to your USB cable; and a speaker. The top of the iPod offers a Sleep/Wake button that is used to power on and off certain features. The iPod's front has a large touchscreen, a single Home button at the bottom, and a camera at the top center. Turn your iPod touch over to see the rear camera at the top corner. On the left side of the iPod are the volume control buttons.

Preparing for a Fresh Start

You've unpacked your iPod but haven't yet turned it on. Now is a good time to review the data on your computer. When you eventually connect your iPod to iTunes, it synchronizes itself to your media library and, depending on your computer, to your bookmarks, your calendars, and so forth. Before you go forward, here are some items you may want to either expand or clean up so your iPod starts its life with the freshest possible data:

- **Contacts:** iPod can sync with Outlook or Outlook Express on Windows, Address Book or Entourage on a Macintosh, and Yahoo! Address Book and Google Contacts on the Internet. To prepare for your first sync, review your existing contacts to make sure they're up-to-date with current phone numbers and e-mail addresses. If you use another program to manage contacts, consider migrating your contacts to one of these solutions. If you would rather not, that's OK, too.

- **Calendar:** Your iPod can also sync with computer-based calendars. The touch supports iCal and Entourage calendars on the Mac and Outlook calendars on Windows. Get your calendars into shape before your first sync, and you'll be ready to monitor your schedule.

- **Bookmarks:** Spend a little time reviewing and cleaning up your Internet Explorer or Safari bookmarks. Some housecleaning now makes it much easier for you to find your favorite web sites from your iPod touch.

- **Music:** iPod touch models offer relatively small storage space when compared to, for example, iPod classic's generous 160GB hard drive. To make the most of this limited space, set up playlists for your favorite songs and podcasts. Since, in all likelihood, you won't be able to synchronize your entire library to your new iPod, invest time now in weeding through your media to find those items you most want to have on hand.

- **Videos:** iPod touch can import any videos you have in iTunes that you've purchased from the iTunes Store. It also imports any videos you have on your computer in your iTunes library as long as you've converted those videos to an iPod-compatible format. Compatible formats are MP4, MOV, and M4V.

- **Books and PDFs:** Make sure any ePub books or PDFs you have on your computer have been added to your iTunes library. This allows you to sync them with Apple's iBooks app.

CAUTION: Make sure you've authorized your computer in iTunes (**Store ➤ Authorize Computer**) before synchronizing your music. If you don't, your music won't be copied to your iPod. Also note that you can't copy music from more than five accounts.

■ **_Software and operating system_:** Make sure you've updated to iTunes 10.5 or newer. And, if you're using a Mac, make sure you've updated your operating system to at least OS X 10.5.8. If you're using Windows, you need to make sure you are using Windows 7, Windows Vista, or Windows XP Home or Professional with Service Pack 3 or newer. You can download the latest version of iTunes from Apple at www.apple.com/itunes/download.

■ **_iTunes Account_:** If you plan to purchase music using the iPod's iTunes Music Store, Apple requires a current iTunes account. If you don't already have one, you can sign up for a U.S. account, as described next.

Creating a New Apple Account

Creating a new Apple account requires a U.S. address and credit card. Here are the steps you'll need to follow in order to create that account:

1. Launch the iTunes application, and wait for it to load.

2. Click the iTunes Store entry in the column on the left side of the window, and wait for the store screen to load. You must be connected to the Internet for this to happen, because all the storefront information is stored at Apple.

3. Click the Sign In button at the top-right corner of the screen. iTunes opens the sign-in dialog box (see Figure 1–4), which will allow you to either sign in with an existing account or create a new one.

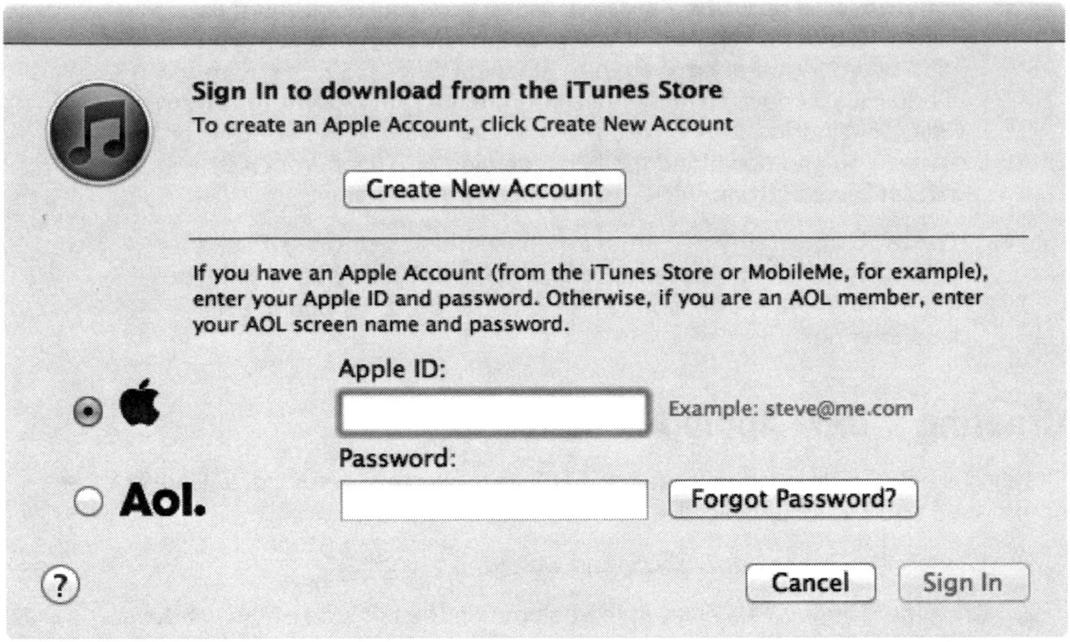

Figure 1–4. *The iTunes sign-in dialog box allows you to sign in to iTunes with your existing account or begin the process of creating a new account. This figure shows the Sign In screen on a Mac. It will be the same, though Windows-looking, on a PC.*

4.   Click Create New Account. The screen clears, and a message welcoming you to the iTunes Store is displayed. Click Continue.

5.   Review the terms of service, and then click Agree. A new dialog box appears, prompting you to create your account.

6.   Enter your e-mail address and a password (you must enter the password twice for verification). Also enter a question and answer that will help verify your identity and the month and day of your birth. Review the other options on the page, and adjust them as desired before clicking Continue. Again, the screen will clear, and you'll move on to the final account-creation step.

7.   Enter a valid U.S. credit card and the billing information for that credit card. These must match to finish creating your account. When you have entered the information, click Continue.

After following these steps, you will receive a confirmation e-mail at the address you specified while signing up. The e-mail welcomes you to the iTunes Store and provides you with the customer service web address (www.apple.com/support/itunes/store).

Configuring Your iPod touch

With iOS 5, Apple has cut the cord from your iPod touch to your computer. This new "PC Free" world of iOS devices is a new era in computing technology. Oh, you still have to plug the iPod into your computer or charger to recharge the battery all right, but now you no longer need to plug the iPod into your computer to begin using it. You can buy it in the store, open it up right there, and go through a simple setup procedure right on the iPod.

Follow the steps in this section to set up your iPod right out of the box:

1. Take your iPod touch out of its packaging.

2. Press the power button on top of the iPod touch to turn it on. You'll see the screen in Figure 1–5. If your iPod does not automatically power on and display this screen, press and hold the Sleep/Wake button. With the main screen facing toward you, you can find this button at the top left of the iPod. After a few seconds, the iPod should wake up and display the white Apple logo as it powers on. If the iPod does not respond and does not display either the white Apple logo or the Connect to iTunes screen, contact the store where you purchased the iPod.

Figure 1–5. *The iPod setup welcome screen*

3. Slide the configure slider to begin setting up your iPod.

4. On the next screen you'll get a choice to enable or disable location services. Location services allow the iPod touch and its apps to estimate your current location. After you have chosen to enable or disable location services, tap the "next" button.

5. The Wi-Fi Networks screen appears next. Select your wireless network and enter your Wi-Fi password. This will allow you iPod to join your Wi-Fi network and make use of its Internet connection for a number of things, like connecting to iCloud or using the Maps app.

6. On the next screen you can choose to set up your iPod touch as a new device or restore it from an iCloud or iTunes backup. If you've never owned an iPod before, select "Set Up as New iPod touch." If you are restoring from a previous iPod touch, select the iCloud or iTunes backup options.

Figure 1–6. *The iPod touch restore option screen.*

7. On the next screen, enter your Apple ID. You have an Apple ID if you've ever bought anything from the iTunes Store. If you don't have an Apple ID, tap the

Create a Free Apple ID button. Alternately, you can skip this step. When finished entering your Apple ID, tap the "next" button. You'll have to agree to Apple's Term and Conditions. Read them if you want, then tap Next again.

8. Once you've entered your Apple ID you are taken to the Set Up iCloud screen. We'll talk all about iCloud in Chapter 2. For now just choose if you want to use iCloud or not, then tap Next.

9. If you've chosen to use iCloud, the backup screen appears next. Select whether you want to back up your iPod touch to iCloud or to your computer, then tap Next.

10. As part of iCloud, Apple lets users track their iOS devices and Macs using a feature called Find My iPod touch. Select whether you want to allow you iPod touch to be found using your iCloud account. This free service is part of your iCloud account and allows you to track down your iPod touch should it become lost or stolen. We'll talk more about Find My iPod touch in Chapter 11. Click Next after you've made your selection.

11. On the next screen, choose whether you want to send anonymous diagnostics to Apple to help them improve the iOS and iPod experience. Tap the Next button after making your selection.

12. After you've successfully navigated all those setup screens, you'll see the one pictured in Figure 1–7. Congratulations! You've set up your iPod touch. Simply tap the "Start using iPod touch" button to begin playing with your new favorite toy!

Once you've set up your iPod touch, you can begin using it right away if you have most of your media stored in the cloud through iCloud. However, if you are still storing most of your media on your computer, you'll need to pair your iPod touch with your computer in order to get yoru music, movies, and tv shows on it.

Figure 1–7. *Completing the iPod touch setup process*

Pairing Your iPod touch to Your Computer

As we mentioned earlier, a big feature of iOS 5 is that it's "PC Free." That means it has the ability for your iPod touch to sync wirelessly with your computer. But before you can sync wirelessly, you must pair your iPod to your computer. This must be done through the USB cable that came with your iPod touch. You need to do this only once.

To pair your iPod touch to your computer, follow these steps:

1. Locate the two ends of the USB cable that was included with your iPod touch. One is thin and marked with a standard three-pronged USB symbol. The other is wide and marked with a rectangle with a line in it.

2. Orient your iPod. On the back of your iPod, the Apple logo and the word *iPod* show you which way is up (Figure 1–8). The dock connector is at the bottom of your iPod touch.

Figure 1–8. *Orient your iPod by locating the Apple symbol and the word* iPod *on its back. In this figure you can see the dock connector. It's the long, thin, rectangular opening on the bottom.*

3. Connect the wide end of the USB cable to the bottom of your iPod touch. Be gentle but firm, without twisting or forcing the connection. Connect the thin end to a spare USB 2.0 port on your computer (for a direct-connected sync) or a USB power adapter (for a Wi-Fi sync).

   iTunes launches, and your iPod chimes softly.

4. Since this is the first time you are pairing your iPod touch with your computer, the iPod Setup Assistant appears in iTunes (Figure 1–9). The iPod setup assistant asks you whether you want to enable your iPod touch as a new device or whether you want to restore it and its contents from the backup of an older iPod touch. Be aware that these steps may vary slightly as Apple updates and changes iTunes.

Set Up Your iPod

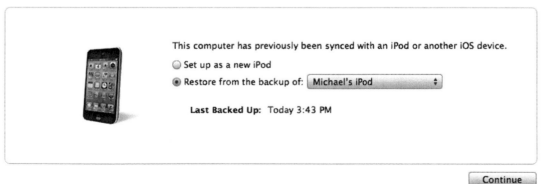

Figure 1–9. *The iPod Setup Assistant lets you name your iPod and decide which items to automatically synchronize to it.*

5. Choose between "Set up as new iPod" or "Restore from the backup of." You won't see the "Restore from the backup of" option if you've never owned an iPod touch before. If you have, this option allows you to move all your personal settings of the old iPod over to the new one. If you are setting up this iPod for the first time and have never owned a previous one, choose "Set up as new iPod," and click the *Continue* button.

6. The next screen allows you to name your iPod and choose what items to automatically sync to it. If you want to name your iPod something other than "your name's iPod," enter a new name into the "The name of my iPod is" field. Do not press Enter or Return, and do not click the Done button.

7. We recommend you uncheck both boxes: "Automatically sync songs to my iPod" and "Automatically sync photos to my iPod." It's far easier to manage these choices manually.

8. Click the Done button. iTunes closes the Setup Assistant.

Once you've paired your new iPod touch, you're ready to perform your first synchronization. In the iTunes source list, which is the light blue column on the left side of the iTunes screen, locate the Devices section, and click the name of your iPod. This opens its Preferences window (see Figure 1–10). The tabs along the top of the Preferences window allow you to set each of the options associated with your iPod. We go into what each of these tabs does in detail in Chapter 2.

> **TIP:** Click your iPod's name a second time to open a text edit field that allows you to edit the name. You can name your iPod more creatively than the default (your name and "iPod").

Figure 1–10. *iTunes lets you manage the content loaded onto and synchronized with your iPod. Each tab at the top of the screen offers a variety of controls, allowing you to choose the information that is loaded onto your touch at each sync.*

Syncing the iPod touch to Your Computer

After you have initially paired your iPod touch to your computer, you can choose to sync your iPod touch wirelessly or directly (by connecting it to your computer) for all future syncs. However, if you want to sync wirelessly, you first have to enable wireless syncing.

Do this by checking the box that says "Sync with this iPod over Wi-Fi connection" (Figure 1–11) on your iPod touch's Summary page in iTunes. After you've done this, the steps to sync your iPod wirelessly or through a USB cable are pretty much the same.

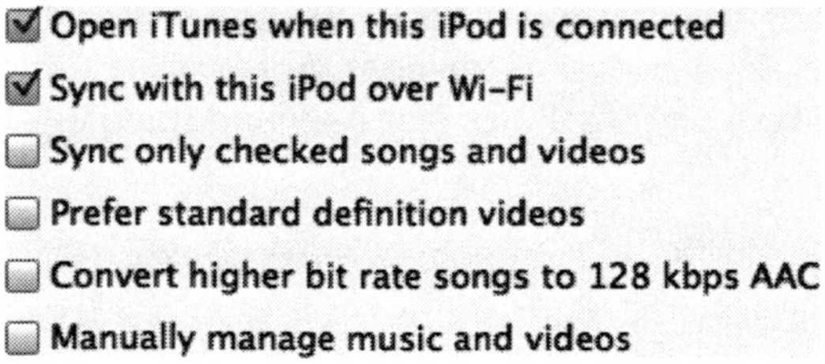

☑ Open iTunes when this iPod is connected

☑ Sync with this iPod over Wi-Fi

☐ Sync only checked songs and videos

☐ Prefer standard definition videos

☐ Convert higher bit rate songs to 128 kbps AAC

☐ Manually manage music and videos

Figure 1–11. *Check "Sync over Wi-Fi connection" to enable Wi-Fi syncing.*

To sync via a USB cable, follow these steps:

1. Plug your iPod touch in to your computer via the USB-dock connector cable. Your iPod begins syncing.

2. Unplug the iPod when the sync is finished.

To sync wirelessly, follow these steps:

1. Both your iPod touch and computer must be turned on and connected to the same Wi-Fi network.

2. When your iPod appears under the Device header in the iTunes source list, click the Sync button in iTunes to begin your sync.

3. Don't leave the Wi-Fi network until the sync notification in your iPod touch's status bar disappears (Figure 1–12). When it does, you know your sync is complete.

Figure 1–12. *The rotating arrows in the status bar tell you your iPod touch is syncing to your iTunes library.*

No matter which way you choose to sync, you can continue to use your iPod while it syncs to your library. We discuss all your syncing options in detail in the next chapter.

Insuring and Repairing Your iPod

Your iPod is covered under Apple's Limited Warranty for 90 days. This includes one complimentary support incident within the first 90 days of product ownership.

You can add iPod touch AppleCare for $59. This extends your hardware repair coverage to two years in total from the date of purchase. If you're interested, you can purchase AppleCare online at the Apple Store (http://store.apple.com).

Once the warranty expires, iPod touch repair costs vary depending on the unit's defect. Taxes and $29.95 for shipping and handling are also added to the cost. Apple will replace your iPod touch battery for $79 (plus taxes and $6.95 for shipping and handling) if your unit is out of warranty.

You can find a complete list of ways to contact Apple Support at www.apple.com/support/contact/.

> **CAUTION:** If you plan to hack your iPod touch, be aware that unauthorized modifications will void your warranty. Apple also excludes coverage for damages from accidents (such as dropping your iPod onto a concrete floor), unauthorized service (such as trying to replace your own battery), and misuse (don't use your iPod as a hammer).

Regarding insuring your iPod, check with your renter's or home insurance carrier to see how much you'll need to pay for an iPod touch rider (a rider is placed on top of an existing policy, adding coverage for a specific item not covered under the standard plan). Allstate, GEICO, and State Farm quote about $5 to $20 per year on top of an existing policy.

If you can, be sure to back up your iPod by synchronizing it to iTunes *before* bringing it in for service. Apple restores your touch to factory condition, which means you'll lose any data stored on it during the repair and service process.

> **NOTE:** Unlike with an iPhone, Apple does not offer loaner iPods when you bring in your iPod for service.

Accessorizing Your iPod

If you like accessorizing things, then you'll be in heaven with all the accessories that are available for the iPod touch! You can choose from a virtually unlimited number of cases, headphones, screen protectors, car-integration kits, home speaker systems, and more. If we talked about every accessory available, this book would be the size of five phone books!

Although there are almost limitless accessories, generally there are a few things everyone who buys an iPod touch should think about owning:

- *Case:* It's always good to have a case to protect your investment. Griffin makes a number of beautiful cases, as does Belkin. The hard part about buying a case is not finding one, it's choosing one!

- *Armband:* If you are a cyclist or a runner, an armband is a must for your iPod touch. Again, you've got a wide variety to choose from.

- *USB power adapter:* Your iPod charges any time it's connected to a computer's USB 2.0 port. However, you may go on a trip and not have your computer with you. In this case, it's wise to purchase a USB power adapter. These adapters plug into any wall outlet and charge your iPod on the spot.

- *Car charger:* Like to go on long drives? Think about investing in a car charger for the iPod touch. Like the USB power adapter, a car charger lets you power up your iPod wherever the road takes you.

■ *iPod speaker system:* If you throw a lot of parties or just like listening to music around the house, an iPod speaker system is a must. An iPod speaker system is simply a set of speakers with a built-in iPod dock. Simply drop your iPod into the speaker's dock and listen to the glorious music that comes out. Like all iPod accessories, you can choose from a wide variety of iPod speaker systems.

For all these accessories, a good place to start shopping is `http://store.apple.com`. You can also walk into any Best Buy or Walmart to get a sense of what's out there for your iPod touch!

Summary

In this chapter, you've seen how to select and purchase your iPod touch. You've discovered what's involved in setting up an iTunes account, activating your iPod, and pairing your iPod touch to your computer. To wind things up, here is a quick overview of some key points from this chapter:

■ There are several models of the iPod touch, but whichever unit you choose, you'll probably want to buy it in person at a store, unless you need an online-only feature such as engraving.

■ To use your iPod, you no longer need to own a computer. You can buy your iPod and configure it right out of the box. However, it's always helpful to sync your iPod with iTunes on a computer so it is loaded with all of the media you already own.

■ iPods are not cheap. Protect your investment by insuring your touch, and consider adding AppleCare for two years of coverage (from the date of purchase) against hardware repairs.

■ Your iPod touch purchase entitles you to one complimentary support incident within the first 90 days of product ownership.

■ There are almost as many accessories for the iPod touch as there are songs in the iTunes Store. You may have to do a lot of browsing before you know which accessories are right for you.

Chapter **2**

Putting Your Data and Media on the iPod touch

In Chapter 1, I briefly discussed syncing your iPod touch with your music, movies, photos, and other data via iTunes. In this chapter, I explore the many options you have in syncing data with your iPod touch.

The first time you sync your iPod touch with your iTunes library, you need to do it via the USB docking cable. After that, you can sync it with your iTunes library via the USB cable that came with it or do so wirelessly as long as the iPod touch is on the same wireless network as your computer. Once connected via either of these ways, your iPod appears in the list on the left side of the iTunes window (you can see it later in Figure 2–3). This light blue column, called the *source list*, is divided into several sections for your media library, the iTunes Store, your devices, and your playlists.

If you do not see your iPod in this list, make sure you've physically connected your iPod through the USB cable and that the cable is firmly inserted into both the computer and the iPod if you are doing a hardline connection, or make sure that your iPod touch and computer are both connected to the same wireless network. Next, make sure your iPod is powered on. Your iPod will be listed when it's active or asleep, but it won't show up when it's powered down.

The iPod touch iTunes Device Window

When the iPod touch is plugged into your computer, it automatically appears in your iTunes source list under Devices. Click the name of your iPod touch in the source list to open its preferences in the main iTunes window (see Figure 2–1). You'll see a series of tabs along the top of the window that allow you to set options associated with your iPod touch. The tabs you'll see (from left to right) are Summary, Apps, Ringtones, Music, Movies, TV Shows, Podcasts, Books, Photos, and Info.

Figure 2–1. *iTunes allows you to manage the content loaded onto and synchronized with your iPod touch. Each tab at the top of the window offers a variety of controls, allowing you to choose what information is loaded onto your iPod touch at each sync.*

Along the bottom of the iPod touch preferences window you'll see a long, colorful Capacity bar (see Figure 2–2). This bar appears regardless of what tab you have selected. The bar displays the total storage capacity of the iPod touch and breaks down the amount of data you have on the iPod touch in color-coded squares along the Capacity bar. Blue is for Audio, purple is for Video, yellow is for Other, green is for Apps, pink is for Books, orange is for Photos, and gray is for the remaining free space you have on your iPod touch.

Figure 2–2. *The Capacity bar is a visual representation of the different types of files occupying space on your iPod touch.*

NOTE: The Capacity bar breakdown is pretty self-explanatory. Still, some people are thrown by yellow—the color that represents "Other." What is "Other," exactly? Other includes database files (which keep track of your music, video, and podcast libraries), which can be 100MB to 200MB in size; album artwork (which can be 500KB per track); and preference files for the applications you have on your iPod touch. Preference files let the apps remember in-app settings you've configured every time you launch them.

A Word on Syncing Your Data

The current iPod touch devices hold a lot of data. But many of us have music or movie libraries that are far larger than even the storage in the most capacious iPod touch. Apple devised sync preferences to help organize and select your most important data and move it to the iPod touch.

If you have a 32GB iPod touch and a 40GB music library, not only will you *not* be able to fit all your music onto the device, but if you settled for 32GB of your music library, that would mean you'd have no room for photos, movies, books, or apps. The following tabs that I discuss can help in selecting what to sync to your iPod touch.

Although you most likely won't be able to fit all of your music, photos, and movies onto the iPod touch, you don't have to do so. You can keep changing what you put on the iPod touch. For example, once you've watched a movie on your iPod touch, you can remove it and replace it with another one. Also, some files are larger than others. Although movies are typically the largest, don't worry about syncing all of your contacts, calendars, and book collections onto your iPod touch. These are all text-based files, and text takes up very little storage.

Where Do You I Get My Media From?

The iPod touch is a great device for consuming media. But where do you get that media? The easiest and most direct way to get movies, music, TV shows, and books onto your iPod touch is through the iTunes Store (see Figure 2–3). In the iTunes Store, you can buy music (a song or an entire album), rent or purchase movies, download your favorite TV shows by the episode or subscribe to a Season Pass, and download free podcasts and iTunes U content.

Figure 2–3. *The iTunes Store is the world's largest music store. You can also download movies, TV shows, apps, podcasts, and books from it.*

You can also import music and movies from your own collections. Importing music from CDs is straightforward using iTunes, as is importing video. One way to get movies onto your iPod touch is to rip them from your DVD collection.

> **NOTE:** *Ripping* a DVD means copying content from the disc into a format that's playable on other devices, including iPod touch devices. To load video from your DVDs onto your iPod touch, download a copy of HandBrake from `http://handbrake.m0k.org` (for both Windows and Mac), and convert your DVD content to an iPod touch–friendly format. HandBrake is free and easy to use. Insert your DVD into your computer, run the application, and follow the directions in the program. After your movie has finished ripping, you must then add it to iTunes by dragging and dropping the movie file onto your Movies library in the source list.

The only way to get applications onto your iPod touch is by using the iTunes App Store. You can easily browse for apps from the desktop version of iTunes or in the dedicated App Store app on the iPod touch (we'll talk about that app in a later chapter).

There are several ways to get e-books for the iPod touch. Perhaps the easiest is to buy them through Apple's iBookstore (see Chapter 8 for details), which is part of the free iBooks app Apple offers for download. Another way is to download from the collection of more than 30,000 free e-books at Project Gutenberg (`www.gutenberg.org`) and drag the books from your downloads folder into iTunes. There are also many other e-book stores that you can buy from. For a good list of websites that sell e-books, go to www.epubbooks.com/buy-epub-books.

> **NOTE**: E-books come in many formats. The format compatible with the iPod touch's iBooks app is ePub. Make sure when buying an e-book outside the iBookstore that it is in ePub or PDF format, or else you'll need to find another app that reads the format your e-book is in. Books from Amazon's Kindle Store are an example of this. Kindle books can be read on the iPod touch, but not in the iBooks app. You need to download Amazon's Kindle app for the iPod touch to read e-books purchased from Amazon or view them in Amazon's browser-based Cloud Reader (www. read.amazon.com).

Remember to Apply Your Changes

After making any of the choices we discuss in the following sections, note that they do not become finalized until you click the gray Apply button to the right of the Capacity bar (see Figure 2–4). Don't worry if you forget to click it, because iTunes automatically reminds you before you navigate away from the iPod touch preferences window. Don't panic if you make a change in the preferences by mistake; you can always click the Revert button that sits above the Apply button.

Figure 2–4. *The Revert and Apply buttons (boxed) allow you to accept or negate any of the changes you have made in iTunes' iPod touch preferences window.*

The Tabs

The tabs (see Figure 2–5) running along the top of the iPod touch preferences window are how you navigate all your iPod touch settings. There are 10 tabs in total: Summary, Apps, Ringtones, Music, Movies, TV Shows, Podcasts, Books, Photos, and Info. To begin configuring the settings under any tab, just click the tab to select it.

Figure 2–5. *The tabs. Learn 'em, love 'em.*

The Summary Tab

The Summary tab (see Figure 2–6) is the first tab visible in the iPod touch preferences window. It displays an overview of your iPod touch including its name, capacity, currently installed firmware version, and serial number. From this page, it's also possible to check for firmware updates, restore your iPod touch to a pristine factory-installed condition, and set options to help you manage the way your data is synced. The page is broken up into three boxes: iPod, Version, and Options.

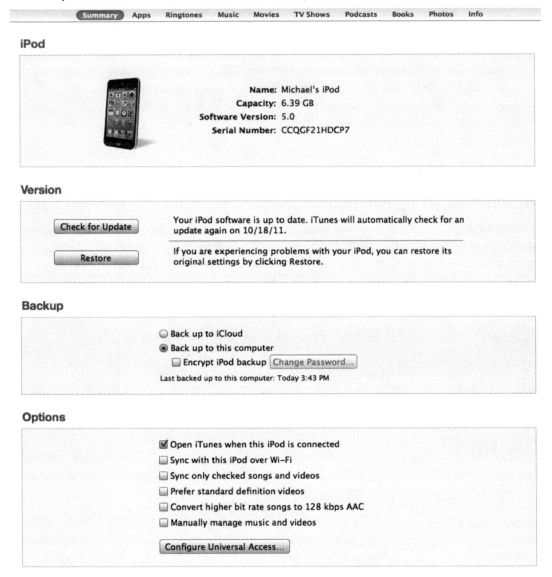

Figure 2–6. *The Summary tab provides an overview of your iPod touch's make and model.*

iPod

In this box, an image of your iPod touch is displayed along with its name, capacity, software version, and serial number.

The only things that could ever change in this box are your iPod touch's software version number and your iPod touch's name. When you perform a software update on the iPod touch, the new version number appears in this box. It's an easy way to tell which version of iOS (the operating system used on Apple's iPod touch devices, iPhones, and iPads) you are using. If you change the name of your iPod touch by double-clicking its name in the iTunes source list (see Figure 2–7), the name change is updated here. Your iPod touch's capacity and serial number will never change.

Figure 2–7. *Double-click your iPod touch's name in the iTunes source list. You can rename it to anything you want. The name change will be reflected on the Summary tab.*

NOTE: You bought a 32GB iPod touch, but you notice that the capacity states your iPod touch has only 29.28GB of storage. What gives? Whenever you buy an electronics device that offers storage capacity, the advertised amount of storage is always more than the actual storage available to you. Why? Several reasons. One is because the device's operating system must be stored on the same disk as your files. Without the OS, your device could not function. In this case, the iPod touch's OS takes up almost 2GB of space. Another, more technical reason is because storage size can be measured in binary or decimal measurements. Binary says 1KB is equal to 1,024 bytes, while decimal says 1KB is equal to 1,000 bytes. When advertising storage space, companies choose to use the decimal measurement, which ends up showing more space than is actually available to you.

Version

The Version box allows you to manually check for iOS software updates by clicking the Check for Update button. Next to the button is text notifying you if your iPod touch software is up-to-date or if there is an update available. Sometimes iTunes notifies you that there is a software update available before you've even clicked the Check for Update button. It knows this because iTunes automatically checks for iOS updates once a week. You'll also see text to your right that tells you when the next time iTunes is going to automatically check for an update. If there is an iOS software update available, always install it. Sometimes updates provide new features; other times they provide simple bug fixes. Apple rigorously tests these updates before releasing them to the public, so it's usually safe to assume the updates will improve your device (whether you notice it or not).

> **NOTE:** Just what is iOS? iOS is the name Apple gave to the operating system that runs on all of its touchscreen mobile devices (iPhones, iPod touch devices, and iPads). The latest version of iOS is iOS 5. Versions before iOS 4 were referred to as "iPhone OS" 1, 2, or 3 since the iPod touch's operating system was based on it. Thankfully, Apple decided to take "iPhone" out of the OS name; it just makes referring to the operating system easier. This book explores everything you can do with your iPod touch running iOS 5.

Below the Check for Update button is the Restore button. Clicking the restore button allows you to restore your iPod touch to a factory-new condition. You will rarely, if ever, use this feature. The only time to restore your iPod touch is if you are having technical difficulties with it or if you decide to sell the iPod touch or give it away and want to make sure all your personal data is removed from the device. Before the restore commences, you'll be shown a dialog box asking you to confirm the restore (see Figure 2–8).

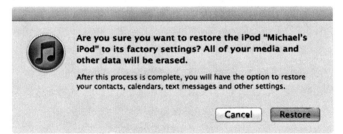

Figure 2–8. *After a restore, you have the option of putting all your data back onto the iPod touch.*

Backup

Every time your iPod touch syncs to iTunes, a backup of all the files and settings on your device is created. This backup is handy if you ever need to restore your iPod touch. Once the restore is complete and you've synced your iPod touch to iTunes again, you have the option of restoring the iPod touch from this backup, which, once completed, enables you to retain all your old settings and files.

The Backup section of the Summery tab is where you decide where you want that backup to reside. If you want to store the backup on iCloud so you can access it from any iOS device wirelessly (such as when you want to restore), select *Back Up to iCloud*.

Alternately, you can choose to save your backups to your computer. If you want to do that, select *Backup to this comptuer*. You can also choose to encrypte backups to the computer or not. With the "Encrypt iPod backup" option selected, your backups, and thus all your data, are encrypted and protected by a password. To back up from an encrypted data file, you must know the password to the file. Next to this selection is a Change Password button, which allows you to change the password to your encrypted data at any time.

> **NOTE:** Do not forget your password! If you encrypt your backups and you forget your password, your backed-up data cannot be restored, and you will have to resync all your data from scratch. You'll also have to reconfigure all the settings on your iPod touch to the way you had them, including rearranging the iPod touch's app icons to their desired locations. If you have lots of custom settings on your iPod touch, this can take a long time. Remember your passwords!

All iPod backups stored on iCloud are automatically encrypted and the only thing you need to access them is your iCloud password. Also note that with iOS 5, your iPod will atuomatically backup whenever it's plugged in to a power connection and is on your Wi-Fi network.

Options

You have several preferences in the Options box. To enable or disable any of the features, simply check or uncheck the box next to it.

- **Open iTunes when this iPod is connected:** This option is selected by default. It tells your computer to open iTunes when it detects that your iPod touch is connected via USB. If this option is not selected, iTunes doesn't open when you connect your iPod touch, and no data is synced to your device until you manually open iTunes and click the Sync button next to the Capacity bar.

> **NOTE:** Even though iTunes does not launch or sync your data when this box is not selected, the iPod touch is still charged.

- ◼ *Sync with this iPod over Wi-Fi :* This box must be checked if you want to sync the iPod touch with your iTunes library over a Wi-Fi connection. This is why you need to sync your iPod touch via a wired connection (the USB-dock connector cable) the first time, so you can select this Sync over Wi-Fi connection box. Without this box being checked, your iTunes library has no way of knowing that it should be syncing with your iPod over Wi-Fi.

- ◼ *Sync only checked songs and videos:* When this option is selected, iTunes only syncs the songs in your library and playlists that have a check mark next to them in the iTunes library (see Figure 2–9).

- ◼ Let's say you have a Greatest Hits playlist set to sync with the iPod touch. In the playlist you have two copies of Michael Jackson's "Man in the Mirror" from two separate albums. You want to have only one copy of the song on the iPod touch, but you don't want to remove the extra copy from the playlist. If you deselect one version of "Man in the Mirror" in the playlist and have "Sync only selected songs and videos" selected, the playlist syncs to your iPod touch minus the extra "Man in the Mirror," but the song remains in your playlist in your iTunes library.

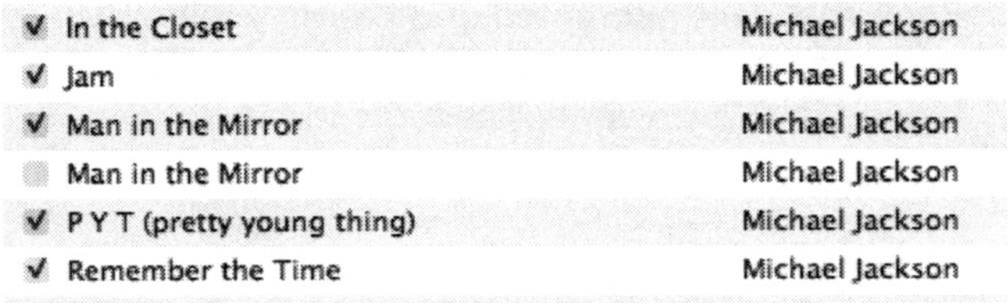

☑ In the Closet	Michael Jackson
☑ Jam	Michael Jackson
☑ Man in the Mirror	Michael Jackson
☐ Man in the Mirror	Michael Jackson
☑ P Y T (pretty young thing)	Michael Jackson
☑ Remember the Time	Michael Jackson

Figure 2–9. *Selected songs and an unselected song in iTunes*

- ◼ *Prefer standard definition video:* When this box is checked, only the standard definition version of any video in your iTunes library that has both standard- and high-definition copies is synced. It's a good idea to keep this checked if you don't have a lot of space on your iPod touch. A standard-definition version of a movie can save you up to four times the space of a high-definition movie.

- ◼ *Convert higher bit rate songs to 128 kbps AAC:* Digital music comes in many formats and sizes, with the most popular being MP3 and AAC. Depending on how you obtained your music, whether buying it from the iTunes store or ripping your collection from old CDs, your songs most likely have different encoding settings. A song encoded at 256Kbps takes up twice the space as a song encoded at 128Kbps. With the "Convert higher bit rate songs to 128 kbps AAC" option selected, any music synced to your iPod touch is converted on the fly to the 128Kbps AAC format. The advantage of doing this is to save space on your iPod touch by reducing higher bit rate songs to a perfectly acceptable 128Kbps.

> **NOTE:** Unless you are an extreme audiophile with a gifted ear, you probably won't notice a difference between 128Kbps AAC file and 256Kbps versions of a digital music file.

- ▥ ***Manually manage music and videos:*** With this option selected, music and videos are never automatically synced with your iPod touch. The only way to add music and videos on the iPod touch under this option is by dragging the songs or videos from the iTunes library onto the iPod touch in the iTunes source list. Likewise, with this option selected, the only way to remove music or videos from your iPod touch is by clicking the drop-down triangle next to the iPod touch in iTunes' source list, navigating to your playlists selecting the song or video, and then pressing the Delete key on your computer's keyboard.

> **NOTE:** Manually adding or removing music or video from your iPod touch does not affect the files on your computer. Whenever a file is added to or deleted from the iPod touch, it is just a copy of the file in your iTunes library. The original file always resides in your iTunes library until you delete it from there.

- ▥ *Configure Universal Access:* The last thing on the Summary page is a Configure Universal Access button. Clicking this button opens a Universal Access box (see Figure 2–10) for setting visual and audio device assistance options for people who are hard of sight or hearing.

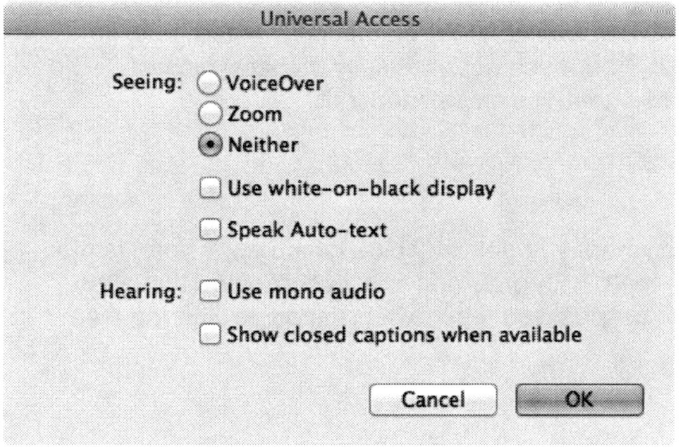

Figure 2–10. *The Universal Access settings*

- ▥ *Seeing:* You have the option of selecting one of three radio buttons: Voice Over, Zoom, or Neither.

- *VoiceOver* makes your iPod touch speak the name of a button or its function when the user touches it. It also speaks text. We explore the VoiceOver features in Chapter 15 of this book.

- *Zoom* allows the user to zoom into parts of the screen that normally don't support a magnifying or zoom function. When this option is selected, the user can double-tap any part of the iPod touch's screen with three fingers to automatically zoom in 200 percent. When zoomed in, you must drag or flick the screen with three fingers. Also, when you go to a new screen, Zoom always returns to the top middle of the screen.

- *Use white-on-black display*: Selecting this option inverts the colors of the iPod touch's screen so text appears white on a black background. The iPod touch's entire screen will look like a photograph negative.

- *Speak Auto-text*: With this option selected, any autocorrection text (like the spell check pop-ups that appear when you are typing) is spoken aloud.

- *Hearing*: There are two accessibility features for the hearing impaired.

- *Use mono audio*: When this is selected, the stereo sounds of the left and right speakers are combined into a mono (single) signal. This option lets users who have a hearing impairment in one ear hear the entire sound signal with the other ear.

- *Show closed captions when available*: When this is selected, any video you have on your iPod touch automatically displays closed captions if that video has captions embedded in it.

The Apps Tab

This is my favorite tab. It's the place where you get to decide which apps you want to put on your iPod touch and arrange them with drag-and-drop simplicity. This tab is composed of two main sections: Sync Apps (see Figure 2–11) and File Sharing (see Figure 2–13). Let's get started.

Figure 2–11. *This is where you choose what apps to put on your iPod touch and how to arrange them.*

Sync Apps

Under the Sync Apps heading is a scrollable list of all the applications you have in your apps library in iTunes. You can sort the list by name, kind, category, size, or date downloaded. There's also a search field in the upper-right corner of iTunes if you're one of those people who has downloaded thousands of apps and can't scroll through all of them quickly.

In the apps list there is a check box to the left of the app's icon. To the right of the icon is the app's name, and below that are the app's category listing and the file size of the individual application. Any app that has a selected check box means the application is set to sync with the iPod touch. Below the apps list is a a check box labeled "Automatically sync new apps." When this is selected, any new apps you've downloaded through iTunes are automatically synced with your iPod touch on the next connection.

Next to the apps list is a a visual representation of the screen of your iPod touch. To the right of that are one or more smaller black screens with icons representing apps that are already on, or set to be synced with, your iPod touch. You'll also see a completely gray screen below the last black one.

The easiest way to get apps on your iPod touch is to find them in the apps list and simply drag them onto the virtual screen. As soon as you do, the app's check box is automatically selected in the app list.

You can drag around the apps on the virtual iPod touch screen until you've arranged them in the order you like. It's also possible to grab the smaller black screens and move them up or down in the list, rearranging entire pages of apps on your iPod touch. The black screen at the top of the list is the home page on your iPod touch, and each one below that is a subsequent swipe away. The gray screen at the bottom is an extra screen should you want to create a new screen with apps.

To remove an app, hover your computer cursor over the app, and a little *X* appears in the upper-left corner. Click the *X*, and the app disappears from the screen. On the next sync, the app is removed from your iPod touch. Don't worry; you can always get an app back by dragging it to the virtual iPod touch's screen or by clicking the app in the list to the left.

> **NOTE:** Apps that Apple ships on the iPod touch cannot be removed from the device—they can only be repositioned.

Creating Folders

There's a way to create folders of apps on your iPod home screen as well. Folders help you avoid constantly swiping screens to the left or right and make it easy to group similar apps together. To create a folder in the Apps tab, drag one app onto another on the virtual iPod screen and release it. A folder is created with the two apps in it, and you can name the folder whatever you want. Drag more apps to the folder and release them to add them . In the folder in Figure 2–12, I've created a folder called Travel, and it contains some of my favorite travel apps.

To remove apps from the folder, drag them out or click the *X* that appears when you move your pointer over the app's icon. Folders contain up to 12 applications, and there can be up to 20 folders on a page. Similarly, each screen holds 20 apps (or folders of apps) including the ones docked at the bottom of the screen. The dock holds anywhere between zero and four apps. Any apps placed in the dock appear at the bottom of the iPod touch no matter what app screen you've swiped to. Since the docked apps always appear at the bottom of any app screen, it's best to put the ones you use most frequently down there for quick access.

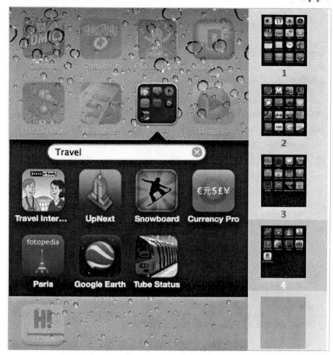

Michael's iPod   **41 apps**

Select apps to be installed on your iPod or drag to a specific home screen.
Drag to rearrange app icons or home screens.

Figure 2–12. *Creating a folder full of apps*

File Sharing

Starting with iOS 4, Apple introduced a way to easily share files between the iPod touch and your computer. Beneath the File Sharing heading is an Apps box and a Documents box (see Figure 2–13). Any apps that are currently on your iPod touch that support drag-and-drop file sharing appear in the Apps list here. To share a file with an application, select the application in the Apps list, find the file on your computer you want to share, and drag it into the Documents list. You can also click the Add button at the bottom of the Documents list to browse for the file on your computer.

To transfer a file from your iPod touch back to your computer, select the file in the Documents list, click the "Save to" button at the bottom, and choose where you want to save the file on your computer. Alternatively, drag the file from the Documents list to your desktop.

To delete a file from an app that contains it, select the file in the document list, and press the Delete key on your computer. iTunes prompts for confirmation when deleting or replacing files. Click the Delete button in the confirmation dialog to complete the deletion. At this time, you cannot delete folders or read the contents of files stored in folders in the documents list.

As long as a file is shared inside an app, it is always backed up when you sync your iPod touch to your computer.

File Sharing

The apps listed below can transfer documents between your iPod and this computer.

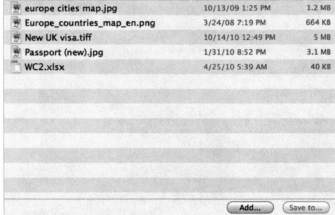

Figure 2–13. *Apps that support drag-and-drop file sharing and their enclosed documents*

> **NOTE:** Just because you can drag a file to an app's Documents box doesn't mean that the app can open it. Apps are limited to working with files that the iPod touch supports. For example, the iPod touch does not support Microsoft's WMV video files. If you drag a WMV movie to an app, the app contains it but is still not able to play it. There is a workaround to this, however. If you download an app called Yxplayer (http://itunes.apple.com/us/app/yxplayer/ id373751560?mt=8), those WMV files are playable!

The Ringtones Tab

You might see this tab and wonder why it's there (Figure 2–14). After all, you have an iPod touch and not an iPhone. Well, the Ringtones tab is here because you can now make FaceTime video calls over Wi-Fi. When you receive a call, a ringtone notifies you. The Ringtones tab allows you to import custom ringtones you've purchased from the iTunes Store.

Figure 2–14. *The Ringtones tab*

To sync ringtones, select the Sync Ringtones box. Next, choose whether you want to sync all of your ringtones or just selected ones. If you choose "Selected ringtones," the Ringtones box appears, listing all of the ringtones you have stored in iTunes. Check the ringtones you want to sync.

The Music Tab

The Music tab is pretty easy to understand (see Figure 2–15). Make sure the Sync Music check box is selected at the top. In the box below it are two radio buttons.

Figure 2–15. *The Music tab allows you to select which songs, playlists, and artists you want to sync to your iPod touch.*

Entire music library: When this is selected, the entire music library is synced to your iPod touch. Note that your entire library is synced only if you have the storage space available on your iPod touch. If you have more music than the iPod touch can hold, the remainder of the music stops syncing once the iPod touch is full.

Selected playlists, artists, albums and genres: Selecting this option displays four boxes listing all of the playlists, artists, and genres in your iTunes library. Go through and select the check boxes of the playlists, artists, and genres you want on your iPod touch.

Include music videos: Selecting this check box transfers any music videos associated with playlists, artists, or genres to the iPod touch.

Include voice memos: If you select this check box, any voice memos stored in your iTunes library are synced with your iPod touch.

Automatically fill free space with songs: This check box appears only if you've chosen the "Selected playlists, artists, and genres" radio button. If it's selected, once all your other files (movies, books, photos, and so on) have been synced to your iPod touch, any leftover free space is filled with music. I don't recommend selecting this option. It severely limits your ability to create any new documents on your iPod touch since there won't be any space left in which to store them.

The Movies Tab

The iTunes Store offers a large collection of movies for rent or purchase that you can download and sync to your iPod touch. The Movies tab, shown in Figure 2–16, provides several ways of getting your movies onto the iPod touch.

Figure 2–16. *The Movies tab allows you to select which movies you want to sync to your iPod touch.*

To sync your movies, first make sure the Sync Movies check box is selected (see Figure 2–16). Three checkboxes are displayed on the Movies tab:

Automatically include: If this check box is selected, you'll be able to access a drop-down list of preset options to make your movie syncing experience easier. From the drop-down list, you can choose to sync all your movies (not a good idea because one hour of video can take up to half a gigabyte of space) or decide to save some space.

If you'd like to go the space-saving route, select the 1, 3, 5, or 10 "most recent movies" preset. You also have the option of selecting the "all unwatched" movies preset, which adds all the movies in your library that have not been watched yet. Other preset options include syncing 1, 3, 5, or 10 of your "most recent unwatched movies" or 1, 3, 5, or 10 of your "least recent unwatched movies."

Movies: If the "automatically include" check box is selected and the drop-down list is set to anything but "all," you also have the option of selecting additional movies from your iTunes library. With the "automatically include" box unchecked, you can manually select as many of your movies as you want (see Figure 2–17).

Movies

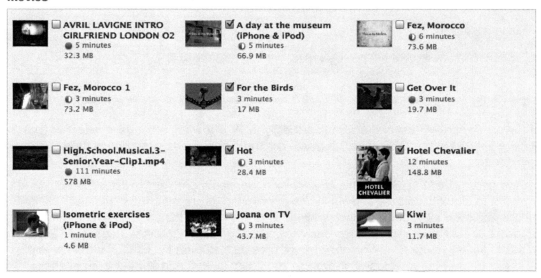

Figure 2–17. *The Movies check box allows you to select individual movies to sync to your iPod touch.*

Include Movies from Playlists: This box, shown in Figure 2–18, provides the option of including movies found in your iTunes playlists.

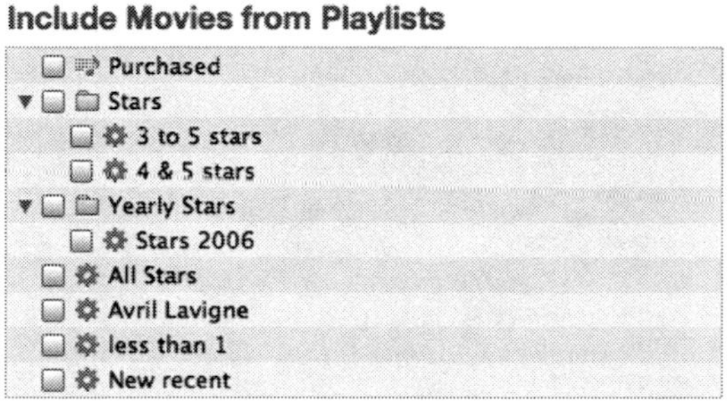

Include Movies from Playlists

- ☐ ➡ Purchased
- ▼ ☐ 🗀 Stars
  - ☐ ⚙ 3 to 5 stars
  - ☐ ⚙ 4 & 5 stars
- ▼ ☐ 🗀 Yearly Stars
  - ☐ ⚙ Stars 2006
- ☐ ⚙ All Stars
- ☐ ⚙ Avril Lavigne
- ☐ ⚙ less than 1
- ☐ ⚙ New recent

Figure 2–18. *This box allows you to sync movies from your iTunes playlists.*

The TV Shows Tab

The iTunes Store offers large collections of TV shows available for purchase and download. All of these shows can be synchronized to your iPod touch for viewing. You can purchase individual episodes *à la carte* or buy a Season Pass. With the latter choice, you pay for the entire season at once, often at a slight discount, and new episodes are automatically downloaded as they become available.

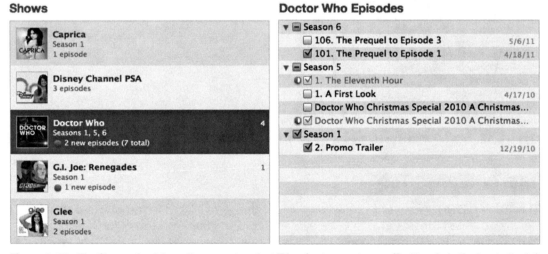

Figure 2–19. *The TV Shows tab allows you to select the shows you want to sync to your iPod touch.*

To sync TV shows, first make sure that the Sync TV Shows check box is selected (see Figure 2–19). On the TV Shows tab below are three check boxes similar to those on the Movies tab.

Automatically include: Select this check box to access a drop-down list of preset options to simplify your TV show syncing experience. From the drop-down list, you can choose to sync all your TV shows; again, this is not a good idea if you have a lot of shows because one hour of video can occupy up to half a gigabyte of space. There is also an "all unwatched" option and several presets including syncing only the newest shows, the newest unwatched shows, or the oldest unwatched shows. With all these options, you can apply the preset to all shows or just selected TV shows.

The Shows and Episodes boxes: If the "automatically include" check box is selected and set to anything but "all," you also have the option of selecting additional TV shows from your iTunes library (see Figure 2–20). With the "automatically include" check box deselected, you are able to manually select as many of your TV shows as you want.

Figure 2–20. *The Shows check box allows you to select TV series to sync to your iPod touch. In the box to the left you can select the episodes to sync.*

Include Episodes from Playlists: This box gives you the option of including any TV show episodes found in your iTunes playlists (see Figure 2–21).

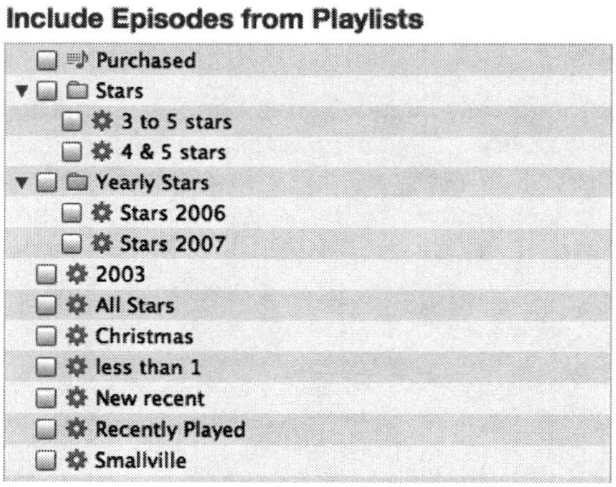

Include Episodes from Playlists

Figure 2–21. *This box allows you to sync any TV shows found in your iTunes playlists.*

The Podcasts Tab

Many people use iTunes to subscribe to their favorite podcasts. *Podcasts* are audio programs delivered over the Internet, much as TV shows are delivered over the airways. Numerous podcasts are available, with topics ranging from entertainment and advice to how-to shows, politics, news, and much more. iTunes monitors your podcast subscriptions and can automatically download new shows when they become available. The Podcasts tab gives you control over which shows are synchronized to your iPod touch.

Figure 2–22. *The Podcasts tab allows you to select the podcasts to sync to your iPod touch.*

The Podcasts tab (see Figure 2–22) has a similar look and feel to the Movies and TV Shows tabs. To sync podcasts, first make sure the Sync Podcasts check box is selected. Below the check box are three boxes on the Podcasts tab.

Automatically include: Select this check box to access a drop-down list of preset options and customize your podcast syncing experience. From the drop-down list, you can select to sync all your podcasts. Syncing all your podcasts won't take up as much room as movies and TV shows do if the podcasts in question are audio-only. However, if you are downloading video podcasts, the same space requirements apply as with movies.

In addition to the "all" option, there are "all unplayed" and "all new" options as well as several presets including syncing only the newest podcasts, the most recent/least recent unplayed podcasts, or the most recent/least recent new podcasts. These presets can be applied to all or just selected podcasts.

The Podcasts and Episodes boxes: If the "automatically include" check box is selected and set to anything but "all," you also have the option of selecting additional podcasts from your iTunes library in this box (see Figure 2–23). With the "automatically include" check box deselected, manually select as many or as few of your podcasts as you want.

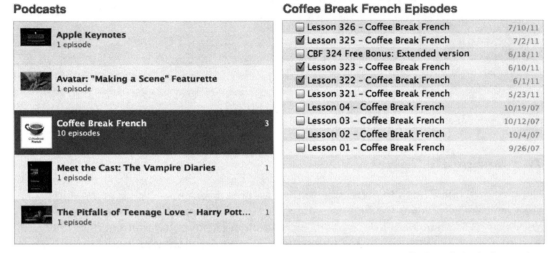

Figure 2–23. *The Podcasts check box allows you to select podcasts to sync to your iPod touch. In the box to the left you can select which episodes of the podcast series to sync.*

Include Episodes from Playlists: This box (see Figure 2–24) provides the option of including any podcast episodes found in your iTunes playlists.

Include Episodes from Playlists

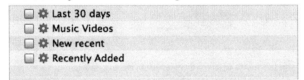

Figure 2–24. *This box allows you to sync any podcasts found in your iTunes playlists.*

The Books Tab

One of the coolest features of the iPod touch is the ability to buy and read e-books or view your own PDFs in the iBooks app. We'll delve into the iBookstore and the iBooks app in Chapter 8, but for now all you need to know is that the Books tab in the iPod touch preferences window is where you control what books and PDFs are synced to your iPod touch (Figure 2–25).

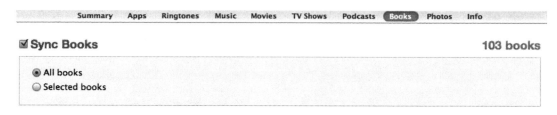

Figure 2–25. *The Books tab allows you to select which books you want to sync to your iPod touch.*

Make sure the Sync Books check box is selected. In the box below it are two radio buttons: "All books" syncs every book in your iTunes library, and "Selected books" allows you to sync only the books and/or PDFs selected in the Books box further down the page (see Figure 2–26).

> **NOTE:** Even if you have 300 books in your iTunes library, you might as well sync them all. An e-book takes up very little storage. As a matter of fact, *War and Peace*, one of the largest ever written (and also one of the greatest), takes up only 1.2MB of storage. That's more than 50 percent less than a single three-minute 128Kbps AAC music file. Illustrated books take up more space, but even then they won't take up any more storage than a few MP3s would. Don't worry about a cluttered library, either. You'll learn how to organize your books in Chapter 9.

Books

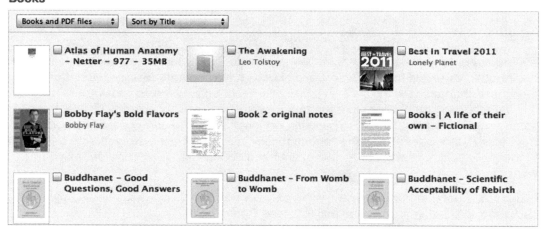

Figure 2–26. *The Books check box allows you to select individual books to sync to your iPod touch.*

Below the Books box is a check box in front of Sync Audiobooks (see Figure 2–27). Again, there are two options: "All audiobooks" or "Selected audiobooks."

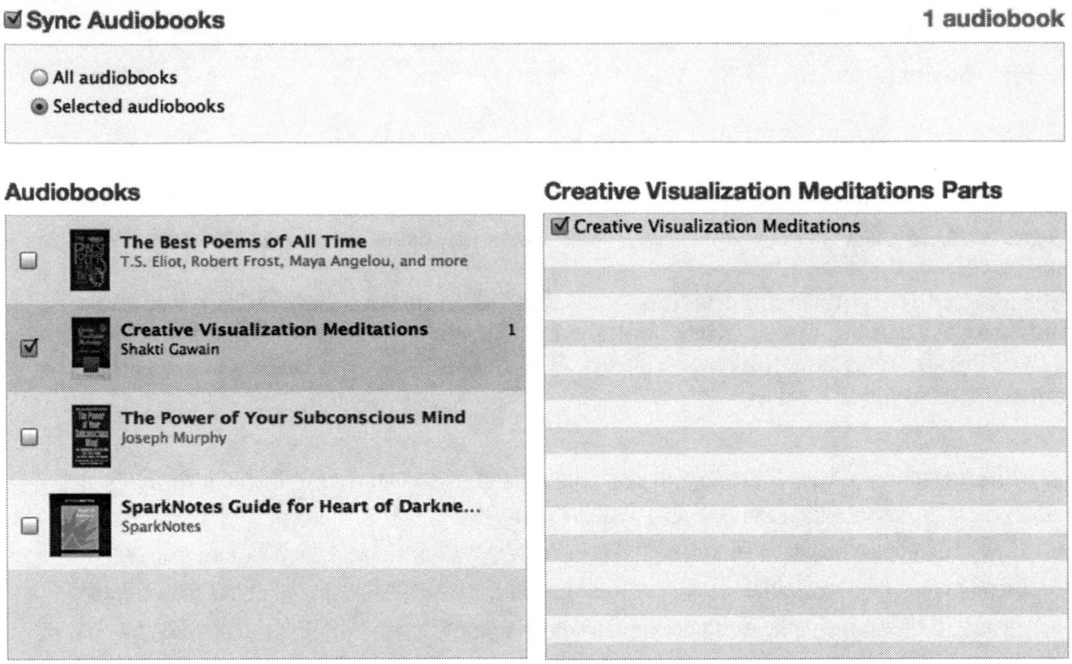

☑ Sync Audiobooks   1 audiobook

○ All audiobooks
◉ Selected audiobooks

Audiobooks   **Creative Visualization Meditations Parts**

☐ **The Best Poems of All Time**   ☑ Creative Visualization Meditations
     T.S. Eliot, Robert Frost, Maya Angelou, and more

☑ **Creative Visualization Meditations**   1
     Shakti Gawain

☐ **The Power of Your Subconscious Mind**
     Joseph Murphy

☐ **SparkNotes Guide for Heart of Darkne...**
     SparkNotes

Figure 2–27. *The Sync Audiobooks interface*

With "All audiobooks" selected, the audiobooks in your iTunes library are synced with your iPod touch. If you choose "Selected audiobooks," you're presented with the familiar layout you've seen on the other media tabs.

The Audiobooks and Parts boxes: In the Audiobooks box, you can manually select which audiobooks you want to sync. Some audiobooks have separate files, or *parts*, that designate chapters (see Figure 2–27). You can select only the parts you want to sync for any audiobook in the Parts box. If the "automatically include" check box is selected and set to anything but "all," you also have the option of selecting additional audiobooks from your iTunes library. With the "automatically include" check box deselected, feel free to manually select as many or as few of your audiobooks and their chapters as you want.

Include Audiobooks from Playlists: This box gives you the option of including any audiobooks found in your iTunes playlists (see Figure 2–28).

Include Audiobooks from Playlists

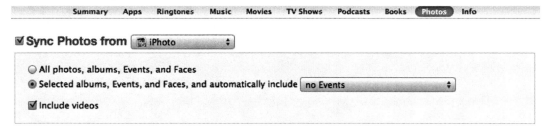

☐ 🎵 Purchased
▼ ☐ 📁 Stars
    ☐ ⚙ 3 to 5 stars
    ☐ ⚙ 4 & 5 stars
    ☐ ⚙ Last 150 stars
☐ ⚙ All Stars
☐ ⚙ New recent
☐ ⚙ Recent starred 25
☐ 🎵 Test

Figure 2–28. *This box allows you to sync any audiobooks found in your iTunes playlists.*

> **NOTE:** Unlike e-books, audiobooks can be quite large since they are basically very long audio files. If you have dozens of audiobooks, you may want to transfer only a select few to save space.

The Photos Tab

The ability to view my photos on the iPod touch was pretty low on my list of reasons to buy one. Ironically, viewing photos is now one of my favorite things to do with my iPod touch. I'll discuss viewing photos on your iPod touch in Chapter 11, but for now I'll say that the experience is so much better than viewing photos on your desktop. There's nothing like physically holding digital photos in your hand and swiping through them on the gorgeous display of the iPod touch.

To get photos onto your iPod touch, make sure the "Sync Photos from" check box on the Photos tab is selected (see Figure 2–29), and then choose where you want to sync your photos from. On the Mac, your options will be iPhoto 4.0.3 or newer, Aperture 3.0.2 or newer, or any folder on your computer. On a Windows computer, your options will be Adobe Photoshop Elements 3.0 or newer or any folder on your computer.

| Summary | Apps | Ringtones | Music | Movies | TV Shows | Podcasts | Books | Photos | Info |

☑ **Sync Photos from** 🖼 iPhoto ⇕

  ○ All photos, albums, Events, and Faces
  ◉ Selected albums, Events, and Faces, and automatically include [no Events ⇕]
  ☑ Include videos

Figure 2–29. *The Photos tab allows you to select which photos you want to sync to your iPod touch.*

In the box below the check box, there are three options:

All photos, albums, events, and faces: Selecting this option syncs every photo from your selected photo application or folder onto the iPod touch. Again, I recommend against this if your photo collections are as large as mine (I have somewhere around 80GB of travel photos on my Mac). If you have only a few thousand photos, load 'em up!

> **NOTE:** The first-generation iPod touch devices do not have a built-in camera, but you can still add photos from another digital camera to your iPod touch via the Camera Connection Kit. The $29 kit (available at www.store.apple.com) includes two adapters—one for connecting a camera through a USB 2.0 cable and the other for reading SD memory cards.

Selected albums, events, and faces, and automatically include: Selecting this option displays boxes for albums, events, and faces further down the page (see Figure 2–30). From these boxes you can choose which iPhoto photo albums and events to sync. You can also choose whether you want to sync faces. Faces is a feature in iPhoto that uses facial recognition capabilities to create collections of photos in which a certain person appears.

When you select any of the check boxes next to a certain album, event, or face, the photo count of that selection is displayed to the right. Choosing the "Selected albums, events, and faces, and automatically include" option, you are presented with a drop-down list of options allowing you to select all, none, or a preset date-specific range of iPhoto event collections.

Include video: When this check box is selected, any videos made with your digital camera that appear in any of your selected albums are transferred to the iPod touch. Keep in mind that video can quickly use up storage space.

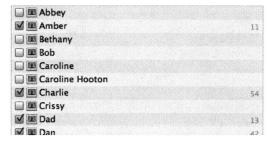

Figure 2–30. *Choose which iPhoto photo albums, events, and faces to sync.*

The Info Tab

The last tab is the Info tab (see Figure 2–31), and it's all about you. This is the tab that allows you to get your most personal information synced with the iPod touch, including contacts, calendars, and e-mail. This tab has five sections: Sync Address Book Contacts, Sync iCal Calendars, Sync Mail Accounts, Other, and Advanced.

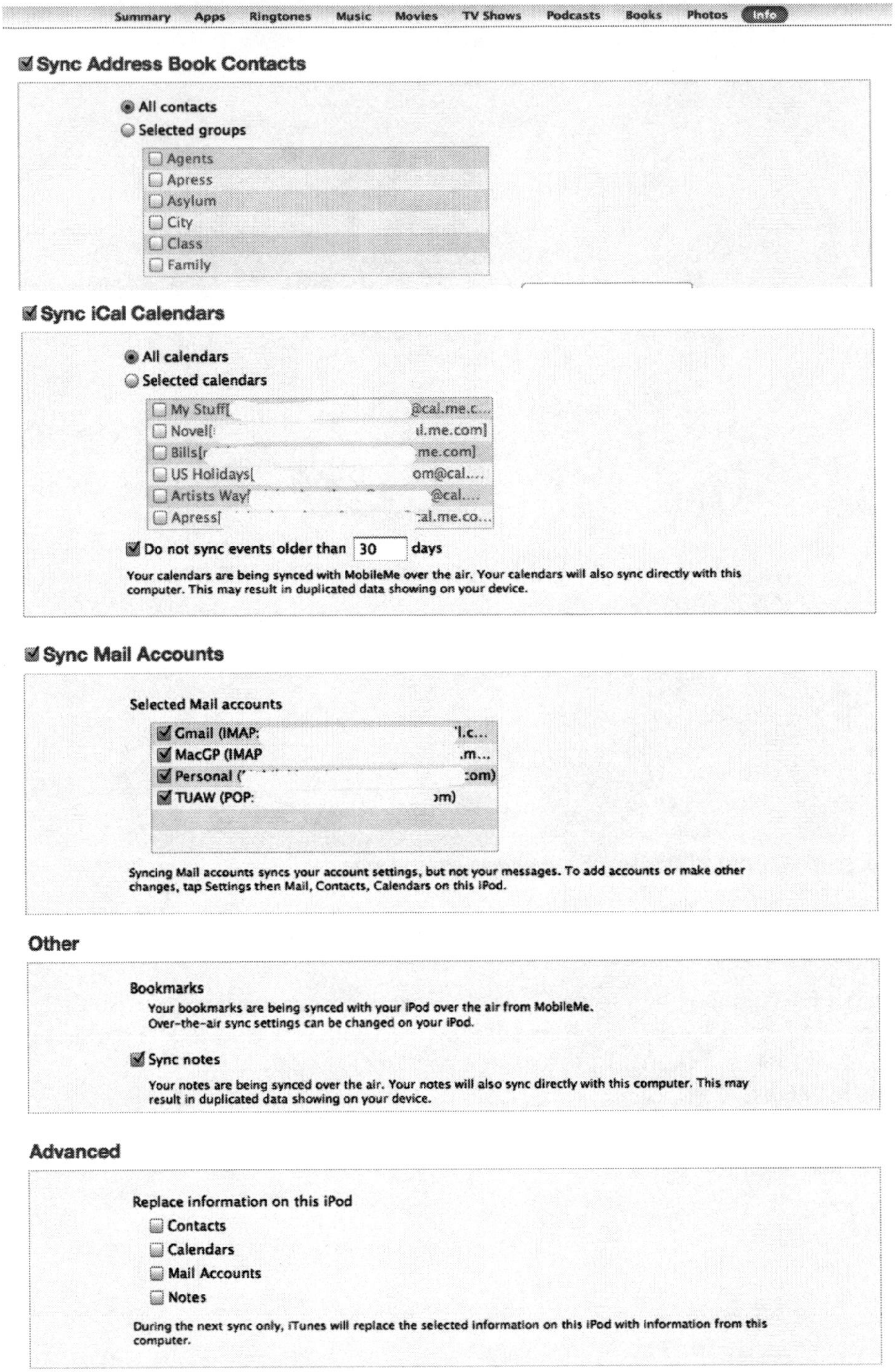

Summary   Apps   Ringtones   Music   Movies   TV Shows   Podcasts   Books   Photos   **Info**

☑ Sync Address Book Contacts

◉ All contacts
◯ Selected groups

▢ Agents
▢ Apress
▢ Asylum
▢ City
▢ Class
▢ Family

☑ Sync iCal Calendars

◉ All calendars
◯ Selected calendars

▢ My Stuff[@cal.me.c...]
▢ Novell[il.me.com]
▢ Bills[r   me.com]
▢ US Holidays[om@cal....]
▢ Artists Way[@cal....]
▢ Apress[:al.me.co...]

☑ Do not sync events older than 30   days

Your calendars are being synced with MobileMe over the air. Your calendars will also sync directly with this computer. This may result in duplicated data showing on your device.

☑ Sync Mail Accounts

Selected Mail accounts

☑ Gmail (IMAP: 1.c...
☑ MacGP (IMAP   .m...
☑ Personal ('   :om)
☑ TUAW (POP:)m)

Syncing Mail accounts syncs your account settings, but not your messages. To add accounts or make other changes, tap Settings then Mail, Contacts, Calendars on this iPod.

Other

Bookmarks
Your bookmarks are being synced with your iPod over the air from MobileMe.
Over-the-air sync settings can be changed on your iPod.

☑ Sync notes
Your notes are being synced over the air. Your notes will also sync directly with this computer. This may result in duplicated data showing on your device.

Advanced

Replace information on this iPod
▢ Contacts
▢ Calendars
▢ Mail Accounts
▢ Notes

During the next sync only, iTunes will replace the selected information on this iPod with information from this computer.

Figure 2–31. *The Info tab allows you to sync your mail accounts, contacts, calendars, bookmarks, and notes.*

If you have been using Outlook on Windows or Mail, iCal, and Address Book on a Mac, then you'll already have everything you need to sync your information to your iPod touch. You just need to tell the iPod touch how you want to sync that information.

> **NOTE:** If you are using Apple's iCloud service (www.icloud.com), the Sync Address Book Contacts and Sync iCal Calendars options are unselected after your first iPod touch sync, and a message states that your contacts and calendars are being synced over the air via iCloud.

Sync Address Book Contacts

To sync your address book contacts, you need to be using one of the following applications: Address Book, Microsoft Entourage 2004, Microsoft Entourage 2008, or Microsoft Outlook 2011 on a Mac or Windows Address Book, Microsoft Outlook 2003, or Microsoft Outlook 2007 on Windows.

Select the Sync Address Book Contacts check box (see Figure 2–32), which gives you the option of syncing all the contacts in your address book or just those from selected groups.

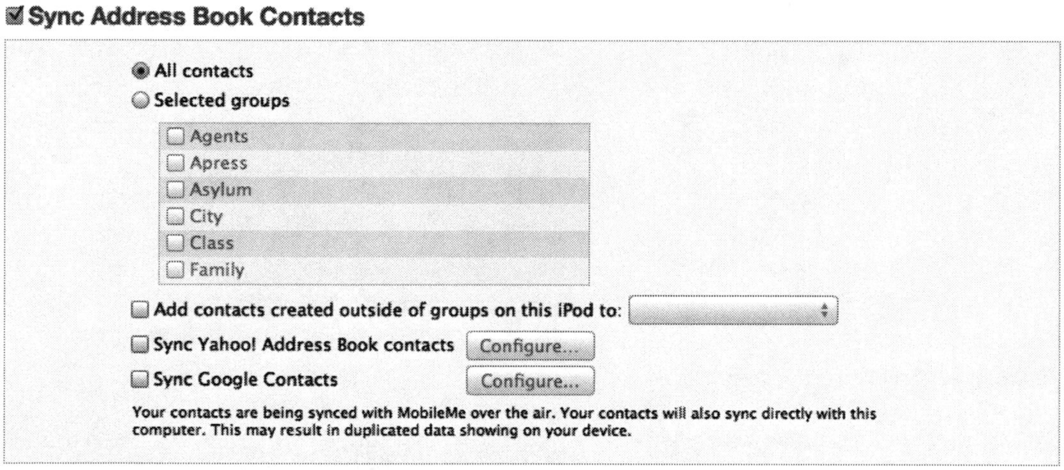

☑ **Sync Address Book Contacts**

Figure 2–32. *Your address book syncing options*

Add contacts created outside of groups on this iPod to: When this check box is selected, a drop-down list of all your address book groups appears. If you create a new contact on your iPod touch and don't assign the contact to a group, that contact is automatically put into the group you select here.

Sync Yahoo! Address Book contacts: When this check box is selected, Yahoo! Address Book contacts are automatically synced with your iPod touch address book. You must agree with the dialog box that asks you to acknowledge that you are allowing the iPod touch to sync to your Yahoo! account. Next, you are asked to enter your Yahoo! ID and password. Once you've done this, your contacts are set to sync. Clicking the Configure button allows you to enter a different Yahoo! ID.

Sync Google Contacts: When this check box is selected, Google contacts are automatically synced with your iPod touch address book. You must agree with the dialog box that asks you to acknowledge that you are allowing your iPod touch to sync to your Google account. Next, you are prompted to enter your Google ID and password. Once you've done this, your contacts are ready to sync. Clicking the Configure button allows you to enter a different Google ID.

Sync iCal Calendars

To sync your calendars, you need to be using one of the following: iCal, Microsoft Entourage 2004, Microsoft Entourage 2008, or Microsoft Outlook 2011 on a Mac or Microsoft Outlook 2003 or Microsoft Outlook 2007 on Windows.

To set up calendar syncing, select the Sync iCal Calendars check box (see Figure 2–33). Just like with contacts, you then have the option of syncing all your calendars or just selected ones.

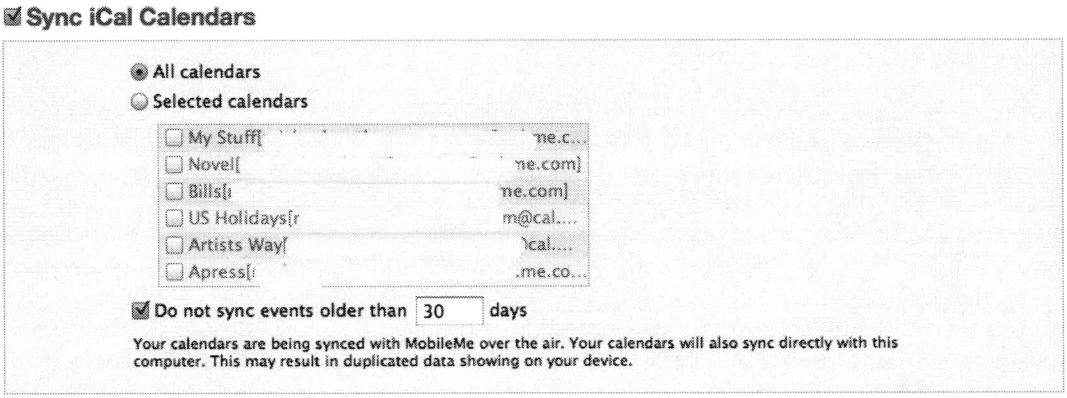

☑ **Sync iCal Calendars**

⦿ All calendars
○ Selected calendars

☐ My Stuff[ne.c...
☐ Novell[ne.com]
☐ Bills[ne.com]
☐ US Holidays[r   m@cal...
☐ Artists Way[   )cal...
☐ Apress[.me.co...

☑ Do not sync events older than [30] days

Your calendars are being synced with MobileMe over the air. Your calendars will also sync directly with this computer. This may result in duplicated data showing on your device.

Figure 2–33. *Your calendar syncing options*

Do not sync events older than: With this check box selected, events that are more than a specified number of days old are not synced. The default number of days is 30, but you can enter anything up to 99,999 days.

> **NOTE:** A great place to find premade calendars for holidays, school events, or your favorite sporting teams is at www.icalshare.com.

Sync Mail Accounts

All of the mail accounts you have set up in Mac OS X's Mail or Microsoft's Outlook appear here (Figure 2–34). You have the option of selecting or deselecting any of the accounts. Accounts that are not selected do not appear in the iPod touch's Mail app.

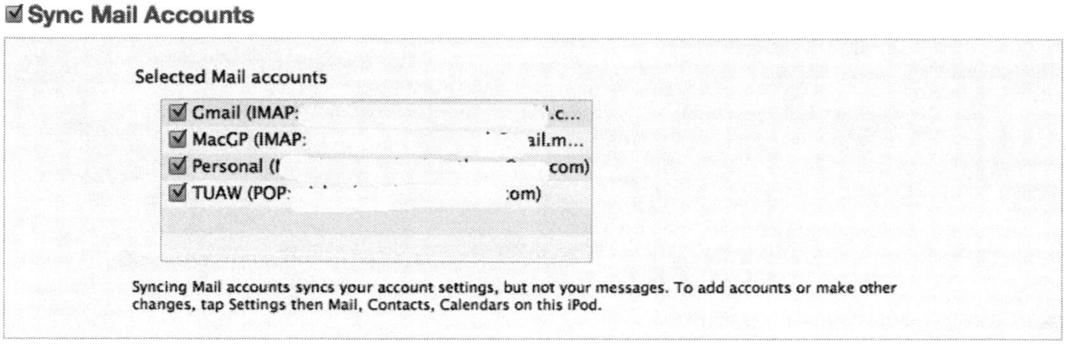

☑ **Sync Mail Accounts**

Selected Mail accounts
- ☑ Gmail (IMAP: '.c...
- ☑ MacGP (IMAP: ' ' · ail.m...
- ☑ Personal (I   ' '   ' ·   com)
- ☑ TUAW (POP: · '   '   :om)

Syncing Mail accounts syncs your account settings, but not your messages. To add accounts or make other changes, tap Settings then Mail, Contacts, Calendars on this iPod.

Figure 2–34. *Your e-mail account syncing options*

Other

Apple should really have named this section "Bookmark and Notes Syncing," but it opted for "Other." Here you can sync bookmarks from the web browser on your computer to the Safari web browser on the iPod touch (see Figure 2–35). Again, if you have a MobileMe or iCloud account, your bookmarks are synced over the air. If not, select the Sync Bookmarks check box, and choose your browser from the drop-down menu. On the Mac, bookmark syncing is supported for Safari. On a Windows computer, bookmark syncing supports Safari and Microsoft Internet Explorer 7 and newer.

Other

Bookmarks
   Your bookmarks are being synced with your iPod over the air from MobileMe.
   Over-the-air sync settings can be changed on your iPod.

☑ Sync notes
   Your notes are being synced over the air. Your notes will also sync directly with this computer. This may result in duplicated data showing on your device.

Figure 2–35. *Your bookmark and note syncing options*

This section also allows you to sync notes to your iPod touch. Note syncing works only with Mac OS X Mail or Microsoft Outlook 2011 on a Mac or Microsoft Outlook 2003 or 2007 on Windows. To enable note syncing, select the check box.

Advanced

When selected, this section allows you to replace contacts, calendars, mail accounts, and notes on the iPod touch with information from your computer (see Figure 2–36). This is a handy feature if your information gets out of sync and you want to make sure that everything you see on your computer matches what is on the iPod touch.

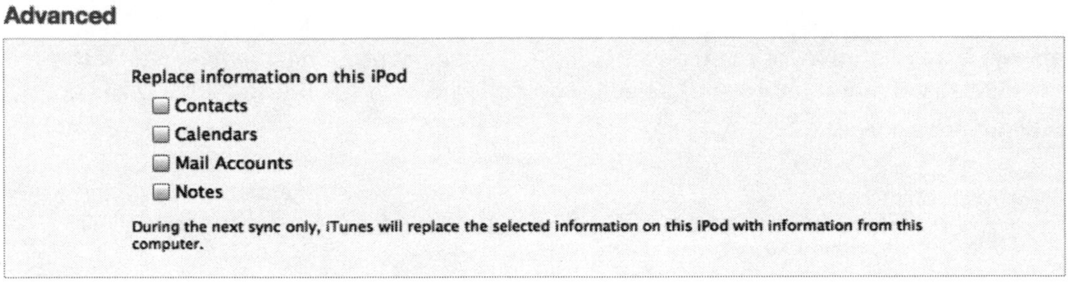

Advanced

> Replace information on this iPod
>   ☐ Contacts
>   ☐ Calendars
>   ☐ Mail Accounts
>   ☐ Notes
>
> During the next sync only, iTunes will replace the selected information on this iPod with information from this computer.

Figure 2–36. *Your advanced syncing options*

When you select the respective check boxes, iTunes overwrites the information on your iPod touch during the next sync only. After that sync, normal syncing resumes between your iPod touch and computer.

> **NOTE:** If your calendars and contacts are being synced via iCloud, you will not be able to select their check boxes in the Advanced section.

iTunes Device Settings

iTunes has several preferences for the iPod touch. To access these on a Mac, launch iTunes and select **iTunes ➤ Preferences** from the menu bar, or select **Edit ➤ Preferences** from the menu bar if you are using Windows. The Preferences window pops up with a series of icons running along the top. The only one we are interested in for the iPod touch is the Devices icon. Click the Devices icon (it looks like an iPod touch), and you'll be presented with the Devices preferences window (see Figure 2–37).

Here you'll find settings for devices that interact with iTunes. These devices can include the iPod touch, iPad, iPhone, Apple TV, and AirPort Express.

Device backups: Any time your iPod touch is synced, iTunes creates a backup of its contents. Any backups of iPad, iPhone, or iPod touch devices are listed here. The name of the device is listed along with the date it was last backed up. Hover your cursor over the name of the iPod touch to view its serial number.

Although iTunes keeps multiple dated, partial backups of your device, it's still a good idea to make copies of your backups on an external hard drive. iTunes places the original backup files in the following locations:

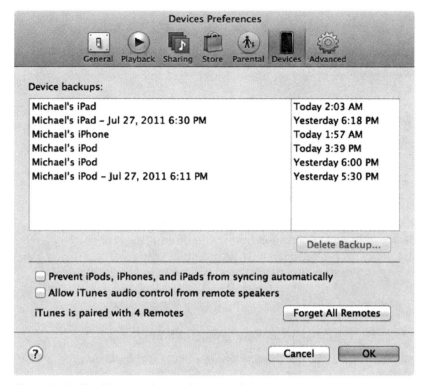

Figure 2–37. *The iTunes Devices preferences window*

Mac: ~/Library/Application Support/MobileSync/Backup/

Windows XP: \Documents and Settings\(username)\Application Data\Apple Computer\MobileSync\Backup\

Windows Vista: \Users\(username)\AppData\Roaming\Apple Computer\MobileSync\Backup\

The list of information backed up by iTunes is a long one:

- Safari bookmarks, cookies, history, and currently open pages
- Map bookmarks, recent searches, and the current location displayed in Maps
- Application settings, preferences, and data
- Contacts
- Calendars
- CalDAV and subscribed calendar accounts
- YouTube favorites
- Wallpapers

- Notes

- Mail accounts

- Autocorrect dictionaries

- Camera Roll

- Home screen layout and web clips

- Network settings (saved Wi-Fi hotspots, VPN settings, network preferences)

- Paired Bluetooth devices (which can be used only if restored to the same iPod touch that did the backup)

- Keychain (This includes e-mail account passwords, Wi-Fi passwords, and passwords you enter into web sites and some other applications. The keychain can only be restored from backup to the same iPod touch. If you are restoring to a new device, you will need to fill in these passwords again.)

- Managed configurations/profiles

- MobileMe and Microsoft Exchange account configurations

- App Store application data (except the application itself and its tmp and Caches folders).

- Per-app preferences allowing use of location services

- Offline web application cache/database

- Autofill for web pages

- Trusted hosts that have certificates that cannot be verified

- Web sites approved to get the location of the device

- In-app purchases

To delete an iPod touch backup, select it from the device backups list, and click the Delete Backup button. Confirm the deletion by clicking the Delete Backup button in the dialog that appears.

Prevent iPods, iPhones, and iPads from syncing automatically: Select this box if you want to disable automatic syncing when the iPod touch is connected to your computer. In order to sync, you'll need to manually press the Sync button at the bottom of the iTunes preferences window for iPod touch.

Restoring

If you ever experience problems with your iPod touch, you can choose to restore it. There are two restore options: restore to factory default and restore from backup.

Restoring to factory default restores your iPod touch to its original factory settings, as if you've just turned it on for the first time. Restoring from backup restores the iPod touch from its last saved backup file.

To restore to factory settings, select the iPod touch from the devices list in iTunes, select the Summary tab, and then click Restore (this deletes all data on iPod touch and restores to factory settings). When prompted by iTunes, select the option to restore your settings.

To restore from backup, right-click (or Ctrl+click) the iPod touch in the devices list in iTunes and select Restore from Backup. The iPod touch is restored from the backup selected from the "Device backups" list.

> **NOTE:** If you've set up password encryption on your iPod touch backups (covered earlier in this chapter), you cannot restore from the encrypted backup if you forget the password. Be sure to choose passwords that are easy to remember!

Welcome to the Cloud

Along side iOS 5, Apple introduced two new cloud-based services: iCloud and iTunes Match. Before we discuss each of those, lets talk about what the "cloud" is exactly.

Cloud computing simply means that your data resides on external servers and not your computer's hard drive. Though you may have created a document on your computer, it's actually synced with an external server, so two perfectly identical copies of it exist simultaneously: one in the cloud and one on your computer.

As we get more devices like iPhones, iPods, Macs, and iPad, its nice to be able to pick up any device and be able to see all our music, documents, and photos on that device no matter if we created them on it or not. This is exactly what could computing allows us to do.

iCloud

Apple's implementation of cloud computing is called iCloud. Put simply, iCloud stores all of your music, documents, TV shows, photos, and more and pushes them all to your different devices automatically. So if you create a document on your Mac in Pages, you can pick up you iPod touch, open the Pages app (if you've downloaded it) and see and edit the document you were just working on on your Mac.

There's actually quite a bit of technology behind iCloud, but Apple doesn't want users to think about that, so they designed it as simply as possible. All you need to do to take advantage of iCloud is set up a free iCloud account at `www.icloud.com`. Once you've done that, open up the Settings app on your iPod touch and select "iCloud." Enter in your iCloud user name and password and you're good to go.

We'll discuss iCloud and all it's feature throughout this book as it relates to the various apps in iOS 5. Until then, here is a brief overview of everything iCloud offers:

- **iTunes in the Cloud:** This feature allows you to download all your paid iTunes song purchases on any device. It will also automatically download a purchased song from one device onto all your other iCloud devices. No syncing needed.

- **Apps and Books:** Like your purchased music, and apps or books purchased from the App Store or iBookstore are download to all your devices automatically.

- **Photo Stream:** Any photo you take with an iCloud-enabled device is automatically pushed to all your other devices be they iPhones, iPod touches, Macs, or PCs.

- **Documents in the Cloud:** As mentioned before, and document you are working on in an iWork app, like Pages, Keynote, or Numbers, will automatically be pushed to all your deices.

- **Backup:** iCloud automatically stores backups of all of your purchased music, TV shows, apps, and books, photos and video in the Camera Roll, device settings, app data, home screen and app organization, messages (iMessage, SMS, and MMS), and ringtones in the cloud. Should you ever need to restore your iPod touch, all your information and data is waiting for you no matter if you are away from your computer.

- **Email, calendars, address book, bookmarks, notes, and reminders:** All iCloud members get a free email account with calendars and an address book as well. In addition to that, iCloud members can sync notes, reminders, and bookmarks across devices.

- **Find My Friends:** This is an app that allows you to share your location and see the location of your friends on a map.

- **Find My iPod touch:** This app allows you to track down your lost or stolen iPod.

As mentioned earlier, we'll discuss all the features of iCloud as they relate to your apps throughout this book. The only thing left to mention here is iCloud's system requirements: Users need an iPhone 3GS or later, iPod touch third generation or later, iPad, iPad 2, a Mac running OS X 10.7 or later, or a PC with Windows Vista or Windows 7 or later. iCloud also requires iOS 5.

iTunes Match

Another new cloud feature Apple introduced alongside iCloud is iTunes Match. iTunes Match is a paid service that costs $24.99 per year. It allows you to move your entire iTunes library to the cloud – even songs that you didn't buy in iTunes.

So, if you've imported years worth of old CD's, iTunes Match will "match" all the songs on your computer, and give you the latest versions encoded in high-quality 256-Kbps AAC DRM-free files. Whatever songs it can't match in yoru library, it will then upload to the cloud, enabling you to automatically access all those songs from any iCloud device. Pretty cool, huh?

Summary

In this chapter, you explored options for syncing media and data with your iPod touch. You discovered where to get your media and how to make sure your iPod touch/iTunes sync preferences stick. To wind things up, here is a quick overview of some key points from this chapter:

- The preference selections and the way your iPod touch connects with iTunes are going to be familiar to you if you've used an iPhone or iPod before; however, there are some important differences with the iPod touch.

- The Capacity bar is always visible in the iPod touch preferences and is an easy indicator of how much storage is available on your iPod touch.

- No change made to the iPod touch preferences is complete until you click the Apply button. Likewise, if you accidentally make a change you don't want, you can always click the Cancel button.

- It is important to manage what data you sync with your iPod touch. Syncing all of your music may not leave enough storage for photos and videos.

- Syncing apps is fun and easy using the visual representation of your iPod touch under the Apps tab. If you have a lot of apps, syncing can be a slow process. Waiting can be a pain, but it's best never to interrupt a sync.

- Syncing of movies, music, TV shows, podcasts, books, and photos is pretty straightforward, and once you've mastered how to sync one form of media, the rest are a cinch.

Chapter 3

Interacting with Your iPod touch

Your iPod touch uses an awesome way to interact with it. As its name suggests, it responds to the language of your touch. Its vocabulary includes taps, drags, pinches, and flicks. With these, you control your iPod as easily as using a mouse or trackpad to control your personal computer. And there's a lot more to interaction than just drags and double-clicks. Your iPod offers Multi-Touch technology. That means it can recognize and respond to more than one touch at a time.

In this chapter, you'll discover all the different ways you can interact with your iPod—from zooming into and out of pictures or using the iPod touch's built-in keyboard to playing with its sensors. You'll learn how all these features work and how to take advantage of some secret ways to interact with your iPod.

Interaction Basics

Personal computers have mice or trackpads. Old-fashioned personal digital assistants (PDAs...remember them?) have styluses. The iPod touch has your fingers. It does not work with mice or styluses. It requires real finger contact. Your iPod touch does not just sense pressure points. It detects the small electrical charge transferred from your fingers. That means you can use your iPod touch with your fingers, your knuckles, or even—if you're feeling up to it—your nose, but you cannot use it with pencil erasers, Q-tips, or those PDA styluses. The electrical charges in your touch make it possible for the iPod touch to detect and respond to one or more contacts at a time, that is, to use Multi-Touch technology.

> **TIP:** If you're feeling really adventurous, you can use a frozen hotdog in place of your finger. Korean winters are very cold, and people were getting frostbite on their fingers from removing their gloves to use their iPhones outside. Some enterprising people in Korea discovered that you could use a frozen hotdog in lieu of your finger and still be able to interact with the iPhone's touch screen—all while keeping their gloves on. Theoretically, a frozen hot dog should work with the iPod touch's screen as well.

The iPod touch Language

How you touch your iPod touch's screen provides your communication vocabulary. Here's a quick rundown of the basic ways you can speak to your iPod touch:

Pressing the Home button: The Home button lives below the touchscreen and is marked with a small square. Press this button at any time while in an app to return to your home screen with its list of applications. Double-pressing the Home button while on another page of apps or inside an app will cause the screen to slide up, and you'll see a row of apps that are currently running in the background. We'll talk more about these multitasking features later in this chapter. While on any page of apps except the first page, pressing the Home button once returns you to the first page of apps. While on the first page of apps, pressing the Home button once takes you to the iPod touch's Spotlight search screen. We'll talk more about Spotlight search later in this chapter.

Tapping: Tap your iPod touch by touching your finger to the screen and removing it quickly. Tapping allows you to select web links, activate buttons, and launch applications. When typing text, you may want to tap with your forefinger or, if it's more comfortable, your thumb.

Double-tapping: Double-tapping means tapping your screen twice in quick succession. Double-clicking may be important on your personal computer, but double-tapping is not actually used all that much on your iPod touch. You can double-tap in Safari (the web browser that ships on your iPod touch) to zoom into columns and double-tap again to zoom back out. In Photos (the iPod touch's built-in photo viewer), use double-tapping to zoom into and out from pictures.

Two-fingered tapping and dragging: The iPod touch's Multi-Touch technology means you can tap the screen with more than one finger at a time. A few applications respond to two-fingered gestures. To do this, separate your forefinger and middle finger and tap or drag the screen with both fingers at once. For example, in Safari, a double-fingered drag allows you to scroll within a web frame without affecting the page as a whole.

Holding: At times, you'll want to put your finger on the screen and leave it there until something happens. For example, holding brings up the spyglass while you're typing, and in Safari, it brings up URL previews.

Dragging: Drag your finger by pressing it to the screen and moving it in any direction before lifting it. Use dragging to scroll up and down in Safari and Music (the application that plays back your iTunes songs). Some applications offer an index on the right side, like the one shown for the Music app in Figure 3–1. To use this index, drag along it until the item you want comes into view.

Figure 3–1. *The index bar (boxed) to the right of the Music app*

Flicking: When you're dealing with long lists, you can give the list a quick flick. Place your finger onto the screen and move it rapidly in one direction—up, down, left, or right. The display responds by scrolling quickly in the direction you've indicated. Use flicking to move quickly through your e-mail contacts list, for example.

> **TIP:** Flicking and dragging will not choose or activate items on the iPod touch's display. Try this yourself by dragging and flicking on the home screen.

Stopping: During a scroll, press and hold your finger to the screen to stop scrolling. Apple's legal text provides a great place to practice flicking, dragging, and stopping. To get there, select **Settings ➤ General ➤ About ➤ Legal**. Have fun with its endless content of legalese that you can flick, drag, and stop to your heart's content. If you don't want to stop a scroll, just wait. The scroll will slow and stop by itself.

Swiping: To swipe your iPod touch, drag a finger from the left side of the screen toward the right. Swiping is used to unlock your iPod touch and to indicate you want to delete list items.

Pinching: On the iPod touch, you pinch by placing your thumb and forefinger on the screen with a space between them. Then, with your fingers touching the screen, move them together, as if you were pinching the screen. Pinching allows you to zoom out in many iPod touch programs, including Photos and Safari.

Unpinching: To unpinch, perform the pinch in reverse. Start with your thumb and forefinger placed together on your screen and, with the fingers touching the screen, spread them apart. Unpinching allows you to zoom into those same iPod touch applications where pinching zooms out.

The iPod touch Sensors

In addition to its touchscreen, your iPod contains two important sensors: a tilt sensor, called an *accelerometer*, and a light sensor. These sensors give your iPod some science-fiction–grade features that set it apart from the crowd of other MP3 players on the market.

Accelerometer Sensor

The iPod uses an accelerometer to detect when your iPod tilts. Some applications, including Safari, update their displays when you turn the iPod on its side. This allows you to use your iPod in both portrait and landscape modes.

If you feel like playing with the accelerometer sensor, try this:

1. Go into Photos (tap its icon—the one with the sunflower on the bottom row of your home screen), and select a favorite picture.

2. Hold the iPod up normally in portrait orientation.

3. Press one finger on the screen, and then tilt the iPod into landscape orientation. The picture will not change.

4. Tap the screen with your middle finger (or any other finger that you're not holding to the iPod). Presto—the iPod finally rotates the display.

> **TIP:** If you've hacked your iPod for third-party software access, take a look at the Butterfly.app game (http://ericasadun.com). It uses the iPod's tilt sensor to manipulate a net around the iPod screen to catch butterflies. The Sensors.app demo displays an arrow that always points up, no matter how you hold your iPod.

Light Sensor

The light sensor is located at the top left of your iPod, on the front touchscreen. It's just below the Sleep/Wake button on the top of your unit, about a half-inch from the left edge of the screen, halfway between the edge and the start of the display. That's about a quarter-inch down. To see it, shine a flashlight beam at the iPod and look for a small, round, light-colored sensor just behind the glass.

This sensor detects whether the room you're in is bright or dark. Whenever you unlock the iPod, it samples the light and adjusts the overall brightness of the display to match. To interact with this sensor, either cover it with a finger or shine a bright light at it when you unlock your iPod. Your iPod adjusts to be very dim (the finger) or very bright (the light) to compensate.

You can toggle the autobrightness feature off and on by adjusting the settings in Settings ➤ Brightness. This screen also offers direct control over your iPod's brightness level. That's handy when you need immediate results instead of playing with unlocking, flashlights, and fingers.

> **NOTE:** As a rule, I leave my brightness set to maximum and the autobrightness feature switched off. This bypasses all light-sensor functionality and leaves my screen bright and usable. The light sensor may be high-end technology, but it's actually pretty annoying in real life.

Gyro Sensor

Apple has added a gyroscope to the latest iPod touch. A gyroscope is a device that allows other devices to "know" where it is on a three-axis orientation. Simply put, the gyro sensor allows the iPod touch to know when you are rotating the device around on an x-, y-, or z-axis. Benefits include advanced motion control in games and superior augmented reality apps.

iPod Power Tricks

You have a lot of different ways to switch your iPod on and off. This section covers some of the most useful methods.

Unlocking Your iPod

If you've just turned on your iPod touch or when your iPod touch has been idle for a while, it automatically locks, and the screen goes dark. When this happens, press the Home button. The locked touchscreen appears, as shown in Figure 3–2. To unlock your iPod touch, swipe the slider from the left to the right. The locked screen clears, and the home screen springs into place.

Figure 3–2. *The iPod touch lock screen*

You can set how long the iPod touch should wait before locking itself. Go to **Settings ➤ General ➤ Auto-Lock**, and choose the number of minutes you want your iPod touch to wait before locking. To disable autolocking, choose Never—and make sure you have a good power source available nearby. Autolocking is a power-saving feature. Disabling it means your iPod touch runs through its battery more rapidly.

For security, you can assign a simple passcode for your iPod touch. A *simple passcode* is just like a four-digit PIN you have for your debit cards. Go to **Settings ➤ General**, tap Passcode Lock, and then tap Turn Passcode On to establish a new simple passcode. Your iPod touch prompts you to enter a four-number code, as shown in Figure 3–3.

Figure 3–3. *Setting your simple passcode*

Enter a code, or tap Cancel to quit without entering a code. After you enter the code, the iPod touch prompts you to reenter it and then enables further passcode lock settings (see Figure 3–4). Those settings include how long the iPod touch needs to be idle before it's locked down; the ability to turn off the simple passcode and create a passcode using letters, numbers, and symbols (see Figure 3–5); and the option to erase all the data on the iPod touch after ten failed passcode attempts.

Figure 3–4. *Additional passcode settings*

Figure 3–5. *Creating a more complex passcode*

To test your passcode, click the Sleep/Wake button once (to put your iPod touch to sleep) and again (to wake it up). The passcode challenge screen greets you, as shown in Figure 3–6. Enter your passcode, and your iPod touch unlocks.

Figure 3–6. *The passcode challenge screen*

To remove the passcode from your iPod touch, go back to the Passcode Lock settings screen (Figure 3–4). Choose Turn Passcode Off, and reenter the passcode one more time to confirm that it's really you making this request.

So, what happens if you lose your passcode or a mean-spirited colleague adds one to your iPod touch without telling you? You'll need to connect the iPod touch to your home computer and use iTunes to restore the iPod touch software. You can restore your iPod touch by selecting the Summary tab in iTunes and clicking Restore. For more information about restoring your iPod touch, see Chapter 2.

The lock screen can also perform other functions including controlling the iPod touch's music player and camera. If music is playing on the iPod touch when the screen is locked, you can double-press the Home button to display music controls at the top of the screen. You can also quickly access the iPod touch's camera from the lock screen. You'll learn more about these controls in Chapters 6 and 13.

Putting Your iPod to Sleep

For iPods, sleep mode offers a power-saving way to use your device. Press the Sleep/Wake button once. The screen turns off, and your iPod locks and enters its low-power mode. You can still listen to music, and you can still double-tap the home screen to bring up your playback controls, but you cannot do much else.

To wake up your iPod again, press the Home button once, and then swipe to unlock.

Powering Your iPod Off and On

To power off your iPod, press and hold the Sleep/Wake button for about five seconds. The slider shown in Figure 3–7 appears. To power down, swipe the slider to the right. To cancel, either tap Cancel or just wait about ten seconds; the iPod automatically returns you to the previous screen if you don't power down within that time.

Figure 3–7. *This screen appears after you hold down the Sleep/Wake and Home buttons for about five seconds. To power down, simply swipe the slider from left to right. Your iPod shuts itself down and powers off. To power back on, press and hold the Sleep/Wake button for about two seconds, until you see the white Apple icon.*

When your iPod is powered off, it ceases to function. You cannot listen to music. You cannot surf the Internet. You must power your iPod back on for it to do these things.

To power on your iPod, press and hold the Sleep/Wake button for two to three seconds. Release the button when you see the white Apple icon. The iPod starts up and returns you to the home screen automatically.

Rebooting Your iPod

At times, you may need to reboot your iPod. The most common reason for doing this is that you have installed new software using third-party hacking tools.

Although you can reboot just by powering down and then powering back up, Apple provides a much easier way do this. Press and hold both the Home and Sleep/Wake buttons for 10 to 12 seconds. Ignore the power-off indicator (shown in Figure 3–7), and keep holding both buttons until the white Apple logo appears. Once it shows up, release both buttons, and let the iPod finish its reboot. You will return to the home screen automatically.

iPod Recovery Mode and Restoration

Your iPod has a secret setting called *recovery mode*. It's used to tell iTunes to restore your iPod to its factory-fresh condition. It's also used by a number of third-party hacking programs to gain access to your complete iPod file system so you can install software, wallpaper, and so forth.

Do not enter recovery mode lightly. Once you've entered that mode, you cannot change your mind and return to normal iPod use. You must know what you're doing. After you're in recovery mode, you'll need to restore your iPod firmware in iTunes and refresh your iPod's contents from its most recent backup.

To enter recovery mode, press and hold both the Sleep/Wake and Home buttons for about 25 seconds, until you see the screen with the iTunes logo and the end of the USB connector. You may want to watch a clock so you know when 25 seconds have elapsed. It can feel a lot longer when your fingers start getting tired.

You can restore your iPod either from recovery mode or directly in iTunes. When you connect an iPod in recovery mode to your computer, iTunes detects it and asks you to proceed with the restore process. If you want to restore your iPod without manually setting recovery mode, connect the iPod to your computer and launch iTunes. In iTunes, select the iPod from the Devices category in the sources list. Choose the Settings tab, and then click Restore.

When restoring, iTunes walks you through the entire process, offering extensive feedback and refreshing your iPod to a clean firmware installation. When iTunes is finished, it prompts you to decide whether you want to use the most recent backup. Agree if you want to return the iPod to its most previously backed-up state, or disagree if you want to retain the iPod's factory-fresh settings.

The Home Screen

As discussed, when you turn on your iPod touch, you'll be presented with a lock screen. Depending on whether you have a passcode set on your iPod touch, you'll either swipe the "slide to unlock" bar and be presented with a numeric keypad (or keyboard if you are using an alphanumeric password) or be immediately taken to your iPod touch home screen.

The iPod touch home screen (see Figure 3–8) is the first page of apps you have on your iPod touch. The home screen, whose unofficial name is Springboard, provides application-launching abilities. Depending on how many apps you have, you may have several pages that will show in subsequent order when you swipe to the left. The iPod's home screen allows you to launch any application with a single tap.

Figure 3–8. *The iPod touch home screen*

> **TIP:** Since the home screen will be the first page you're taken to when you unlock your iPod touch, it makes sense to keep your most frequently used apps on the home screen for easy access.

From the top of the screen down, you'll see the following elements:

Status bar: A thin bar runs along the top of your iPod touch home screen. This status bar, shown in Figure 3–9, is visible on every page of your iPod touch home screen.

Figure 3–9. *The status bar*

The status bar can show many icons, but the standard layout you'll most likely see is the following. In the upper-left corner, you'll see the word *iPod* next to a Wi-Fi icon. The Wi-Fi icon shows that you are connected to a wireless hotspot and also displays the strength of your wireless signal. The current time is displayed in the middle of the status bar. On the right corner of the status bar is a battery meter icon.

The status bar can also show other status icons:

Airplane mode: An airplane icon designates that airplane mode is enabled. In airplane mode, Wi-Fi and Bluetooth are turned off. Other functions of your iPod touch are still available.

Padlock: A padlock icon tells you that your iPod touch is in orientation lock. We'll talk more about orientation lock in a bit.

Play: This icon, which looks like a triangle pointing to the right, indicates that a song, podcast, or audiobook is playing.

Location Services: This arrowhead-looking icon lets you know that a currently running app is using location services to determine your current location.

Apps page: Below the black status bar is a series of app icons (see Figure 3–10). Each page can hold up to 16 apps or folders in addition to the ones found in the dock. As I'll discuss shortly, apps can be deleted and rearranged without the need to sync your iPod touch with iTunes.

Figure 3–10. *A page full of apps*

Page dots: Just above the app icons in the dock is a series of small, white dots (see Figure 3–11). This series of dots begins with a tiny magnifying glass, which I'll get to shortly. The dots next to the magnifying glass signify the number of pages of apps you have on your home screen. If you see five dots, that means you have five pages of apps. The brightest dot signifies the location of the page you are currently on among all the pages of apps.

Figure 3–11. *The dots signify how many pages of apps you have.*

The dock: At the bottom of the Home screen and every additional page of apps is a long, gray slate known as the dock (see Figure 3–12). The dock can contain up to four apps. No matter what page of apps you swipe to, the dock always displays the same apps. The advantage of this is if you have many pages of apps but frequently check your e-mail, you'll always have quick access to the Mail app if you've placed it in the dock — no matter what page of apps you're on

Figure 3–12. *The dock can hold between zero and four apps.*

Manipulating the Home Screen

You can interact with the iPod touch home screen in several ways:

Navigating the apps pages: If you are on the first page of apps, swiping a finger to the left reveals the next page of apps. Keep swiping to the left to proceed navigating through all of the app pages. To go back to the previous page of apps, swipe your finger to the right. On any page of apps but the first, pressing the Home button once takes you back to the first home screen.

> **NOTE:** Home screens move only left or right. Unlike in many apps, they do not move up or down.

Launching apps: To launch an app, tap its icon. To return to the home screen, press the round, physical home button on the iPod touch's bezel. The app continues to run in the background even though it is not visible.

Manipulating app icons: This is fun. Let's say you want to rearrange the icons on your home page but aren't near your computer to do it through the iPod touch's iTunes preferences page. Simply touch and hold any icon on the home screen. After a few seconds, you see all the icons on the page start to jiggle like they're little mounds of Jell-O (see Figure 3–13). Remove your finger from the app, and the icons continue to jiggle. While jiggling, you can touch and hold any app icon and then simply drag it to a new position on the page. You can also drag icons to and from the dock.

Figure 3–13. *Jiggling icons. In this example, the app Yelp is being moved.*

You can go ahead and swipe to a new page of apps while they are all jiggling and rearrange the apps on that page. You can also transfer apps between pages. Simply touch and hold the app you'd like to move to a different page, and drag it toward the side of the screen where the page is located. After a brief pause, the next page will automatically swipe over, and you can drop the app anywhere you want it. If that page is already full of 16 apps, the app in the lower-right corner will be pushed to the next page automatically.

> **NOTE:** If your dock already has four apps on it, you must remove an app first before adding a new one to the dock. Unlike with home pages, apps in the dock will not automatically be pushed to a new page if you try to add a new app to a full dock.

Creating folders of apps: In Chapter 2 we told you how to create folders full of apps on your iPod touch using iTunes, but you can also create folders of apps right on your iPod. Simply touch and hold an app icon until all the apps are jiggling (see Figure 3–13). Once they are, drag an app onto another app icon and hold it there. After a second or two, an app folder appears. Drop the app inside the folder so it appears next to the app icon you held it over (see Figure 3–14).

Figure 3–14. *Creating a folder full of apps*

You can arrange the apps in this new folder any way you want. You can also name the folder whatever you want. One cool thing Apple did was give the folder the ability to guess the name you want it to be. In the example in Figure 3–14, I created a folder with two games inside. The iPod touch knew both apps were games and appropriately named the folder Games. You can always change the name of the folder, however. Tap anywhere outside the folder to return to the normal apps screen. Drag any app to an existing folder to add it to that folder.

Folders appear as gray boxes with multiple app icons inside (see Figure 3–15). Folders can contain up to 12 applications, and you can have up to 20 folders on a page (16 on a page plus 4 in the dock). To open a folder, tap it, and its contents expand while the rest of the outside app icons are grayed out (see Figure 3–15). To exit a folder, tap anywhere outside of it.

Figure 3–15. *Left, an apps page with two folders, Games and Travel. Right, the same apps page with the Travel folder open.*

Removing apps: In Chapter 2 I told you how to remove apps from your iPod touch using iTunes. You can also remove an app from the iPod touch right on the device. To do this, touch and hold any icon on the home screen, and wait for them all to begin jiggling like they did when you were rearranging apps (see Figure 3–13).

Notice how some of the apps have a little black-and-white *X* in their upper-left corner? Tapping that *X* deletes the app. Don't worry if you accidentally delete an app from your iPod touch. The apps are always stored in your iTunes library, and you can reinstall them at any time.

> **NOTE:** You cannot delete any Apple apps that were factory-installed on your iPod touch, such as Stocks, Mail, and so on. You can, however, delete Apple apps that you installed yourself, such iBooks and Remote.

To delete an app, touch the *X*. A dialog appears on the screen asking whether or not you want to delete the selected application. You'll also see a note saying that deleting the app "will also delete all of its data," as shown in Figure 3–16. *This is important!* If you've created a new document inside the app or achieved a new high score on a game and you delete the app before syncing it to iTunes, any new data associated with that app is deleted.

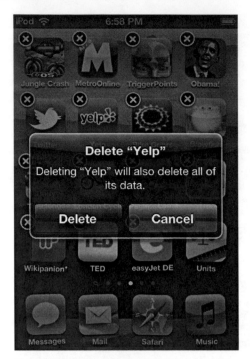

Figure 3–16. *The deletion warning*

NOTE: If you delete an app accidentally and need it back right away, but are not near your computer, use the iPod touch's built-in App Store app to download the app again. If it was a paid application, don't worry; you won't be charged a second time. Your iTunes account knows that you've already paid for it.

If you are sure you want to delete an app, go ahead and tap the Delete button. If you've changed your mind, tap Cancel. When an app is deleted, all the other apps on the page shift to fill the space of the deleted app.

Multitasking and Managing Background Apps

With iOS 4, Apple introduced multitasking features to the iPod touch. Multitasking means you can have more than one app running at a time. In other words, you might be browsing the Web in Safari, and in the background you can have an instant messaging app running. Even though your entire iPod touch screen is devoted to the Safari app, you are still online and notified of new instant messages in the IM app.

To leave an app, press the Home button to return to the home screen, and then find the next app that you want to launch and tap its icon. With the multitasking features built into iOS 5, you don't have to return to the home screen every time you want to launch a different app. Now, no matter what app you are in, pressing the Home button twice displays a row of all the apps that are currently running in the background (see Figure 3–17). These apps are referred to as *background* apps. Any app you have launched on the iPod since turning it on will run as a background app until you close the app for good (discussed in a few pages). This background app bar is a very handy feature, but there is one small caveat: all the apps you see there might not actually be running in the background. Apple also uses this bar to show recently used apps, so even after a reboot, you might see several apps in the bar even though you have not launched them since rebooting.

Figure 3–17. *Some apps that are running in the background while I am in the Weather app*

In Figure 3–17, you can see that I'm in the Weather app. By double-pressing the Home button, the multitasking bar slides the screen up, and you can scroll through all your other background apps. To see more currently running background apps, flick the row of apps left or right. To quickly switch to another background app, tap its icon, and it swaps places with the current app you are in (see Figure 3–18).

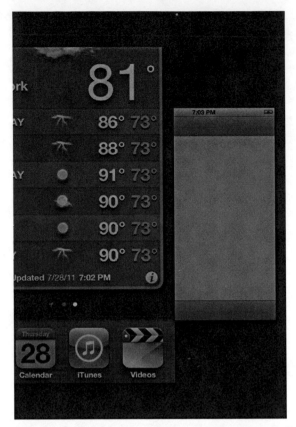

Figure 3–18. *The Weather app swapping places with the Calendar app via the iPod touch's multitasking features*

Quitting an App

The iPod touch's home screen allows you to launch any application with a single tap. Once you've launched that app, it remains open in the background even if you return to the Home screen. To quit the app, double-press the Home button to open the background apps bar. Swipe through the row of apps until you've found the one you want to quit. Now touch and hold the app's icon until it and the other apps in the bar start to jiggle. You'll notice red dots with a white minus sign have appeared in the corner of all the apps in the bar (see Figure 3–19). Tap the red dot to quit the app. To reopen the app, you'll need to launch it from the home screen again.

Quitting applications instead of letting them remain open in the background lowers your CPU usage, keeps your iPod slightly cooler, and puts a little less strain on your battery.

Remember how I mentioned that Apple also uses this background multitasking bar to show recently used apps? Well, if the app isn't running, tapping the minus sign removes the recently used app from the bar. The way Apple has implemented this, you can't really tell which apps are actually running and which are just recently used apps just by looking at the bar.

Figure 3–19. *Tap the red and white minus sign to close an app for good.*

Force Quitting an App

If for some reason an app hangs and your iPod touch becomes unresponsive, press and hold the Sleep/Wake button on the top of your iPod touch. Hold it until the red slider appears (Figure 3–7), release the Sleep/Wake button, and then press and hold the Home button. If all goes correctly, you should be returned to your home screen and can try launching the problematic app again.

> **TIP:** A Back button appears in the upper-left corner of many iPod touch app. Tap this button to return to the previous screen in the app. This is different from pressing the Home button. The Back button moves you between screens within an app. The Home button leaves an app and returns you to the home screen.

Orientation

I mentioned the iPod touch accelerometer earlier in this chapter. In most images of the iPod touch, you'll notice that it is in portrait orientation with the physical Home button at the bottom of the device. Some apps let you hold the iPod touch in either a portrait or landscape orientation. Using different orientations to view an app can increase the usability of the app, depending on what you are doing. Using Safari in landscape mode, for example, provides a wider screen for reading a web page (Figure 3–20).

Figure 3–20. *Safari in landscape and portrait modes*

You've already read that to change orientation, you tilt the iPod to one side or the other. If the app has a landscape mode, it rotates on the screen to enter that mode automatically. The ability to change orientation is nice—except for those times when the orientation changes and you don't want it to, such as when you are reading a book on your iPod touch while laying in bed. A constantly shifting orientation can easily interrupt your reading enjoyment.

Thankfully, Apple has given users the ability to lock the iPod's screen orientation. You can only lock the iPod's orientation into portrait mode, however. To do this, double-press the Home button so the screen shifts up, just like it does when you are quickly changing between background apps. In the space below the dock, swipe your finger left to right until the rewind, play, and forward buttons appear (see Figure 3–21). Next to the rewind button is the orientation lock button. Tap it once to lock the orientation. Unwanted screen rotation solved! Tap the lock button again to disable orientation lock.

Figure 3–21. *The orientation button unlocked (left) and locked (right)*

Spotlight Search

At this point I've explained everything the iPod touch home screen offers, save for one very important feature. Earlier I mentioned a small gray magnifying glass icon next to the row of dots that represent pages of apps (see Figure 3–22). This magnifying glass icon represents the iPod touch's powerful search feature, named Spotlight.

Figure 3–22. *The Spotlight magnifying glass icon (circled) is at the bottom of every home page*

To access Spotlight, swipe to the right of the first page of your home screen. If you are on the first home screen, you can also press the Home button once to be taken to the Spotlight page. You'll be taken to a page that displays a small, white search field at the top with the words *Search iPod* in it. At the bottom of the page is the on-screen keyboard.

Begin typing a search query into the search field, and the space between the search field and the keyboard begins populating with results (see Figure 3–23).

Figure 3–23. *The Spotlight search results page*

At this time, Spotlight isn't as powerful as it can be. If you own a Mac, you know that Spotlight is capable of searching within documents, not just by a document's file name. Currently, Spotlight is only capable of searching the following:

Contacts: First, last, and company names.

Mail: To, From, and Subject fields.

Calendar: Event titles, invites, and locations.

iPod: Song names, artists, and albums. Podcast and audiobook titles and names.

Notes: Although Spotlight can't search the text in the body of an e-mail message, it can search the text in a note from the Notes app.

To select a result, tap it, and you'll be taken to the document or file in the app that the result is found in. At the bottom of the Spotlight results you have the option to search the Web for your query or search Wikipedia. Tapping either option opens the Safari web browser and displays either the default search engine page or the Wikipedia search results page.

Although Spotlight is a nice feature, it does have some limitations. Perhaps the biggest limitation is that you can't search for text in the body of an e-mail. Also, Spotlight isn't smart enough to recognize misspellings, so anything that is mistyped in a note or e-mail subject won't be found.

> **NOTE:** If you have dozens and dozens of apps, instead of swiping through all the home screen pages, just go to Spotlight and search for the name of the app. When the app icon appears, tap it to launch it.

Spotlight Settings

Go to **Settings ➤ General ➤ Spotlight Search** to find a few options for Spotlight. Here you can deselect items to eliminate them from Spotlight search (for example, tap Music to deselect it so song names won't show up when you're searching). You can also use the grip icon to the right of the screen to rearrange the order that search groupings appear in. The grip icon is a set of three horizontal lines that indicates you can drag something up or down in a list.

The iPod Keyboard

Let's start talking about the iPod keyboard by quoting verbatim from one my earliest iPhone e-mail messages (the iPhone uses the same keyboard as the iPod):

> *I would like to sat that the iPhone has turned me into a tupong expert, but that would ne far far far from the truth. The fact is that I type on the iPhone like a cow, working with the iPhone keyboard is norm hard and frustrating. Foe all this Rhine is supposed to be smart and press five, I find that in actual use it is slow and mistake-prone. Will my accuracy improve as I get more experience? Probably. Will my fingers become smaller and less oqlike?almost certainly nor.*

I sent that e-mail within the first 24 hours of iPhone ownership, and I was feeling pretty down on the whole iPhone/iPod keyboard thing. Within a week, however, my typing developed from horrible to readable and, within another week, from readable to pretty darn good.

Bluetooth Keyboard Support

You can use a physical Bluetooth keyboard with an iPod touch. To do so, go to **Settings ➤ General ➤ Bluetooth**, and make sure Bluetooth is turned on. Next, make sure your Bluetooth keyboard is turned on as well. Once it is, it should show up in the devices list on the Bluetooth settings page. Enter the pairing passphrase you see on your iPod touch screen using the Bluetooth keyboard. Once you do so, your Bluetooth keyboard is all set up and ready to use.

Most people won't be using a Bluetooth keyboard with their iPod, but if you find yourself doing a lot of typing, a Bluetooth keyboard might be just the thing for you. With it, you can use some physical keyboard shortcuts such as Cmd+A to select all the text and Cmd+C to copy the selected text or Cmd+V to paste the selected text.

iPod Keyboard Basics

In this section, I'll look at using the on-screen keyboard in Apple's Notes app that comes on every iPod touch. I've opened Notes and clicked the + button in the upper-right corner to create a new note. The keyboard automatically appears at the bottom of the iPod touch screen (see Figure 3–24).

> **NOTE:** Using the keyboard in portrait orientation gives you a smaller keyboard but more space to see what you're typing on the screen. If you switch to landscape orientation, you'll have a larger keyboard but less space to see what you've typed. Play around to see what works best for you.

Though Apple has outdone itself in designing the iPod touch's keyboard, many people still think it's the hardest thing to get used to on their new device. People are so used to typing on physical keyboards that making the switch to a touchscreen keyboard can be difficult, but it does get much better over a relatively short amount of time. The keyboard gets easier to use the more you use it, not just because you get used to it, but because it has a secret.

The secret is that the keyboard, shown in Figure 3–24, is smart. It's so smart that it corrects for a lot of typos and misaligned fingers. It automatically capitalizes the start of sentences. It suggests corrections for misspelled words. It uses predictive technology to make it easier to hit the right keys. So, within a few weeks, you'll master the keyboard's quirks.

Figure 3–24. *The iPod keyboard grows easier to use with experience. Notice the Shift key (arrow pointing up) to the left of the Z key and the Backspace/Delete key (pentagram pointing left with an x in it) to the right of M key. The @123 key switches to a numbers and symbols layout. The Return key finalizes your changes. In some applications, a Return key lets you add carriage returns to your text.*

Here are some of the key technologies that make the iPod touch keyboard work:

Dictionary: The iPod touch has a built-in dictionary that learns frequently used words as you type (see Figure 3–25). It also picks up names and spellings from your address book. This means it gets better at guessing your intentions as it builds its data.

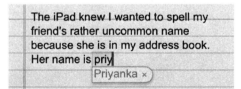

Figure 3–25. *An example of the iPod touch learning words and names from your contacts*

Automatic correction: As you type, the iPod touch looks for words similar to what you're typing and guesses them, placing the guess just below the word you're typing (see Figure 3–26). To accept the suggestion, just tap the spacebar, and the full word is inserted. If you don't want to use the suggested word, tap the X next to the suggested word.

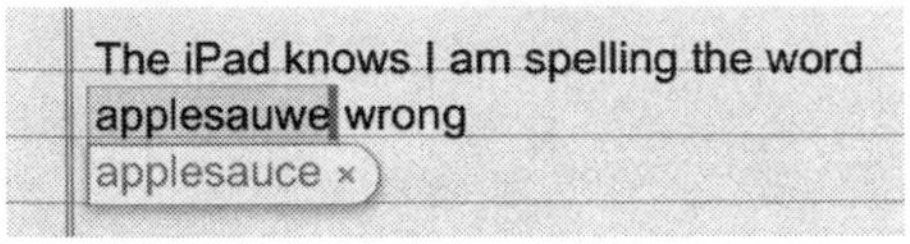

The iPad knows I am spelling the word
applesauwe wrong
applesauce ×

Figure 3–26. *An example of the iPod touch's autocorrection features*

Spell check: If you spell a word wrong or the iPod touch doesn't recognize it, a red line appears below the word. When you tap the word, one or more alternate spellings appear above it (see Figure 3–27). Simply tap the right word, and it inserts itself into the text.

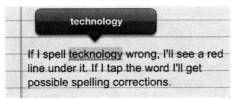

technology

If I spell tecknology wrong, I'll see a red line under it. If I tap the word I'll get possible spelling corrections.

Figure 3–27. *An example of the iPod touch's spell-check feature*

Predictive mapping: The iPod touch uses its dictionary to predict which word you're about to type. It then readjusts the keyboard response zones to make it easier for you to hit the right letters. Likely letters get bigger tap zones; unlikely letters get smaller ones.

More Keyboards

Thought the iPod touch had only one keyboard? Think again. It has more than a dozen (in different languages). It also has two other keyboards you'll frequently access from the primary keyboard on your screen.

On the primary keyboard (see Figure 3–28), you'll notice the .?123 key. Tapping the .?123 key switches your QWERTY keyboard into a numeric keyboard with further punctuation symbols and another keyboard modifier key labeled #+=.

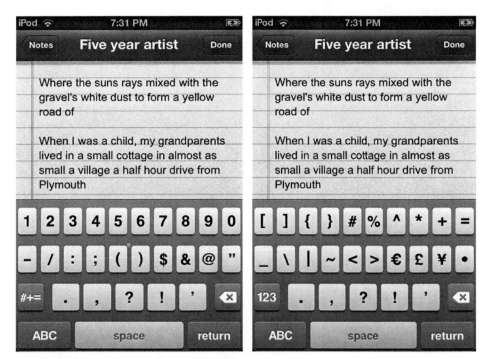

Figure 3–28. *The.?123 and the #+= keyboards*

Tapping the #+= key takes you to a third keyboard with more punctuation buttons. Tap the ABC button to return to the alphabetic keyboard.

Getting Started Typing

When you're new to the iPod, start by typing slowly. Pay attention to those confirmation pop-ups that appear every time you tap a key. I find it easiest to use my forefingers to type. Others prefer to use their thumbs. Whatever method you use, make sure to go at a pace that allows you to keep track of what you're typing and make corrections as you go. Here are a few typing how-tos:

Accepting or rejecting automatic corrections: The iPod displays suggested corrections just below the word you're typing, as shown in Figure 3–29. To accept the suggestion, tap the spacebar. (You don't need to finish typing the word; the iPod puts it in there for you.) To decline the correction, tap the word. The iPod will not make a substitution, even when you press the spacebar.

Using the spyglass: While you're typing, you can adjust the cursor by using the iPod's built-in spyglass feature, as shown in Figure 3–30. Hold your finger somewhere in the text area until the spyglass appears. Then use the magnified view to drag the cursor exactly where you need it.

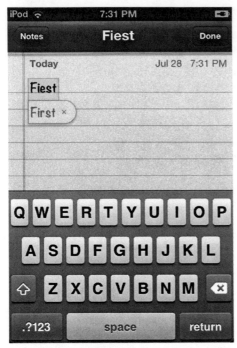

Figure 3–29. *The iPod's suggestions appear just below the word you type. Tap the spacebar to accept the suggestion, or tap the word you're typing to disable automatic correction for that word.*

Summoning the keyboard: To open the keyboard, tap in any editable text area.

Dismissing the keyboard: There is no standard way to dismiss the keyboard, but most programs offer a Done button that indicates you're finished typing. In Safari, press Go rather than Done.

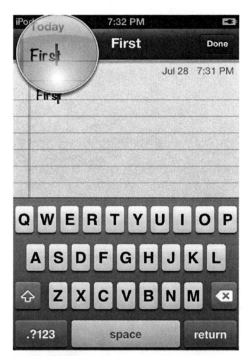

Figure 3–30. *The iPod's spyglass offers a magnified view that makes it easy to position the cursor exactly where you need it to be.*

iPod touch Typing Tricks

Once you get the hang of the keyboard, the iPod touch offers several other ways to make typing easier. This section describes a few of these handy iPod touch typing tricks.

Contractions

When you want to type a contraction like *can't* or *shouldn't*, don't bother putting in the apostrophe. The iPod touch is smart enough to guess that *cant* is *can't*. (Of course, if you're typing about the British Thieves' language, make sure to tap the word itself to decline the change from the noun to the contraction.)

When you're typing in a word like *we'll*, where the uncontracted *well* is a common word, add an extra *l*. The iPod touch corrects *welll* to *we'll* and *shelll* to *she'll* (Figure 3–31).

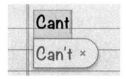

Figure 3–31. *Cant becomes Can't.*

> **TIP:** Other contraction tricks include *itsa*, which gets corrected to *it's*, and *weree*, which gets corrected to *we're*.

Punctuation

At the end of a sentence, tap the punctuation key, and then tap the item you want to use. If you plan to use only one item of punctuation at a time, such as a comma or period, save time by dragging. Drag from the punctuation key (it appears as .?123 in some applications and @123 in others) to the item you want to include. When you start the drag at .?123 or @123, the iPod switches momentarily to the numbers and punctuation view. After selecting your item, the keyboard automatically bounces back to the alphabet.

Another punctuation trick for the end of sentences is to tap the punctuation key, then tap the item you want to use (such as a question mark or period), and finally tap the spacebar. The iPod is smart enough to recognize the end of a sentence and put you back in alphabet mode. During normal typing, you can also double-tap the spacebar to add a period followed by a space. This double-tap trick is controlled in your settings via Settings ➤ General ➤ Keyboard ➤ "." Shortcut.

Accents

Tap and hold any keyboard letter to view inflected versions of that letter. For example, tapping and holding *n* presents the options of adding *n*, *ń*, or *ñ*, as shown in Figure 3–32. This shortcut makes it much easier to type foreign words.

To select a non-English keyboard, go to Settings ➤ General ➤ International ➤ Keyboards, and choose from your iPod's long list of foreign-language variations.

This accents trick also works with other keyboards. For example, when entering a URL in Safari, press and hold the .com button to bring up the .net, .edu, .org, and .us buttons.

Figure 3–32. *Press and hold any key to view its common international alternatives.*

Caps Lock

To enable the Caps Lock function, go to **Settings ➤ General ➤ Keyboard**. When this function is enabled, you can double-tap the Shift key to toggle the lock on and off.

Word Deletion

When you press and hold the Delete key, the iPod touch starts off by deleting one letter and then the next. But if you hold it for longer than about a line of text, it switches to word deletion and starts removing entire words at a time.

Autocapitalization

Autocapitalization means the iPod touch automatically capitalizes the word at the beginning of a sentence. So, you can type *the day has begun*, and the iPod touch is smart enough to capitalize *the*, as in *The day has begun*. This means you don't need to worry about pressing the Shift key at the beginning of every sentence or even when you type *i*, because *i went to the park* will become *I went to the park*. Enable or disable autocapitalization in **Settings ➤ General ➤ Keyboard**.

Shortcuts

iOS 5 allows you to specify text shortcuts that expand into full words or phrases. For example, typing "omw" expands into "On my way!" You can add any kind of text shortcuts you want. Go to **Settings ➤ General ➤ Keyboard ➤ Add New Shortcut**, and then type in the phrase you'd like to add and its shortcut text. Adding your own shortcuts can save time from retyping common phrases used in e-mail or text messages.

Copy and Paste

Apple has created an easy and intuitive way to select a word or block of words, copy them, and then paste them into another location.

Let's copy some text found on a web page in iPod touch's Safari web browser. Before you can copy a word, you'll need to select it. To do that, press and hold your finger over a word. A black contextual menu pops up that gives you Select and Select All options. Select highlights just the single word, while Select All highlights all the words on the page. No matter which you choose, you'll be presented with a grab point at the beginning and end of the selected text (see Figure 3–33). These grab points allow you to adjust which text is selected.

Figure 3–33. *Grab points allow you to select a single word, a sentence, or a whole paragraph to be copied.*

> **NOTE:** If you've selected text to copy in an editable document, you'll see a contextual menu that says Cut, Copy, or Paste. Selecting Cut removes the text. Selecting Copy copies it, and if you already have text copied, you'll be able to paste it over your current selection.

Once you have selected your text, you'll see another contextual menu that says Copy. Tapping Copy will copy the text and make it available in any app that supports text input.

Now let's go back to our note in the Notes app. To paste text you copied from Safari into your note, simply press and hold your finger on the screen until the spyglass pops up. Use the spyglass to adjust the cursor to the location where you want to insert the copied text and let go. Another contextual menu pops up that gives you three options: Select, Select All, and Paste (see Figure 3–34). Tap Paste, and your copied text is instantly inserted.

Figure 3–34. *Simply tap Paste, and your text is inserted automatically.*

Undo and Redo

If you want to undo your last command, such as pasting text, shake your iPod, and the Undo pop-up appears; in this case, it will say Undo Paste (see Figure 3–35). Tap it to undo, which in this case would remove the pasted text.

Shake the iPod again to bring up the Redo pop-up (see Figure 3–35). Tapping Redo Paste repastes the text you just undid.

Figure 3–35. *Shake your iPod to bring up the Undo and Redo pop-up commands.*

Dictionary Lookup

iOS 5 allows you to look up any word in a Note, e-mail, or web page. Select the word and then tap Define from the contextual menu pop-up. The Dictionary panel displays a definition of the word (Figure 3–36). Click the Done button to exit the Dictionary panel.

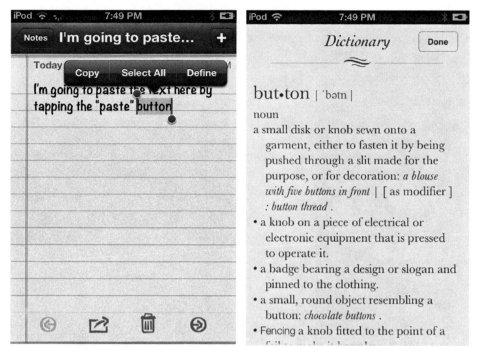

Figure 3–36. *Looking up words with the built-in Dictionary.*

iPod Typing Test

Track the progress of your iPod touch keyboard mastery with one of the iPhone-style typing tests available on the Internet. (Even though they are labeled for iPhones, they work great on your iPod as well.)

Google for *iPhone typing tests wpm*, and you'll find any number of sites offering a words-per-minute test. Load one of these into Safari on your iPod, and you're ready to see how your typing has improved.

Notification Center

The Notification Center is a central location where you can see all of your notifications in one place. These include new e-mails, reminders, tweets, messages, Facebook posts, and more. Basically, if an app can send you any kind of notification, it'll appear in the Notification Center. You can see what the Notification Center looks like in Figure 3–37.

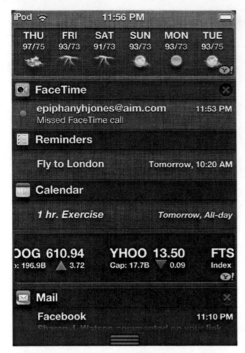

Figure 3–37. *The Notification Center*

In Figure 3–37 you can see the Notification Center is displaying the weather and a stock ticker, as well as select notifications I have set up to be visible in the Notification Center. In this case, those notifications are FaceTime calls, Reminders, Calendar events, and Mail messages.

To access the Notification Center, swipe down with one finger from the top of your iPod touch's screen. It doesn't matter where you are; you can be on a Home screen, in an app or game, or even on the iPod's lock screen. Wherever you are, just swipe down with one finger, and the Notification Center appears.

To scroll through the Notification Center, swipe up or down with your finger. Tap any notification in the Notification Center to go directly to the app that sent the notification. For example, in Figure 3–37, tapping the FaceTime missed call notification launches the FaceTime app and initiates a return call. Tapping the stock ticker takes you to the Stocks app. Tapping an e-mail notification takes you right to that e-mail. Pretty cool, huh?

To close the Notification Center, touch the three grab bars at the bottom of its screen and swipe up.

Types of Notifications

There are many types of notifications in iOS 5 on the iPod touch. They all perform the same task (notifying you of an event), but they all notify you in a different way.

Figure 3–38. *The banner type of notification*

Banners: Banners appear at the top of your screen and go away automatically after a few seconds. They're a short visual cue that allows you to see you have a notification without interrupting your work. The banner notification in Figure 3–38 tells me I've just received an e-mail from "MacGP" and the subject of the e-mail is "Manuscript offer."

Alerts: Alerts are more abrupt than banners. An alert is a pop-up dialog box that requires you to take action before the alert will disappear. You can see an example of an alert in Figure 3–16.

Badges: Badges are red icons that appear in the corner of an app icon. Badges always contain numbers. For example, in Figure 3–8 the "1" badge on the Mail icon means there is one new e-mail waiting.

Sounds: Sounds are audible notifications of an event. You might head a "ding!" when you receive a new e-mail, for example.

Now that you are familiar with the types of notifications, let's look at how to configure them for each app and set up which notifications appear in the Notification Center.

Setting Up Notifications and the Notification Center

To configure notifications, go to **Settings ➤ Notifications** (Figure 3–39). You're presented with a list of all the apps that offer notifications. Beneath an app's name are labels displaying what types of notifications the app is sending you. As you can see, a single app can send multiple types of notifications.

Figure 3–39. *Notifications settings*

The notifications settings screen allows you to sort the order of the apps that appear in your Notification Center. Tap By Time to show the most recent notification at the top of the Notification Center. If you select Manually, you can then tap the Edit button and drag the apps up or down the list. The order that you put them in is identical to the order that they appear in the Notification Center.

The Notifications setting screen also displays two lists. The first is In Notification Center, and the second is Not in Notification Center. Apps appearing in the In Notification Center list appear in the Notification Center when you swipe down from the top of your screen. Apps appearing in the Not In Notification Center list still send you notifications; they just won't appear in the Notification Center list.

There's an advantage to not having all your notifications show in the Notification Center: it reduces clutter. You might not care to see all the Twitter @mentions you've received in your Notification Center, but you may want to still have badge notifications enabled for the Twitter app.

Each app has its own notifications settings. To access them, tap the name of the app in the notification settings (Figure 3–39). The app's individual notification settings appear (Figure 3–40).

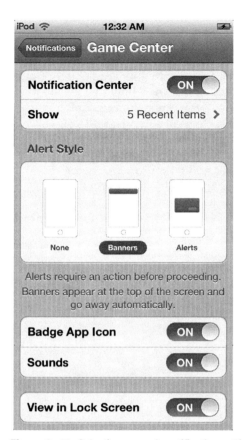

Figure 3–40. *Selecting an app's notification settings*

Figure 3–40 shows the notification settings for the Game Center app. These notification settings are a good representation of the settings you'll find for other apps, but the settings can vary from app to app.

Notification Center: Toggle this to show or hide the app notifications (Game Center in this case) in the Notification Center.

Show: select how many notifications from the app to show in the Notification Center.

Alert style: Choose from between none, banners, or alerts.

Badge App Icon: Toggle this to show or hide red badge notifications.

Sounds: Toggle this to hear/mute audible notifications.

View in Lock Screen: When set to on, an app's notifications appear in the Notification Center on the iPod touch lock screen. If this is set to app, the app's notifications will not appear in the Notification Center when viewed from the lock screen but do appear in the Notification Center when viewed from elsewhere in iOS. Apple gives users this option in order to hide sensitive information (such as e-mails) from prying eyes.

Summary

This chapter has explored most of the ways you can interact with your iPod touch, from taps to buttons to pinches. You've read about the touchscreen and how to communicate with it. You've discovered how to access your home screen, lock it, and rearrange its icons. You've explored your iPod touch's General settings, and you've learned tips and tricks for using the iPod touch's virtual keyboard and setting accessibility options. Finally, you've explored iOS 5's Notification Center. In short, you've been introduced to many of the basic ways you and your iPod touch can communicate with each other. Here are a few key lessons for you to carry away from this chapter:

Chapter 4

Browsing with Wi-Fi and Safari

Every iPod touch has Wi-Fi capability. With it, you can connect to the Internet and view web pages directly on your iPod.

The iPod's mobile version of Safari is a near twin to its computer-based version that runs on both Mac and Windows. The touchscreen displays web pages just as their designers intended. Web sites look like web sites and not like approximations of web sites. When it comes to browsing, there's nothing else like Safari in the handheld market.

In this chapter, you'll discover how to get the most from Safari with all its awesome full-browser powers. You'll learn how to navigate to pages, manage bookmarks, and use both portrait and landscape orientations. You'll also discover some great finger-tap shortcuts, useful Safari web sites, and Safari's handy Reader and Reading List functions.

NOTE: Wi-Fi is a wireless technology. Your iPod touch uses three kinds of Wi-Fi networking technologies: 802.11b, 802.11g, and 802.11n. These three are the most standard connection types available. While there are many minute technical differences between B, G, and N, the primary difference is speed. B is the slowest, followed by G, with N being the fastest.

Getting Started with Wi-Fi

With your iPod's Wi-Fi, you can connect to web sites such as YouTube, the iTunes Wi-Fi Music Store, and so on, and you can pretty much do everything over the Internet that you desire. Read on to learn more about setting up your iPod and connecting to a Wi-Fi network.

Checking Your Wi-Fi Connection

Before you use Safari, you need to have a Wi-Fi connection. You cannot connect to the Internet without it.

You can tell in an instant whether your Wi-Fi connection is up and running. Look at the very top-left corner of your screen. When you see the three semicircle-like arcs next to the word *iPod*, as shown in Figure 4–1, you have a live connection. When the arcs are more blue (and less black or gray), you have the strongest connection possible. Having three blue arcs is ideal. Seeing one or more black—or worse, gray—arcs means that your connection is weak. Try moving closer to the Wi-Fi source. Make sure that you're not obstructing the antenna. Remove your fingers from around the Wi-Fi antenna on your iPod. The small, black rectangle on the back of your iPod shows you where that antenna lives. That's the bit you want to avoid blocking with your hands and body.

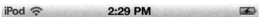

Figure 4–1. *The three arcs shown here indicate a strong Wi-Fi connection. Blue arcs indicate the strongest connection. Black arcs mean a weak connection. Very light gray arcs show the worst connection.*

> **NOTE:** If you use a mobile Wi-Fi hotspot such as the Sprint/Verizon MiFi or a tethering with a mobile phone, your iPod touch will probably show full arcs, but you'll want to check your connection to the Internet on the other hotspot.

Choosing a Wi-Fi Network

If your iPod shows no Wi-Fi service, you'll need to connect to a local network. Navigate to the **Settings ➤ Wi-Fi screen**, shown in Figure 4–2. From here, you can enable your Wi-Fi service and specify whether you want your iPod to search for local networks.

To connect to any network, set Wi-Fi to ON. When Wi-Fi is switched to ON, your iPod scans the immediate area and lists all active networks. When it is OFF, your iPod shuts down Wi-Fi service and does not actively seek connections.

You can connect to any Wi-Fi network listed by tapping its name. As with the network strength indicator in your iPod title bar, the arcs next to each network indicate the strength of its signal.

Figure 4–2. *Set Wi-Fi to ON to connect to local networks. The lock icon next to a network name indicates that you must use authentication to connect.*

Tap the blue circled > icons to see information about each network, including IP addresses, Domain Name System (DNS) server information, and so forth. You'll find all the standard kinds of information you would expect to see on any computer client for any Wi-Fi network. The iPod touch offers the same information and capabilities in a handheld package.

Connecting to a Protected Network

When you see a lock next to the network name on the Wi-Fi Networks settings screen (Figure 4–2), this shows you that the network is protected and requires authentication. When you select a protected network, you must log in to the network before you can use it.

Figure 4–3 shows a typical authentication screen. Enter the network password, and click Join. If you succeed, just go ahead and start using your connection. If you fail, make sure your password is up-to-date and that you typed it correctly. Be aware that you will only briefly see the last letter that you just typed before it changes into a black dot. This is a security feature so people can't read your password over your shoulder. Use extra care, and check the keyboard feedback carefully as you type.

Figure 4–3. *This password-entry screen allows you to join networks using WEP, WPA, or WPA2 authentication.*

You can also add an unlisted network to your iPod network list. Tap Other on your main Wi-Fi settings screen. Enter the network name, choose the kind of encryption in use (None, WEP, WPA, WPA2, WPA Enterprise, WPA2 Enterprise), and then tap Join.

> **NOTE:** The WEP, WPA, and WPA2 acronyms refer to three common data encryption standards, listed in order of their security and strength from weakest to strongest: Wired Equivalent Privacy, Wi-Fi Protected Access, and Wi-Fi Protected Access version 2. Each standard was created to enhance wireless network security. Enterprise WPA encryption is used in business settings.

Asking to Join a Network

Your Wi-Fi Networks settings screen offers an option at the very bottom that prompts you to "Ask to Join Networks," as shown in Figure 4–4. This option allows your iPod touch to automatically scan the local area and search for available networks. When it finds one, it offers to join it—with your permission. If you've already joined that network before, it automatically goes ahead and does so again.

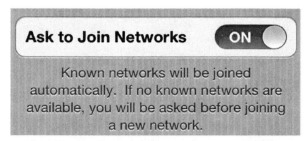

Figure 4–4. *The Ask to Join Networks feature facilitates rejoining known networks and searching for networks in areas where you haven't previously made a connection.*

This option is both a bonus and a possible security problem. On one hand, it's extremely convenient to join networks you already know about and trust. On the other hand, airports and other high-traffic transit areas are known for offering free Wi-Fi services that are easily pirated. Another possible threat comes from Wi-Fi traffic sniffers (also called *packet sniffers*), which are devices that track your online activity while you're connected via Wi-Fi. Both services that masquerade as official service providers and Wi-Fi traffic sniffers are designed to compromise your security and might endanger personal information and passwords. Fortunately, such exploits are rare.

In the end, the decision of when and whether to enable the Ask to Join Networks feature is up to you. For the most part, places like Starbucks and Panera Bread cafes and many airports offer safe connections, but be aware that your iPod activity *can* be tracked.

Getting Started with the Safari Web Browser

Once you're assured of a strong Wi-Fi connection, tap the Safari application icon to open the program. It's the icon on your home screen marked with a white compass on a blue background (see Figure 4–5). The Safari application launches and opens a new Internet browser window.

Figure 4–5. *The Safari icon*

Many elements of the Safari window may look familiar, especially to anyone experienced using web browsers. Familiar items include the address bar, the reload icon, the search field, and the history navigation arrows. Figure 4–6 shows a typical Safari browser window in portrait and landscape modes.

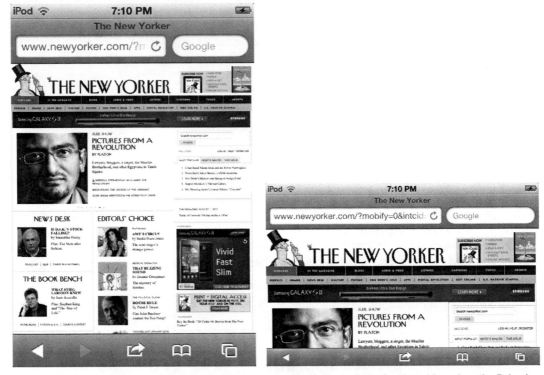

Figure 4–6. *The Safari browser window displays many familiar features, including the address bar, the Reload button, and the History button. Portrait orientation (left) allows you to see further down the page, while landscape (right) provides a wider page view.*

Here are interactive elements you'll find arranged around the screen and what they do:

Address bar: Use the address bar at the top center of the Safari window to enter a new web address (URL).

Reload button: The arrow bent in a semicircle to the right in the address bar is the Reload button. Tap it to refresh the current screen.

Stop button: As a page loads, Safari replaces the Reload button with a small *X* (you cannot see this in Figure 4–6). If you change your mind after navigating to a page, tap this button. It stops the current page from loading any further.

Search field: This is the white field with the word *Google* in it next to the address bar. Tap this field to enter your search query. You can also change your default search provider to Yahoo! Search or Microsoft's Bing using a process I'll describe shortly.

History buttons: Located at the bottom of the screen, the two triangles, facing left and right, navigate through your page history. When grayed out, you haven't yet created a history. The arrows turn from gray to white once you start browsing, and you can move back and forth through your history to the previous and next pages. Each page maintains its own history.

Share button: Found just to the right of the history buttons, this button with an arrow breaking out of a box adds the current page to your bookmark collection as well as gives you other sharing options. You can read more about bookmark creation and management in the "Working with Bookmarks" section later in this chapter.

> **NOTE:** You cannot use the History button to go back to a page you were viewing in another window. Use the Pages button to select another window, and then use the arrows there to navigate through that page history.

Bookmarks button: Tap the book-shaped icon to open your Bookmarks screen.

Pages button: The button at the bottom right that looks like two squares superimposed on one another allows you to open the page-selection browser and select one of your Safari sessions. You can open up to eight browser windows at a time. With more than one session active, a number appears on this icon. It indicates how many sessions are in use. You can read more about viewing and adding pages in the "Working with Pages" section later in this chapter.

Safari lets you do all the normal things you expect to do in a browser. You can tap links and buttons, enter text into forms, and so forth. In addition, Safari offers iPod-specific features you won't find on your home computer; for example, tilting the iPod on its side moves the browser window from landscape to portrait orientation and back. The following how-to sections guide you through Safari's basic features.

> **NOTE:** Although Safari allows you to browse the Web in full resolution, some web sites detect that you're surfing with an iPod and (wrongly) present a lighter, mobile version of their web pages. This should change as the iPod's capabilities become better known and web sites become accustomed to receiving iPod touch visits.

Entering URLs

Tap the address bar to open the URL-entry screen, as shown in Figure 4–7. The navigation section appears at the top of your screen, and a keyboard opens from below. Between these, the screen dims, and you can still see part of the current page.

Figure 4–7. *The URL-entry screen allows you to enter the address that you want Safari to visit.*

Tap the white URL field, and use the keyboard to enter a new URL. Apple provides both the forward slash (/) and a .com key to help you type, but not a colon (:) key. Safari is smart enough to know about `http://`, so you don't need to type it each time.

> **TIP:** To access secure web pages, make sure to type the full address, including the `https://` prefix. Mobile Safari assumes any address without a prefix uses `http://`. By typing the full address including `https`, you make sure you connect to the right page.

When you're finished typing, tap Go, and Safari navigates to the address you've entered. To return to the browser screen without entering a new URL, tap Cancel instead.

As you type, Safari matches your keystrokes to its existing collection of bookmarks. The space between the top of the keyboard and the bottom of the URL field turns white and displays a list of possible matches. To select one, just tap it. Safari automatically navigates to the selected URL. This matching ability is much more useful in portrait orientation than in landscape orientation, because there's more space to view matches.

When entering URLs, you can use the tap-and-hold trick discussed in Chapter 2 to invoke the spyglass. Use the spyglass to move the insertion point and edit URLs to fix any mistakes made while typing.

> **TIP:** When you see a white *X* in a gray circle in a text-entry field, you can tap it to clear the field.

Searching the Web

A search bar appears just to the right of the address bar, as shown in Figure 4–8. Tap it to begin entering text into the URL field. As you do, search suggestions start to appear between the search field and the keyboard. To use a search suggestion, tap it—you don't need to finish typing the entire query. To start a search query of your own, tap the Search button next to the spacebar. Safari navigates to the search page of your selected search engine (for example, www.google.com) and searches for that term.

Figure 4–8. *Type in the search field for easy access to the Google, Yahoo!, or Bing search engines.*

If you would rather search with Yahoo! or Bing than Google, use Settings ➤ Safari to change your default search engine.

Searching for Text on a Web Page

Safari also allows you to search for specific text on a web page. To search for text, tap inside the Google search field and enter the word or words on the web page that you are looking for. Next, tap where is says On This Page (X Matches), as shown in Figure 4–8, and then tap the text you entered in the bottom of the search suggestion pop-up.

After tapping the Find command, Safari zooms into the section of the web page with the first occurrence of the text you are looking for and highlights it in yellow (see Figure 4–9). Then, using the search text bar at the bottom of the page, you can tap the arrow keys to find the next or previous instance of the text on the web page. Click Done to leave text search.

Figure 4–9. *Searching for text on a web page*

Entering Text

To edit a text entry (other than in the address bar), tap any text field on the currently displayed web page. Safari opens a new text-entry screen (Figure 4–10). Although this screen is superficially similar to the URL-entry screen (Figure 4–7), it presents a few differences, notably the new text-entry buttons in a black bar above the keyboard:

- A *Done* button hides the keyboard and returns you to the web page after you have entered your text.

- *Previous* and *Next* buttons search for other text fields on your web page so you can jump to them without having to tap into each new field. Simply enter text, tap Next, enter more text, and so forth.

- An *AutoFill* button that uses information from your address book card to fill in relevant information such as your name, phone number, and e-mail address. The AutoFill button saves you time.

To submit a form after you've entered all the text, tap the Go or Search button next to the spacebar instead of the Done button in the text-entry bar. This is like pressing the Enter or Return key on a computer.

Figure 4–10. *Entering text in text-entry fields on a web page. Note the new text-entry bar above the keyboard.*

Following Links

Hypertext links are used throughout the World Wide Web. Text links are marked with underlines and are usually a different color from the main text. Image links are subtler, but they can also move you to a new location.

Tap a link to navigate to a new web page or, for certain special links, to open a new e-mail message or view a map. When a link leads to an audio or video file that the iPod understands, it plays back that file. Supported audio formats include AAC, M4A, M4B, M4P, MP3, WAV, and AIFF. Video formats include H.264 and MPEG-4.

To preview a link's address, touch and hold the link for a second or two. A link screen will slide up, showing you the full URL. Below the URL you'll see four buttons, as shown in Figure 4–11:

Open: Opens the link in the current Safari window

Open in New Page: Opens the link in a new Safari page

Add to Reading List: Adds the selected page to your Reading List (discussed later in this chapter)

Copy: Copies the URL so you can paste it in another document later

Cancel: Returns you to the page you were just on

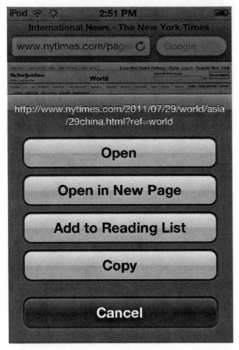

Figure 4–11. *Touch and hold either an image or a text link for a second or two to view the URL link screen. This bubble reveals the link's full URL and allows you to choose whether to continue following the link or to stop.*

Changing Orientation

One of the iPod's standout features is its flexible orientation support. When you turn your iPod on its side, it flips its display to match, as you can see in Figure 4–6. A built-in acceleration sensor detects the iPod's tilt and adjusts the display. Tilt back to vertical, and the iPod returns to portrait orientation. It takes just a second for the iPod to detect the orientation change and to update the display.

The iPod's landscape view offers a relatively wider display. This is particularly good for side-to-side tasks such as reading text. The wider screen allows you to use bigger fonts and view wider columns without scrolling sideways. The portrait view provides a longer presentation. This is great for reading web content with more narrow columns. You don't need to keep scrolling quite as much as you do in landscape view.

Whether in landscape or portrait view, Safari features work the same, including the same buttons in the same positions. In landscape view, you enter text using a wider, sideways keyboard. In portrait view, the smaller keyboard provides more space for you to view possible address completions while entering URLs.

Scrolling, Zooming, and Other Viewing Skills

Safari responds to the complete vocabulary of taps, flicks, and drags discussed in Chapter 2. You can zoom into pictures, pinch on columns, and more. Here's a quick review of the essential ways to interact with your screen:

Drag: Touch the screen, and drag your finger to reposition web pages. If you think of your iPod as a window onto a web page, dragging allows you to move the window around the web page.

Flick: When dealing with long pages, you can flick the display up and down to scroll rapidly. This is especially helpful when navigating through search engine results and news sites.

Double-tap: Double-tap any column or image to zoom in, automatically sizing it to the width of your display. Double-tap again to zoom back out. Use this option to instantly zoom into a web page's text. The iPod recognizes how wide the text is and perfectly matches that width.

Double-drag: When you need to scroll a text entry field in a form or a scrollable frame in a multiframe web site, use two fingers to drag at once. This tells your iPod to scroll just that page element and not the entire web page at once.

Pinch: Use pinching to manually zoom in or out. This allows you to make fine zoom adjustments as needed.

Tap: Tap buttons and links to select them. Use tapping to move from site to site and to submit forms.

Page down: When zoomed in on a column, double-tap toward the bottom of the screen while staying within the column. The page recenters around your tap. Make sure not to tap a link!

Jump to the top: Double-tap the very top of the screen (just below the time display) to pop instantly back to the top of the page.

Stop a scroll: After flicking a page to get it to scroll, you can tap the page at any time to stop that movement. Don't forget that you can also manually drag the screen display to reset the part you're viewing.

Working with Pages

Safari allows you to open up to eight concurrent browser sessions at once. To review your open windows, tap the Pages button (the two squares) at the bottom-right corner of your browser. Safari's pages viewer opens, as shown in Figure 4–12.

Figure 4–12. *The pages viewer allows you to select which browser session to display.*

This viewer allows you to interactively select a browser session:

- To select a window, scroll horizontally from one window to the next. The brightest dot along the line of dots shows which item you're currently viewing. In Figure 4–12, the viewer is showing the second of five open pages. Tap either the window or the Done button to select that window and display it full-screen.

- To close a window, tap the Close button—the red circle with an *X* in it at the top left of each page. The pages viewer slides the remaining pages into the gap left by the closed window.

- To add a new page, tap New Page. Safari creates a new session and opens a new, blank page. You can add up to eight pages, after which Safari complains, "Could not open a new page because there are too many pages open." If you see this message, tap OK to dismiss the alert.

Working with Bookmarks

One of the great things about the iPod is that it lets you take your world with you: contacts, calendars, and bookmarks. You don't need to reenter all your favorite pages on the iPod. It loads them whenever it syncs. The secret to this lies in iTunes.

As we discussed in Chapter 2, iTunes allows you to select the browser whose bookmarks you want to use. (Unfortunately, you cannot sync your iPod with Firefox—shame on Apple for that oversight.) To find these settings, tap the Info tab, and scroll toward the bottom of the window. Choose the bookmarks you want to sync to, and let iPod and iTunes handle the rest.

Selecting Bookmarks

Most standard bookmarks collection contains hundreds and hundreds of individual URLs. That's one reason I really appreciate the Safari's simple bookmarks browser, shown in Figure 4–13. It uses the same folders structure that you've set up on your personal computer. You can tap folders to open them and tap the Back button (top-left corner) to return to the parent folder. To access your bookmarks, tap the bookmarks icon in the lower part of any Safari window.

Identifying bookmarks is easy. Folders look like folders, and each bookmark is marked with a small, open book symbol. Tap one of these, and Safari takes you directly to the associated page.

Figure 4–13. *Use iPod Safari's interactive bookmarks navigation to locate and open your favorite bookmarks. This figure shows folders full of bookmarks (left) and individual bookmarks in those folders (right).*

Editing Bookmarks

As Figure 4–13 shows, an Edit button appears at the bottom left of the Bookmarks screen. Tap this to enter edit mode, as shown in Figure 4–14.

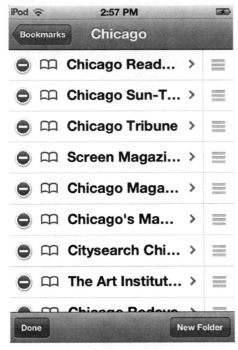

Figure 4–14. *Safari contains a built-in bookmark-management system that allows you to edit and reorder your bookmarks.*

Edit mode allows you to manage your bookmarks on your iPod just as you would on your personal computer:

Deleting bookmarks: Tap the red delete circle to the left of a bookmark to delete it. Tap Delete to confirm, or tap elsewhere on the screen to cancel.

Reordering bookmarks: Use the gray grab handles (the three lines on the far right) to move folders and bookmarks into new positions. Grab, drag, and then release.

Editing names: Tap the gray reveal arrow (the > symbol to the right of each name) to open the Edit Bookmark or Edit Folder screen. Use the keyboard to make your changes. Tap the Back button to return to the bookmarks editor.

Reparenting items: You can move items from one folder to another by tapping the gray reveal arrow and selecting a new parent from the bookmark folder list (just below the name-editing field). Select a folder, and then tap the Back button to return to the bookmarks editor.

Adding folders: Tap New Folder to create a folder in the currently displayed bookmark folder list. The iPod automatically opens the Edit Folder screen. Here, you can edit the name and, if needed, reparent your new folder. Tap the Back button to return to the editor.

Finishing: Return to the top-level bookmarks list (tap the Back key until you reach it), and then tap Done. This closes the editor and returns to Safari.

Saving Bookmarks and Sharing Web Pages

To save a new bookmark, tap the Share button at the bottom of any Safari web page. The Sharing menu appears, giving you six choices (see Figure 4–15).

Figure 4–15. *The bookmark creation menu*

Add Bookmark: Tapping this lets you enter a title for the bookmark and then optionally select a folder to save to (Figure 4–16). Tap the currently displayed folder to view a list of all available folders. The root of the bookmark tree is called Bookmarks. After making your selection, tap Save. Safari adds the new bookmark to your collection. If you want to return to Safari without saving, tap Cancel.

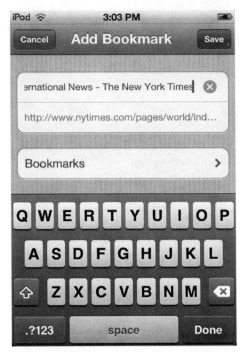

Figure 4–16. *Add Bookmark allows you to rename the bookmark before you save it.*

Add to Reading List: Tapping this adds the current page to your Reading List. I'll talk about Reading List in a moment.

Add to Home Screen: This is a cool feature. Tapping this adds an icon of the web page to your iPod touch home screen. Apple calls these web page icons *Web Clips*. Before you save a Web Clip, you have the option of renaming it. Keep the names short so you can see the entire name under the Web Clip icon on the home screen.

> **NOTE:** Some web sites will have an iPod-optimized site icon when you add a Web Clip to your home screen. Others just show you a thumbnail of the page in the shape of an iPod icon.

The Web Clips look just like app icons, and they allow you to tap to open Safari and automatically be taken to the web page. I keep a home screen on my iPod touch full of my favorite Web Clips so I can quickly navigate to my most frequently visited sites (Figure 4–17). I find this much quicker than using the bookmarks feature in Safari.

Figure 4–17. *A series of Web Clips on the iPod home screen. You can see which sites have dedicated Web Clip icons and which ones make the iPod use a thumbnail of the web page.*

In iTunes, the Web Clips appear in the virtual iPod screen on the Apps tab (see Chapter 2), but you cannot delete them from within iTunes; you can only rearrange them. To delete a Web Clip icon on the iPod, press and hold it until it jiggles, and tap the *X* in the upper-left corner.

Mail Link to this Page: Tapping this button opens a new mail message window in Safari and automatically inserts the link into the body of the message.

Tweet: Tapping this button composes a Twitter message that you can send to all your followers (Figure 4–18). You must have a Twitter account to use this feature.

Figure 4–18. *Tweeting a web page*

Print: This allows you to print the web page to an AirPlay-compatible wireless printer.

Eliminating Clutter with Reader

Safari has an awesome built-in feature that all other mobile web browsers lack. It's called Reader (not to be confused with Reading List, another awesome feature that I'll talk about shortly). Reader allows you to eliminate all the clutter on web pages, such as the ads, the comments, and the links, and read the content of that page as if you were reading it from a piece of paper. You can see Reader in action in Figure 4–19.

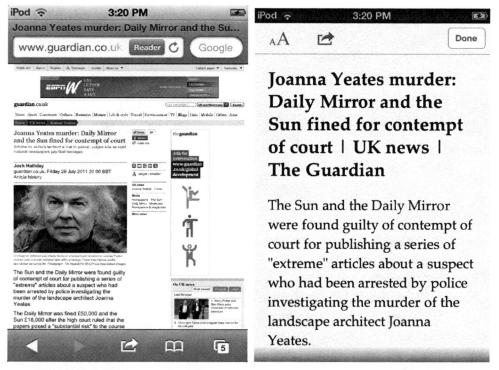

Figure 4–19. *Safari's Reader feature. Left: a web page as it normally appears. Right: the same web page when viewed through Reader.*

As shown in Figure 4–19, viewing the text on a web page through Reader is much easier because all the distractions are eliminated. To activate Reader, click the gray Reader button that appears in the address bar. The Reader document will slide up onto screen. To exit Reader mode, click the Done button. Notice that the Reader button appears only when you are on a web page that has a single article. You will not see a Reader button on the front page of *The New York Times* web site, for example; you'll see it only when viewing single articles on the site.

Building Up Your Reading List

Reading List is another new feature of Safari in Lion. It allows you to save web pages to read when you have the time, even when you're not connected to the Internet. I know, that sounds a lot like adding a bookmark, right? It's similar, but Reading List is more of a temporary bookmark. It's for that cool article you find about a small town in Andorra, which you want to read but don't have time to right now. It's not a bookmark you want to keep forever; it's just something you want to make sure you read.

To activate Reading List, tap the Share button at the bottom of Safari's window (Figure 4–6). The Sharing menu appears (Figure 4–15). Tap Add to Reading List. Your web page has now been added to your Reading List.

To access your Reading List, tap the Bookmarks button in Safari. In the bookmarks screen you'll see a Reading List folder at the top (Figure 4–20). Tap it to view your Reading List. The Reading List panel contains all the web articles you've added to it. You can tap a tab to see all the articles you've added or just the ones you haven't read yet. Simply select an article in the Reading List to read the saved web page.

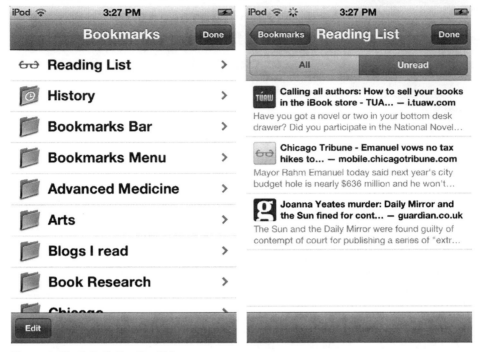

Figure 4–20. *Safari's Reading List*

When you are on the page you want to save to your Reading List, you can save it by taking any of the following actions:

Any saved page will disappear from the Reading List after you have scrolled through its entirety. You can also remove pages from the Reading List by swiping right over the article and then tapping the red Delete button that appears.

One of the best features about Reading List is that it is synced across all your computers and iOS devices (such as the iPad and iPhone) that use Safari. This allows you to find an interesting article on Safari on your iPod touch, save it to Reading List, and then read it on your iPad or Mac when you get home. Just open Safari, and the article appears in Reading List no matter what device you are on. It does this by syncing Reading List via your MobileMe or iCloud account.

Customizing Safari Settings

Like many of the apps on the iPod touch, Safari can be customized to a degree. Customize your Safari settings by navigating to the Settings app on your iPod home screen, and then tap Safari. This screen, shown in Figure 4–21, allows you to control a number of features, mostly security-related. Here's a quick rundown of those features and what they mean:

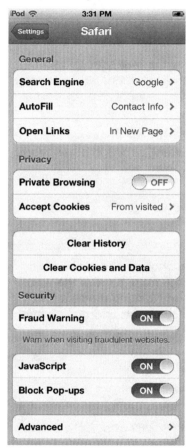

Figure 4–21. *The Safari Settings window is primarily concerned with security features.*

Search Engine: This setting determines which search engine is used for the search field you saw back in Figure 4–8. Choose from Google, Yahoo!, or Bing.

AutoFill: This allows you to turn on AutoFill for use in filling out forms on web pages. In the My Info box, select your address book card to take the AutoFill information from. Here you can also select to turn on Names & Passwords. With this on, Safari will remember login names and passwords to web sites you visit. You might not want to enable name and password saving if you share your iPod with people because they could then easily access your web accounts such as e-mail and bank accounts. Tap Clear All to wipe all saved names and passwords from your iPod.

Open Links: Here you can choose to open links in a new browser page or in the background. When New Page is selected, tapping a link in an e-mail, for instance, causes you to jump immediately to the Safari app. When In Background is selected, tapping a link in an e-mail opens the page in Safari in the background while you remain in the Mail app.

Private Browsing: When private browsing is enabled, your web history is not saved, nor are any of the user names, passwords, web searches, or text you enter on a web page.

Accept Cookies: Cookies refer to data stored on your iPod by the web sites you visit. Cookies allow web sites to remember you and to store information about your visit. You can choose to always accept cookies, never accept cookies, or accept cookies only "from visited" web sites.

Clear History: Tap and confirm to empty your page navigation history from your iPod. This keeps your personal browsing habits private to some extent, although other people might still scan through your bookmarks.

CAUTION: Clearing your history does not affect Safari's page history. You can still tap its Back button and see the sites you've visited.

Clear Cookies and Data: Tap and confirm to clear all existing cookies and cache from your iPod. Your iPod's browser cache stores text and graphics from many of the web sites you visit. It uses the cached information to speed up page loading the next time you visit. As with cookies and history, your cache may reveal personal information that you'd rather not share. Tap Clear Cache and Confirm to clear your cache.

TIP: Clearing your cache may also help correct problem pages that are having trouble loading. By clearing the cache, you remove page items that may be corrupt or only partially downloaded.

Fraud Warning: Turn this preference on, and you'll be presented with a warning before navigating to potentially fraudulent web sites. Unfortunately, fraudulent sites are rampant on the Internet (like bogus PayPal sites). This feature helps you recognize and avoid those sites.

JavaScript: JavaScript allows web pages to run programs when you visit. Disabling JavaScript means you increase overall surfing safety, but you also lose many cool and worthy web features. Most pages are safe to visit, but some, sadly, are not. To disable JavaScript, switch from ON to OFF.

Block Pop-ups: Many web sites use pop-up windows for advertising. It's an annoying reality of surfing the Web. By default, Safari pop-up blocking is ON. Switch this setting to OFF to allow pop-up window creation.

Advanced: This preference gives you control over databases and debugging. Most people will never use this. Some sites like Gmail use databases, which store local information on your iPod touch for offline browsing. Emptying databases can clear up problems you may be having on certain web sites. The debug console helps developers optimizing their web sites for the iPod.

The iPod and Flash Videos

If you've ever watched a video on the Web, chances are the video was encoded using Flash. Ever since Apple unveiled the iPhone to the world, there has been growing tension between Apple and Adobe. The reason is because Apple does not allow Adobe's proprietary Flash plug-in to run on the iPhone—and now the iPod.

Flash, in Apple's estimation, is a slow, buggy, and archaic technology. Steve Jobs even posted a letter on Apple's web site effectively telling the world the same thing (www.apple.com/hotnews/thoughts-on-flash/). His letter was the last nail in the coffin for anyone hoping to see Flash on the iPod or iPhone.

What many people misunderstand when they hear "no Flash on the iPod" is that they think the iPod can't play web videos. There's nothing further from the truth. Sure, if a video is encoded in Flash, you can't view it on the iPod, but most videos on the Web (about 75 percent of them, Steve Jobs says) are encoded in Flash but also in a new, universal web standard called HTML5. HTML5 videos don't require a plug-in to play. HTML5 is also much less power hungry than Flash—an important feature when dealing with mobile devices that consume battery power.

The world is moving to HTML5, and Apple chose to support it—and open standards— instead of Adobe's aging and proprietary Flash. Most of YouTube's videos have already been re-encoded to support HTML5, and many other major web sites have chosen to drop Flash in favor of the new HTML5 web standard. Apple even has a dedicated page to spotlight the advantages of the new HTML5 web standard: www.apple.com/hmtl5/.

Summary

Safari on the iPod puts the power of a real Internet browser into your pocket. There's nothing half-cocked or watered down about it. You can browse the real Web and read real sites without major compromise. It's such an amazing step forward in technology that you'll find yourself shaking your head with disdain when you remember the time when your iPod could only play music.

Here are a few tips to keep in mind as you move on from this chapter:

- iPods work in more orientations than just vertical. Go ahead and flip your iPod on its side. Your Safari pages will adjust.

- Nope, there's no Flash support. There never will be. And you don't need it.

- Web Clips are a great way to access your favorite web sites right from your iPad's home screen.

- Lost your address bar? Use the "double-tap to the top" trick.

- Safari's page management tool lets you navigate back and forth between several Safari windows at once. This functions like the way tabs function on desktop browsers.

- Don't confuse Reader and Reading List. Reader lets you strip away ads and read a web page's text as if you were reading a newspaper. Reading List allows you to save interesting articles to come back to at your leisure.

Chapter 5

Touching Your Photos and Videos

With the iPod's Photos application, you can free your photos from your home computer and pass them around the room like you used to do with photos of old. Hand your iPod to your friends, and they can swipe through your photos in their hands without the need to huddle around a computer screen. In this chapter, you'll discover how to navigate your photo collections and share them with friends and family. You'll also become familiarized with all the video capabilities of the iPod touch.

The iPod touch's wide-screen playback offers beautiful, clear images at higher resolutions than ever before. Its touchscreen provides intuitive interaction controls. Its wireless Internet capabilities allow you to access a huge range of content—from YouTube to the Internet Archive to your own personal computer. Video on your iPod isn't just about buying a TV show on iTunes and synchronizing it. With your iPod touch, video has entered the Internet age. This chapter introduces you to both the expected and unexpected ways you can use video on your iPod.

Working with Photos

Before you can view your photos on the iPod touch, you first need to transfer them to the device. There are many ways you can do this: syncing photos from your computer, saving photos from e-mailed messages, saving images found on web pages, capturing screenshots, and taking photos with the iPod touch's camera. We discuss all but taking photos in this chapter. Taking photos and all of the iPod's camera features are covered in Chapter 13.

Syncing Photos from Your Computer

We discussed syncing photos to your iPod touch in Chapter 2, but let's touch upon it briefly again. iTunes can synchronize your iPod touch with pictures stored on your computer. This allows you to bring your photo collection with you and share it using the iPod's unique touch-based interface. Who needs to carry around thick and heavy physical photo albums when you have an iPod touch with its thin body and vibrant display?

To get started, connect your iPod touch to your computer, and launch iTunes. Select your iPod touch from the source list (the blue column at the left side of the iTunes window), and open the Photos tab. Check the box labeled "Sync photos," and then choose the location of the photos you want to sync (see Figure 5–1). Your choices depend on your operating system.

On a Windows computer, your options are Adobe Photoshop Elements 3.0 or newer or any folder on your computer, such as My Pictures. On the Mac, your options are iPhoto 4.0.3 or newer, Aperture 3.0.2 or newer, or any folder on your computer. On a Mac you'll also need iPhoto 5.0 or newer, if you want to sync videos you've taken with your digital still camera.

Figure 5–1. *Syncing your photos through iTunes 10*

After you choose where to sync your photos from, choose to sync your entire photo collection (a good choice for relatively small libraries) or individual albums (better for large libraries that might not fit on the iPod touch's limited storage space). In the latter case, pick only those albums you want to copy to your iPod touch.

If you are using a Mac and iPhoto or Aperture, you'll also have the option to sync Faces (iPhoto '09 or later) and Events (iPhoto '08 or later) albums. Faces are smart photo albums that contain all the photos that have a selected individual's face in them. iPhoto does this by using built-in facial recognition software. The software "learns" as you tell it that it has or hasn't matched the right image to the person. In my tests, Faces in iPhoto doesn't get the right match all of the time, but its accuracy isn't too bad. Events are another type of smart album that groups photos together that were taken on the same day. This helps eliminate clutter and keeps your photo library organized.

To finish, click Apply to save your changes and then sync.

Saving Photos from Mail and Safari

You can also store photos on your iPod touch without importing them from your computer or taking them with the iPod's camera. If someone e-mails you a photo, you'll see the photos appear in the body of the e-mail message in the iPod touch's Mail app. Tap and hold your finger on any photo, and a pop-up appears allowing you to save that one photo or all the photos contained in the e-mail (see Figure 5–2). The photo or photos you've selected to save appear in the Camera Roll in the iPod touch's Photos app.

Similarly, in the iPod touch's Safari web browser, you can tap and hold your finger on any photo in a web page and select the Save Image pop-up that appears (see Figure 5–2). That photo is saved to the Camera Roll in the iPod touch's Photos app.

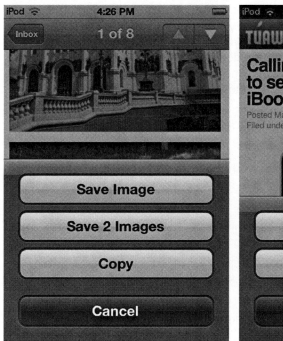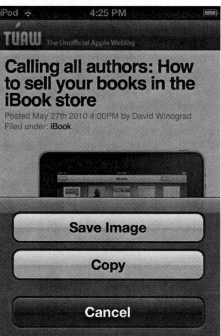

Figure 5–2. *Saving photos from an e-mail (left) or a web page (right)*

NOTE: Many third-party apps (like web browsers and magazines) also allow you to save images to your iPod touch. Some apps may have their own, unique way of saving images, but most methods should be fairly similar to the way you save images in Mail or Safari.

Navigating Your Photos in the Photo App

Now that you have photos on our iPod touch, let's start exploring the Photos app. To launch the app, tap the Photo icons on the home screen. It's the one with a yellow sunflower on it (Figure 5–3).

Figure 5–3. *The Photos app icon has a yellow sunflower on it.*

This is where the fun begins. When you touch your digital photos for the first time, you feel like you've finally stepped into the 21st century—that promised utopian future where technology merges with our fondest memories and we can go back and relive and explore them like never before. When you start pinching, dragging, and expanding your photos and albums, you'll feel like a child again who's just been given his first bag of marbles, spread them on the ground, and is staring wide-eyed at the colors and shapes that he can control before him.

To launch the Photos app, tap its icon on the home screen (see Figure 5–3). Once launched, the Photos app displays a list of albums, as shown in Figure 5–4.

Running along the bottom of the app is a toolbar that allows you to switch between the different ways your photos are organized. To select a view, tap its button in the toolbar.

NOTE: Did you know you can take screenshots of your iPod touch? A screenshot, or a screen capture, is an image taken of whatever appears on the iPod touch's screen at the moment you are taking it. To take a screenshot, press and hold the power button on the iPod touch, and then press and release the home button while still holding the power button. The iPod touch's screen flashes white, and you'll hear a shutter click sound effect. Once you hear the sound, you can let go of the power button. The captured screenshot appears in the Camera Roll album. You can use screenshots to save images of entire web pages or show off that high score in a video game. Most of the images in this book were taken using the iPod touch's screen capture function.

Albums: This view displays your photos in their albums as you've arranged them on your computer (see Figure 5–4). You will also see a Camera Roll album if you've saved images from the Web or if you've received them in e-mail on your iPod touch. If your iPod has a camera and you've taken any photos with it, they also appear in the Camera Roll along with any screen captures you may have taken.

Figure 5–4. *The Photos app in album view*

NOTE: If you are using iCloud's Photo Stream feature, you'll see another album titled "Photo Stream." Any photo you take with your iPod touch will appear here and be pushed to your other iOS devices and Macs and PCs automatically.

Events: This view displays your photos in events (see Figure 5–5). Events are used in Aperture 2 and iPhoto '08 and newer as a way to automatically arrange your photos by the date they were taken. This helps people automatically keep large photo libraries in easy-to-navigate shape. Events is a Mac-only feature. You will not see this tab if you are syncing your iPod touch with a Windows computer.

Figure 5–5. *Events view*

Faces: This view displays your photos grouped into an individual's "face" album (see Figure 5–6). If you are using iPhoto '09 or Aperture 3 on a Mac, the programs have built-in facial recognition software that creates albums of individuals and groups all the photos they appear in. It's an amazing and fun way to see all the photos of a certain friend or family member. Faces also works to some extent on cats and dogs. You will not see this tab if you are syncing your iPod touch with a Windows; Faces is a Mac-only feature.

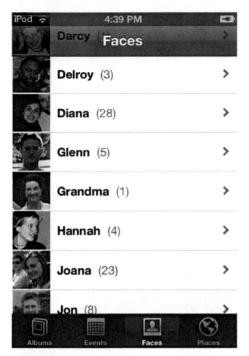

Figure 5–6. *Faces view*

Places: Many cameras today, including the one on the iPod touch, feature geotagging, which codes the photo with the location coordinates where it was taken. What the Places tab does is take the coordinates of your photos and display them on a Google map (see Figure 5–7). This is arguably the snazziest feature of Photos on iPod touch because it lets you navigate your photos on a map that you can view from a global level to a street level. It's an especially cool feature for travelers: you can see at a glance where you have been and just how much of the world is left to explore.

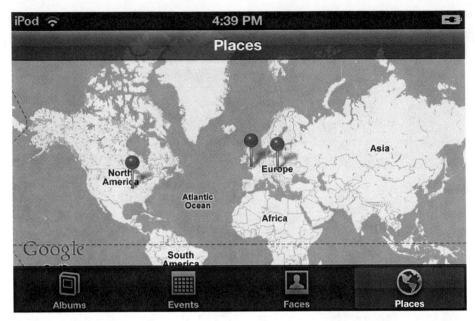

Figure 5–7. *Places view*

Red pins appear on the map signifying the geographic location of your photos. You can pinch and zoom on the map to get closer. As you do, you may see more pins appear on the map, signifying greater accuracy of the photo's coordinates (see Figure 5–8).

Figure 5–8. *Note that more pins appear as you zoom into an area of the map, signifying greater accuracy of the photo's coordinates.*

Tap a pin to see an album pop-up appear (see Figure 5–9). Tap the blue-and-white > to view that Places album. You can then explore all the photos that were taken in that location. Places requires an Internet connection to display the Google map.

Figure 5–9. *Tap a pin to see an album and thumbnail of photos that were taken at that location.*

As you can now see, the iPod touch's Photos app organizes your photos into four views for easy navigation. It is important to note that you may not see all the views on your iPod touch. The view categories you see depend on whether you are using a Mac or a Windows computer, whether you have chosen to sync albums from each category view, and whether your photos are tagged with geocoordinates.

As long as you have one photo on your iPod touch, you'll always see the Albums tab. To see Events, or Faces, or Places, you'll need to sync them from your computer. You don't need to do anything to sync Places; its tab will appear automatically if you have any photos tagged with geocoordinates.

Touching and Viewing Your Albums and Photos

Now that you know how to navigate your photo collections, let's learn how to touch and view them. Remember all the gestures covered in Chapter 3? When viewing a collection of albums or a single image full-screen, the iPod touch allows you to interact with that album or photo using a number of these gestures.

Touching and Viewing Albums

For this section, an *album* will refer to a regular album, an Events album, or a Faces album, since the interactions with these are all the same. As you can see in Figure 5–4, there are a series of albums. To open the album, tap it, and you'll be taken to the album page (Figure 5–10).

Figure 5–10. *Photos inside an album*

You'll notice the menu bar at the top of the screen. It displays the name of the album, with a back button that takes you to the category view you were previously in. It also shows a Share button (the arrow in the box in the top-right corner), which allows you to present your photos and share them with others (we'll talk the Share button a little later).

To exit the album, tap the back button (which is named after the category the album is in; in Figure 5–10, the album "Favorite photos" is contained in the Albums category, Albums being the back button in this example).

Remember, while on the Places tab, the red pins on the map act as albums containing all the photos taken there. Tap the pin to be presented with an album thumbnail (see Figure 5–9), and then tap the thumbnail to view the album of that location.

Touching and Viewing Photos

When in an album, you see thumbnails of the photos it contains (see Figure 5–10). To view a photo full-screen, tap the photo once to view it full-screen. As you can see from Figure 5–11, you can view the photo in portrait or landscape mode.

Figure 5–11. *Viewing a photo in landscape and portrait mode*

Once you display a photo full-screen, you have several ways to interact with it:

- Pinch to zoom into and out of the photo.
- Double-tap to zoom into the photo. Double-tap again to zoom out.

■ When your image is displayed at the normal zoomed-out size, drag to the left or right to move to the previous or next image in the album. When zoomed into an image, dragging the photo pans across it.

While viewing individual photos, flip your iPod touch onto its side to have your photo reorient itself. If the photo was shot using landscape orientation, it fits itself to the wider view. Tap any image once to bring up the image overlay, as shown in Figure 5–11. The image overlay features a menu bar at the top and bottom of the screen.

The image overlay menu bar at the top of the screen displays the number of the selected image out of the total number of images in the album and the back button to return to the album. At the bottom of the screen is the Share button and also back, play, and forward buttons. The back and forward buttons move the photos in your album back or forth one at a time. The play button allows you to start a slide show, which we will discuss next.

Viewing Your Photos as a Slide Show

When viewing the contents of any album or a single image in any album, you'll see the Share and Slideshow buttons at the bottom of the screen. As the name suggests, the Slideshow buttons display the contents of a photo album, one image after another. We'll discuss the Share button after describing the slide show features.

Playing a Slide Show

Playing slide shows on your iPod touch is as easy as tapping a single button, namely, the play button that resides at the bottom center of the screen. When you tap it, your slide show begins displaying one photo in the selected album after the next. To stop a slide show, tap the screen.

Slide Show Settings

You do have some limited settings for controlling how your slide show is presented. To adjust these settings, you need to leave the Photos app and launch the Settings app on the home screen. Once in the Settings app, navigate to the Photo settings (Figure 5–12).

Figure 5–12. *The slide show's settings*

The Photos app slideshow settings:

Play Each Slide For: Here, you can set the amount of time each slide remains on the display. Your choices are 2 seconds, 3 seconds (the default, which works really well for most people), 5 seconds, 10 seconds (which starts to get boring fast), and 20 seconds (which is probably recognized officially by Amnesty International as torture for most humans; seriously, don't do this to your friends and family).

Repeat: When set to ON, the slide show plays continuously. In other words, when you get to the last slide in the slide show, it begins again at the first one.

Shuffle: Show your pictures in a random order by switching Shuffle from OFF to ON. When Shuffle is disabled, your pictures display in album order.

I'll talk about the Photo Stream setting in Chapter 13.

Slide Show Tips

Slide shows are an awesome way to share your photos with your friends and family. Remember, however, that our images are associated with our personal memories, so they are always going to be more pleasant for us to watch than for others. All you have to do is remember a time you were stuck looking at someone else's photos and the seconds ticked by as if they were hours. To keep slide shows exciting for your viewers, keep a few things in mind:

- *Shorter is better*: The average shot (a clip of video displayed between cutting away to another shot) in a movie or TV show is less than two seconds nowadays. Back in the 1950s, the average shot was 30 seconds long. Watch an episode of *Friends* and then an episode of *I Love Lucy*, and you'll see exactly what we mean. *Lucy* seems to trudge along so slowly by today's standards. As the world—and media—got faster, our attention spans shrunk. This applies to viewing still images too. People can take in a lot from an image in just two or three seconds. If they are forced to look at an image any longer, they start to get bored. Keep the time a single image is displayed short. Also, keep the entire length of the slide show short. When you watch a movie trailer in the cinema, its time is exactly two minutes and twenty seconds—a perfect amount to whet the appetite, show people the best shots, and leave them feeling fulfilled but not exhausted.

- *Transitions help too*: A transition is the effect that occurs when moving from one image to the next. It adds some visual flare to the change of images. Photo's slide shows allow you to choose between five transitions. Use them as eye candy to keep your audience entertained, but don't use any of the flashier ones if your slide show is really long. Stick to dissolve; others will get tiring.

- If you are having a party, a great way to show off your photos without wrangling up all your guests and forcing them to sit and watch is to project your slide show on a TV and set it to repeat. That way, your slide show is constantly playing in the background, and your guests can continue to catch glimpses of it as they mingle. Images on slide shows playing in the background are great conversation starters and allow you to play much longer slide shows and display individual images for longer, since you don't have to worry about a captive audience. If you are going to play your slide shows in the background, you can choose to show several thousand images for as long as five or ten seconds each; the entire show could run for hours, and it won't get boring or tedious.

Sharing Your Photos

You have a number of ways to share photos you have on your iPod touch. To access all the ways you can share your photos, bring up a photo full-screen, and tap the Share button, which looks like an arrow breaking free from a small box (see Figure 5–11). You'll be presented with a pop-up menu of sharing options (see Figure 5–13).

Figure 5–13. *The sharing photos menu*

E-mail Photo: Tap this to see an e-mail compose window appear on the screen. You'll notice the photo has been copied into the body of the e-mail already. Enter the recipient's e-mail, a subject, and some body text, and then tap Send; your photo is on its way!

Alternatively, you can e-mail up to five photos at a time from within the Photos app. While in an album, tap the Share button, and you'll see the album menu renamed to Select Photos. Tap up to five photos that you want to send, and then tap the Share button at the bottom of the screen (see Figure 5–14). A pop-up menu appears with a button that says E-mail. Tap this button, and an e-mail compose window appears on the screen with the photos in the body of the message.

Figure 5–14. *You can e-mail up to five photos at a time from within the Photos app.*

Tweet: Tapping Tweet opens a Twitter upload screen. This allows you to tweet your picture directly to your Twitter account. You can also add a short message to the photo and your current location (see Figure 5–15).

Figure 5–15. *Tweeting a photo*

Assign to Contact: This option allows you to assign a photo to an address book contact. Tap Assign to Contact, and then select the contact's address book entry from the pop-up menu. Move and scale the thumbnail of the photo that appears, and then tap the Set Photo button.

The next time you view the contact in the iPod touch's Contacts app, the image you selected for them appears next to their name. This image syncs with their contact info in Address Book, Entourage, and Outlook on a Mac, and Outlook on a Windows computer.

Use as Wallpaper: Tap this button to use the selected image as wallpaper on your iPod touch. Move and scale the image, and then tap Set. From the pop-up menu (see Figure 5–16), you can select whether you want to use the image for the iPod touch's lock screen, the home screen, or both. This isn't the only way to set your iPod touch's wallpaper options. We'll talk about the other way in Chapter 15.

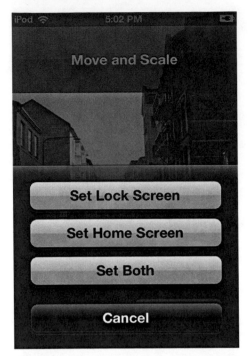

Figure 5–16. *The wallpaper menu bar options let you select which screen you want to use the photo as wallpaper for.*

Print: Tapping this prints your selected photo to an AirPrint wireless printer. Alternatively, you can print multiple photos from within the Photos app. While in an album, tap the Share button, and you'll see the album menu renamed to Select Photos. Tap as many photos as you want to print, and then tap the Share button at the bottom of the screen (see Figure 5–14). A pop-up menu appears with a Print button. The photos are sent to your wireless AirPrint printer.

Copying Photos

You can copy up to five photos at a time in your photo albums. To do this, go into a photo album, and tap the Share button. Tap up to five of the photos in the album. A check mark appears on each selected photo (see Figure 5–17). After you have selected all your photos, tap the Copy button in the lower-right corner of the screen. This saves the images to your clipboard for use in pasting into other things (such as an e-mail or document) later.

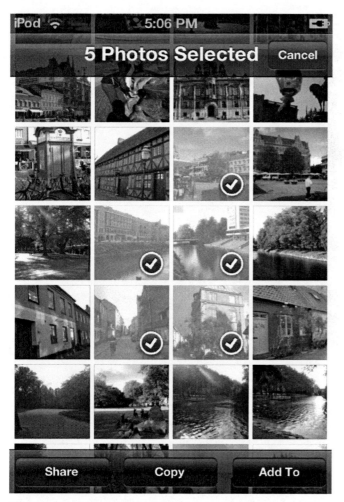

Figure 5–17. *Copying photos. You can copy only up to five at a time.*

Adding Photos to an Album

You can add photos on your iPod touch to other albums on your device. You can also create new albums right on your iPod touch. To add photos to an existing album or create a new album, go into a photo album, and tap the Share button. Tap all the photos that you want to move to an existing album. A check mark appears on each selected photo (see Figure 5–17). After you have selected all your photos, tap the Add To button in the lower-right corner of the screen. The pop-up menu shown in Figure 5–18 appears.

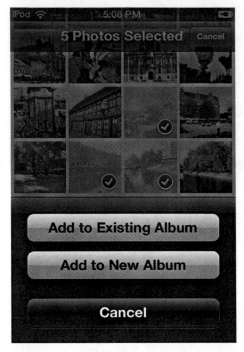

Figure 5–18. *Adding photos to new or existing albums*

To add photos to an existing album, tap Add to Existing Album and then choose the album you want to add your photos to from the album list that appears on the screen. To create a new album with photos on your iPod touch, tap Add to New Album and then enter the name of the new album in the dialog box that appears. The new album appears in your albums list.

Deleting Your Photos

Apple made it so you can only delete photos that are part of the Camera Roll album. This album contains any photos you have saved from the web or an e-mail or that you took with your iPod touch's camera. Apple disabled deletion of photos from your other albums synced to your iPod touch because they didn't want users accidentally deleting photos they had stored on their computer.

To delete the photos, navigate to your Camera Roll album, and tap the Share button. Tap the photos you want to delete to make a check mark appear on them, and then tap the red Delete button (see Figure 5–19). Alternately, while displaying a photo full-screen in your Camera Roll album, you'll notice a garbage pail icon next to the Share button (see Figure 5–20). Tapping this button causes a Delete Photo confirmation pop-up to appear. Tap Delete Photo to delete the selected photo from your iPod touch.

Figure 5–19. *You can only delete photos on the iPod touch from the Camera Roll.*

Figure 5–20. *The trash can icon in the lower-right corner of a photo in the Camera Roll album.*

To delete other photos on your iPod touch, you must delete them on your computer first and then resync the iPod touch.

Editing Your Photos

With iOS 5, Apple has introduced photo editing to the Photos app. The photo-editing features aren't too advanced, but they do allow you to make some nice adjustments to your photos. Apple has including four editing tools: rotate, enhance, redeye reduction, and cropping. To edit a photo, select a photo from your albums, and then click the Edit button in the top-right corner to enter Edit mode.

Figure 5–21 shows you what edit mode looks like in the Photos app. Your four editing tools are displayed along the bottom of the screen.

Figure 5–21. *Editing a photo. The tools, from left to right: rotate, enhance, redeye reduction, and crop.*

Rotate: Rotating a photo is something almost everyone has done or needs to do. Usually when a photo needs to be rotated, it's because you took it in portrait, or vertical, orientation with your camera, but it was imported in the standard landscape, or horizontal, orientation. Tap this button (it looks like a curved arrow) to rotate the photo in 90-degree increments. Click the yellow Save button when you've finished rotating your photo.

Auto-Enhance: Sometimes you might take a beautifully composed photo, but the color or exposure may be off. When this happens, there's no need to panic! The Photos app has a one-click fix for most photos with ailments such as poor saturation or contrast. It's called the Enhance button, and it works almost like magic. Tap the Enhance button (it looks like a magic wand) to auto-enhance your photo. Enhancing a photo can really bring out details that would normally have remained hidden without doing advanced manual adjustment techniques on it in a dedicated photo-editing app. Click the yellow Save button when finished enhancing your photo.

Red-eye reduction: Ah, red-eye -- the scourge of photographers everywhere. We're all familiar with red-eye. It's the thing that makes us look like demons in photographs: the red halo that appears in people's eyes that is caused by the way the human eye reflects the camera's flash. Luckily, most of the cameras on the market today offer built-in red-eye reduction, but the iPod touch does not. However, if your iPod touch takes photos in which your friends look like they're about to unleash some heat vision, the Photo app's red-eye reduction tool makes it easy to eliminate the red tint.

To eradicate red-eye in your photos, tap the red-eye tool (it looks like a red dot with a line through it). Next, tap each eye of the person (Figure 5–22). Like magic, their red eyes gain a more natural color. Click the yellow Apply button when finished.

Figure 5–22. *Reducing red-eye in your photos. In this photo, the right eye has had red-eye reduction applied, while the left eye has not.*

Crop: You can crop your photos to remove unwanted portions of them. To crop a photo, tap the Crop button (it looks like a square), and crop gridlines appear (Figure 5–23). Drag the gridlines around until you've selected the portion of the photo you want to crop. Click the yellow Crop button to apply the crop.

Figure 5–23. *Cropping a photo*

You can also constrain the aspect ratio of the crop so you'll know the exact ratio between the height and width of the photo once you are done cropping it. To constrain a photo's aspect ratio, click the Constrain button at the bottom of the crop screen (Figure 5–23). The Constrain screen appears (Figure 5–24).

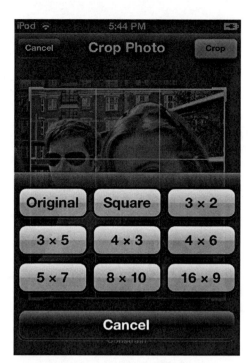

Figure 5–24. *Constraining a crop's aspect ratio*

Tap the desired aspect ratio. That locks the crop box to that specific ratio. You can then drag the constrained crop box around knowing that no matter where you crop, the photo has the selected ratio. Tap the yellow Crop button when ready to crop your photo, and then tap the yellow Save button to save your cropped photo.

iPod Video Applications

Video forms such a basic component of your iPod that you shouldn't think about it as just a single application. Apple provides the base technology used by several different programs. You'll find several applications that support video playback on your iPod (see Figure 5–25).

Figure 5–25. *Your iPod touch provides not one but three different applications that support video playback: Safari, YouTube, and Videos.*

Videos: The Videos application appears on the home screen of your iPod. The icon looks like a traditional clapperboard, with a black-and-white striped top over a blue base. This application plays back TV shows, movies, podcasts, iTunes U lessons, and music videos you've synchronized from your home iTunes library.

YouTube: You'll find the YouTube application icon next to the Videos app in Figure 7-1. The icon looks like an old-fashioned TV, complete with a greenish screen and brown dials. YouTube connects to the Internet and allows you to view videos from YouTube.com. You can navigate to http://youtube.com in Safari on the iPod and browse YouTube videos that way, but the iPod's YouTube app wraps http://youtube.com in such a nice and easy-to-navigate package, you'll find it is leaps and bounds better than using YouTube in a web browser.

Safari: Safari, which you read about in depth in Chapter 4, offers a third way to view videos. Like its computer-based equivalents, the Safari app allows you to watch embedded movie files. Safari's icon looks like a light blue compass with a needle pointing to the northeast.

In addition to the three apps that play video that come with the iPod, there are thousands of other apps that play video. You can discover all these apps in the iTunes Store. Some of my personal favorites are the BBC News app to view news footage and the Weather Channel app to watch weather-related news stories and Doppler video.

> **NOTE:** Apple's iPod touch officially supports H.264 video, up to 720p, 30 frames per second, in .m4v, .mp4, and .mov file formats.

For all that the iPod brings to video, it has limits. Your iPod plays H.264 MPEG-4 video, and that's pretty much it. As we talked about in the previous chapter, you cannot use your iPod to view Flash/Shockwave videos or animation. You cannot play AVI videos. You cannot play DivX, Xvid, or any of the other dozens of popular formats. If your video isn't in MPEG-4 H.264 format, your iPod won't understand it.

Video Playback

iPod video is primarily a wide-screen feature, unlike audio, which plays back in both portrait and landscape orientations. You must usually flip your iPod on its side to view TV shows, video podcasts, movies, and music videos. Select any video—from Safari, YouTube, or Videos—to begin playback, and then flip your iPod on its side to watch. The Home button goes to your right. Safari and YouTube provide exceptions to the landscape-only rule; in those applications, you can also watch videos in portrait orientation.

Depending on the app you are watching it in, you may see more options for the video being played or for the app itself. However, most apps display the same elements in the video interface, meaning once you know how to control video playback in one app, you know how to do it in the rest of them. Here is a quick overview of those controls, which are shown in Figure 5–26.

Figure 5–26. *The iPod's video playback controls allow you to control playback as you watch.*

Play/Pause: Play/Pause appears as either a right-pointing triangle (Play) or a pair of vertical lines (Pause). Tap this button to pause or resume video playback.

Rewind: The Rewind button appears as two triangles pointing left to a line. Tap it to return to the start of the video, or press and hold the button to scan backward.

Fast-Forward: The reverse of Rewind, the Fast-Forward button's triangles point to the right instead of the left. Press and hold this button to scan forward. Tap it to skip to the next video track.

Scrubber bar: The scrubber bar appears at the top of your screen. It is a long line with a small knob that you can drag. (The volume control is the thicker bar at the bottom.) Drag the playhead along the scrubber bar to set the current playback time.

Zoom: The Zoom button looks like two arrows pointing away from each other, at the top-right of your screen. Either double-tap the screen or tap the Zoom button to switch between full-screen mode and original aspect ratio. To get back into the original aspect ratio's view, double-tap the screen again, or tap the zoom button again. You'll note that the zoom button changes slightly when viewing a video full-screen: the arrows have turned into a letterbox icon. When viewing in full-screen mode, you use the entire iPod screen, but some video may be clipped from the top or sides of the video. In original aspect ratio, you may see either letterboxing (black bars above and below) or pillarboxing (black bars to either side), which results from preserving the video's original aspect ratio.

Volume: The volume control is the large line below the play/pause buttons. Drag the volume control knob to adjust playback volume. Of course, you can always use the dedicated physical volume button on the side of the iPod as well.

Audio tracks and Subtitles: If alternate audio tracks or subtitles are available in the video you are watching, you'll see an icon that looks like a speech bubble, appear in the play/pause bar. Tap this icon to select from a pop-up list of audio tracks and subtitles.

Done: The Done button appears on all video application screens. Tap Done to exit video playback. Press the physical Home button on the iPod's bezel to quit the app and return to your home screen.

While you're playing a video, the iPod automatically hides your video controls after a second or two. This allows you to watch your video without the distraction of on-screen buttons. Tap the screen to bring back the controls. Tap the screen again to hide them, or leave them untouched for a few seconds, and they once again fadeaway.

YouTube

The YouTube app requires an Internet connection, so as long as you have a Wi-Fi connection, you're all set. But to take full advantage of the YouTube app, you'll want to have a YouTube account. You don't *need* a YouTube account to use the app, but having one makes the app that much more powerful. With a YouTube account, you can view and bookmark your favorite videos; subscribe to YouTube users videos; see all the videos you've uploaded to YouTube with the tap of a button; and share, rate, and flag videos—all from within the YouTube app. Creating a YouTube account takes only a few minutes and can be done at www.youtube.com/create_account.

To launch the application, tap the YouTube icon, which looks like a retro-styled TV set (see Figure 5–27). When launched for the first time, the application displays the Featured screen, as shown in Figure 5–28. This screen showcases YouTube's notable videos.

Figure 5–27. *The YouTube app*

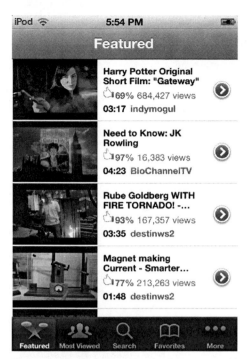

Figure 5–28. *YouTube's Featured screen provides a video showcase.*

Here are a few items you'll find on most YouTube video-listing screens:

Play a video: Tap the image or name of a video to begin playback. Your iPod connects to YouTube, downloads the video, and plays it for you.

View a video's info screen: Tap the More Info button (the blue circle with the right arrow) to learn more about the video. Read more about the info screen later in this chapter, in the "Viewing Video Info Screens" section.

Select another listing screen: Choose any button along the bar at the bottom of your screen. You'll jump to the associated built-in YouTube screens: Most Viewed, Search, Favorites, and so on. Each of these screens helps you find and view YouTube videos. You can customize this buttons bar to change the buttons it contains.

Playing YouTube Videos

To play a video, tap the name or image of the video. The video appears in full-screen, as shown in Figure 5–29.

Figure 5–29. *Playing a YouTube video*

From this screen you can interact with the video in the following ways:

Scrubber: At the top of the screen you'll see the scrubber bar. This allows you to *scrub*, or advance or go back, through a video. The silver dot symbolizes where you are in the video, and the white part of the scrubber bar symbolizes how much of the video has downloaded. You can skip ahead to undownloaded portions of the video, and the YouTube app starts downloading the video from that point on.

Bookmark: The bookmark button looks like a book and allows you to save a video to your favorites for easy, quick access.

Rewind, play/pause, and fast-forward: These standard buttons allow you to rewind, play or pause, and fast-forward through a video.

Share: This Share button allows you to send an e-mail with a link to the YouTube video in the body of the message. You can also add the video to your Favorites or tweet a link to the video. This allows you to share your favorites immediately after you watch them.

Volume slider: Located at the bottom of the screen, this allows you to adjust the volume of the video to the most comfortable audio levels.

Done: Tap this button in the upper-left corner to exit the video and return to its Info page.

Finding YouTube Videos

Each button on the buttons bar offers a different way to list YouTube videos. To find videos, tap any of these buttons:

Featured: This screen lists videos reviewed and recommended by YouTube staff. These are usually pretty high quality and worth checking out.

Most Viewed: This screen lists the most popular videos of the day, week, or all time. The All Time screen is great, because it's interesting to see a list of the planet's most-viewed videos.

Search: On this screen, enter a keyword or two, and then tap Search to look through YouTube's entire collection.

Favorites: This screen is for a collection of videos you've selected and bookmarked. Easy access to your favorite videos is always a plus because it saves you time from searching for them again.

More: Choose from six more viewing choices or customize the display:

Most Recent: Showcases YouTube's newest items. Some might be good; others not.

Top Rated: Lists YouTube's collection of videos that have garnered the most viewer support. This is the wisdom of the masses, so starred videos might not equal quality in every case.

History: Displays recently viewed items. This is handy if you remember you watched a hilarious video but can't remember the exact name of it.

My Videos: Displays all the videos you've uploaded to YouTube. This feature requires you to be logged in to your YouTube account.

Subscriptions: Allows you to subscribe to another YouTube user's videos so you can keep up-to-date with the latest videos they've posted. Any subscriptions you have show up on this screen. Tap the name of the user to see all their videos displayed to the left of the list. This feature requires you to be logged in to your YouTube account.

Playlists: Creates playlists of videos. When signed in, you can see any playlists you've created on YouTube.com. Playlists are handy because it lets you group related videos together (for example, exercise videos).

Edit lets you choose which items appear on your shortcuts bar and which appear on the More screen.

On each of these screens, you can scroll up and down the listings and play back any video by tapping its name or icon.

Customizing the YouTube Buttons Bar

The buttons bar at the bottom of your screen is fully customizable, so it can provide quick access to the categories you view the most. Tap **More ➤ Edit** to make changes. Available categories appear in the screen above the bar, as shown in Figure 5–30. Select the ones you want to use, drag them down to the buttons bar, and then tap Done.

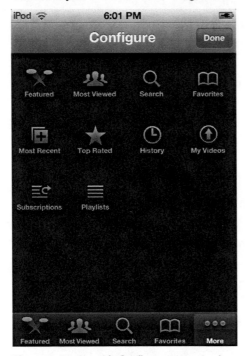

Figure 5–30. *Use this Configure screen to choose which buttons appear in the bar at the bottom of the YouTube application.*

Here are a few pointers about how this customization works:

- The buttons bar always contains four category buttons plus the More button. You cannot add more buttons or remove buttons to display fewer options.

- You cannot replace More with another button.

- If you replace a button with an item already in the buttons bar, the two items switch positions.

- There is no "revert to defaults" option. The original order is Featured, Most Viewed, Search, and Favorites.

- The items you do not include in the buttons bar appear as a list when you tap More. You can select them from that list. It's an extra step, but all the options are still available.

Viewing Video Info Screens

Video information screens provide a detail view for each video. Figure 5–31 shows a typical info screen. Here, you'll find the name of the video, its rating (in stars, from zero to five), the number of times the video has been viewed, its run time, and more. Scroll down the screen to find YouTube's suggestions for related videos.

Figure 5–31. *A video info screen offers information about the video and the option to bookmark the video.*

Here is also where you'll find the Add to Playlist and Share buttons.

Add to Playlist: Adds the video to one of your YouTube playlists

Share Video: Creates an e-mail with a link to the YouTube video in the body of the e-mail. You can also tweet a link to the video.

To get more information about the video, tap the blue-and-white arrow button. Doing so takes you to the More Info screen (Figure 5–32). From this screen you can read more about the video; read comments; and rate, comment, or flag the video. Tap the More Videos tab to see move videos from the user.

Figure 5–32. *A video's More Info screen*

The Videos App

Gone are the days when keeping entertained on long car trips required a portable DVD player and a case of discs. The iPod touch's Video app lets you carry around your favorite movies, TV shows, and podcasts in your pocket and switch between them with a tap of your finger. Let's explore the Videos app now.

The Videos application icon (Figure 5–33) is colored blue and has a traditional, striped clapperboard top. Tap it to launch the program. This opens the screen shown in Figure 5–34.

Figure 5–33. *The Videos app*

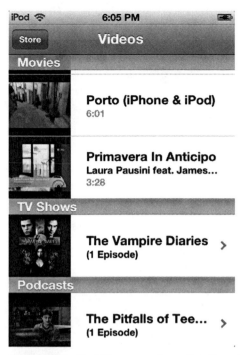

Figure 5–34. *The Videos app offers a list of music videos, TV shows, and movies you've synchronized to your iPod.*

As you can see, the Videos interface couldn't be simpler. It displays a series of thumbnail images representing the music videos, TV shows, podcasts, and movies you've synchronized to your iPod (synchronizing these items is discussed in Chapter 2). Tap any item to begin playback. Your screen clears, and the video loads and automatically begins playing. Tap Done to return to the list screen, or press Home to quit and go to your home screen.

Tapping the Store button in the top-left corner of the screen takes you to the iTunes Store app (discussed in Chapter 7) where you can buy music and videos.

If you tap a TV show or podcast, you'll be taken to an additional page (Figure 5–35) that lists all the episodes for the TV show or podcast that you have on your iPod before the video begins playing. From this screen, tap the episode you want to play or tap the Get More Episodes… button to be taken to the show's iTunes Store page where you can download additional episodes.

Figure 5–35. *A TV show's page in the Videos app*

Deleting Videos on the Go

The iPod allows you to recover space on the go by deleting videos after you've watched them. To take advantage of this feature, go to the Videos screen and swipe through the name of any video. A red Delete button appears to the right of the video name. Tap Delete to remove the video, or tap anywhere else on the screen to cancel and keep the video.

Choose your videos wisely. Even with newer iPods with expanded memory, videos can quickly eat up your free space. And don't be shy about deleting your videos on the go. You can always sync them back on your home computer.

Getting Videos

The easiest way to get videos on your iPod touch is to buy or rent them from the iTunes Store. Check out Chapter 7 for more details on buying and renting movies. You can also rip DVDs you own using desktop applications like Handbrake (http://handbrake.fr). Keep in mind local laws may prevent you from ripping DVDs, even if you own them.

Video Settings

You can adjust several settings that affect your video playback. These settings are accessed through the iPod touch's Settings application (see Figure 5–36) and affect how your video is played on your iPod and when your iPod is connected to your TV.

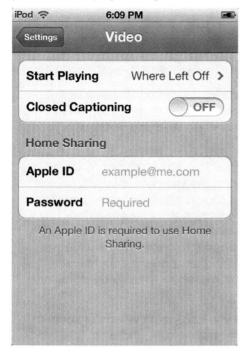

Figure 5–36. *The Video app's settings*

For your iPod video settings:

Start Playing: choose whether to start playing videos from the beginning or where you left off.

Closed Captioning: If your video contains embedded closed captions, you can view them by switching on the Closed Captioning option. Switch the option from OFF to ON.

For your Home Sharing settings, enter your Apple ID and password to enable video home sharing on your iPod touch. Home sharing allows you to stream videos from iTunes on your computer and watch them on your iPod touch. Your iPod touch and computer must be connected to the same wireless network and iTunes must be open on your computer for your iPod to see its videos.

NOTE: Unfortunately, the iPod touch does not allow you to turn off your screen and continue listening to the audio track from your video. Tap the Sleep/Wake button, and your video playback ends. You can, however, diminish the screen brightness levels in **Settings ➤ Brightness**. This is not much of a win. Your iPod continues using (energy-consuming) video decoding to play back video as well as audio.

Watching Videos on the Web with Safari

Video on the iPod isn't limited to special-purpose applications. You can also watch MPEG-4 movie files with the iPod's Safari application. Chapter 4 introduced Safari. Here you'll see how you can connect to video on the World Wide Web and watch it in your Safari browser.

Many web sites besides YouTube feature embedded video. For example, go to virtually any news site, and you're sure to find embedded video. As we mentioned in Chapter 4, the iPod, and thus Safari, does not support Flash playback, which limits the iPod's ability to display every single video on the Web. However, many web sites serve HTML5 and MPEG-4 videos, and these are fully iPod-compliant. HTML5 is particularly exciting because it's an open web standard that allows developers to create fully interactive content that is optimized and compatible to today's (and tomorrow's) touchscreen devices. HTML5, unlike Flash, does not require that the user download and install a special plug-in to view video content.

For example, the web site TED (www.ted.com) where you can watch videos of some of today's greatest minds talk about science, education, technology, and art is fully iPod-compatible, and it achieves this by being written in and having the videos encoded in HTML5. Figure 5–37 shows this site's video of author Elizabeth Gilbert talking about creativity playing back in the iPod's Safari web browser.

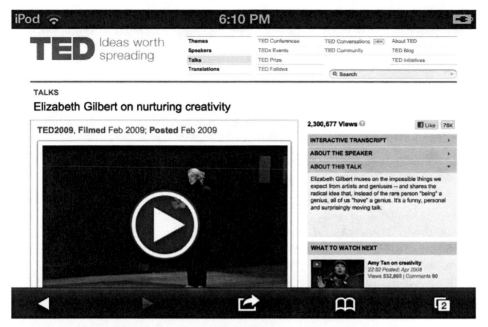

Figure 5–37. *Many videos on the Web can be played natively in the Safari web browser.*

Tap an embedded video to begin playing it. The video opens in the usual video playback window (see Figure 5–26). Depending on the speed of your Internet connection, it may take a few seconds before the video begins playing. Watch the video, and when you're done, tap the Done button in the video playback screen to return to the Safari web page.

Streaming Video to Your Apple TV with AirPlay

Just as Home Sharing allows you to stream video from your iTunes library on your computer to your iPod touch, another technology called AirPlay lets you stream video from your iPod touch to your AppleTV.

An Apple TV is an inexpensive (US$99) set-top box that you plug into your HDTV. With this box, you can rent movies and TV shows from the iTunes Store directly on your TV. The Apple TV connects to the Internet wirelessly and also communicates with your computer, iPod touch, iPhone, or iPad wirelessly as well. Once you have your Apple TV set up, start watching a video on your iPod, and then tap the AirPlay icon (Figure 5–38) that appears in a video's control bar to instantly stream that video to your TV.

Figure 5–38. *The AirPlay icon that appears in a video's control bar when your iPod touch detects nearby AppleTVs*

AirPlay is a really cool feature because you can start watching a video on your iPod on your commute home from work, and when you get home, you can finish watching the video on your TV with the tap of a button.

Video Accessories

As far as video goes, there are several iPod touch accessories besides the AppleTV you should consider purchasing:

Stands: Several companies make them, and they range in price from $5 to $30. Whatever stand you choose, if you are planning to prop the iPod up while watching video, make sure it holds the iPod in landscape mode.

iPad Dock Connector to VGA Adapter ($29): Yes, its name says "iPad," but it works just fine with the iPod touch. The VGA end of the adapter can be connected to external monitors, some TVs, and PC projectors. You'll need this or the cables below to connect your iPod to your home television.

Apple Component AV Cable ($49) and *Composite AV Cable* ($49): These also work with the iPod, providing two more methods of linking external monitors and projectors to the device.

Apple Digital AV Adapter ($39): This cable allows you to attach your iPod touch to your HD TV through the HDMI port. You can then play your videos and slideshows in crystal-clear digital quality on your TV.

Don't worry if you don't know the difference between VGA, Composite, Component, and HDMI. All three are types of physical video connectors that link devices to TVs.

VGA is a 15–pin connector that you can still find on the back of many PCs. It supports resolutions up to 2048x1536.

Composite is a video connector that channels three video source signals through a single connection. It's the oldest of the three technologies but still supports a resolution of up to 720x576i.

Component is a video connector that takes three video source signals and outputs them through three different connections. It's basically a Composite cable with three heads, but Component offers a much better resolution, up to 1920x1080p (otherwise known as "Full HD").

HDMI is the new standard for high-definition televisions. It kind of looks like a USB cable and allow you to connect devices to your TV through a pristine digital connection.

Many modern TVs support all four connections. Check your TV's manual to see which yours supports.

Summary

This chapter introduced you to the iPhotos app of the iPod touch and showed you how to navigate your photo collections in a variety of ways. I also demonstrated how your iPod's wide-screen video features and interactive touchscreen are in a class of their own. They offer clear, easy-to-watch video on a (relatively) large screen. In this chapter, you've seen how to watch video from YouTube, the Videos application, and Safari. Here are a few points you should take away and consider:

- The iPod touch's Photos application offers some of the most instantly appealing ways to show off the power of your iPod touch. You can scroll through your albums, zoom in and out with a pinch or double-tap, and flip the unit on its side. These features all deliver the iPod touch wow factor.

- You aren't limited to just viewing photos on your iPod touch; you can also apply simple edits to them to make them look their best!

- You have several ways to navigate your photos: by album, by face, by event, or by place. By far the coolest way is Places, which shows you your photos on a map, based on the location where they were taken.

- Consider investing in an inexpensive business card holder as a stand for your iPod touch. It makes watching slide shows on your iPod touch a lot easier, especially for more than one person at a time. A video-out cable from Apple increases the fun by sending the slide shows to a TV screen.

- Pick the YouTube listings that you like best. The buttons bar at the bottom of the screen is fully customizable. If you prefer to view the Top Rated videos over the Most Viewed, feel free to drag that option to your bar.

- Use the red Clear button at the top-right corner of the History screen to erase your YouTube viewing history. People don't have to know you've been watching that skateboarding dog

Chapter 6

Touching Your Music

The latest iPod touch is the best iPod that Apple has ever shipped. Despite that the iPod touch has become much more than just a music player, it still lets you rock out to your tunes better than any other multimedia device. This chapter introduces you to the iPod's music player and shows you how to get the most use out of it.

The Music Application

Your iPod's Music app brings all the functionality and ease of use you expect from a music player, but it delivers that functionality in a distinctive touch-based package. Figure 6–1 shows the Music application icon. It's easy to spot, since it is bright orange and marked with a music note. Tapping this icon launches the music player and allows you to access and play the songs you've synchronized to your iPod.

> **NOTE:** Do not confuse the Music and iTunes applications on your iPod. Music is used to play your music tracks. iTunes connects you to the mobile iTunes Wi-Fi Music Store where you can shop for and purchase music and video tracks and is not a general music player.

Figure 6–1. *Launch the Music application by tapping its icon.*

If you've used iPods before, expect to be pleasantly surprised. If you're new to the world of iPods, expect to be blown away. The iPod touch interface simplifies browsing, locating, and playing music and videos. Here are just a few ways the iPod touch gives you your best music experience yet:

Touch screen: With the iPod's touch screen, there's no need for scroll wheels. Flick through your lists, and tap the items you want to play.

Cover Flow: If you like Cover Flow in iTunes, you'll love it on the iPod.

Alphabet index tool: The iPod application uses the same kind of alphabet index you saw in Chapter 2 (see Figure 2-1). It makes searching through long alphabetized lists a breeze.

Customizable button bar: Do you prefer to search by genre or album, rather than artist or song? Just drag the items you use the most onto the configurable button bar.

And that's just a taste of the ways the Music app changes the way you use your iPod. Read on for more details on how this program works.

Browsing Media on the iPod

Tapping the orange Music icon on your Home screen takes you to the music player application. This program gives you access to all the audio media files you have synchronized to your iPod, including songs, podcasts, and audiobooks. At the bottom of the screen you'll see blue and black buttons labeled Playlist, Artists, Songs, Albums, and More (see Figure 6–2). Tapping any of these buttons enables you to sort through your music. Tapping the Store button in the top-left corner of the screen takes you to the iTunes Store app (discussed in the next chapter) where you can buy music and videos.

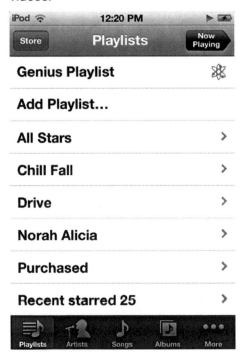

Figure 6–2. *The music player screen*

The More screen offers the best place to start exploring your media collection. Locate the More button at the bottom right of the screen, and tap it to load the screen shown in Figure 6–3.

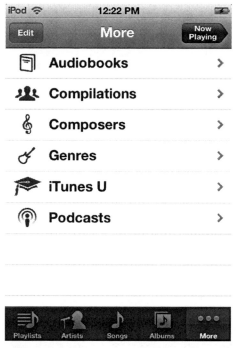

Figure 6–3. *The More screen provides an excellent jumping-off point for exploring your media. The Now Playing button appears on all category screens, including this one, and instantly takes you to the track currently playing.*

From the More screen, you can see every kind of category used to sort your songs: Playlists, Artists, Songs, Albums, Audiobooks, Compilations, Composers, Genres, iTunes U and Podcasts. Some of these appear in the black bar at the bottom of the screen, while others appear in the list in the center of the screen. Tap any item to open that collection. For example, tap Artists to see a list of your media sorted by artists, or tap Audiobooks to view the audiobooks loaded on your system.

The black bar is your shortcuts bar or, more officially, your browse buttons bar (a name I find especially awkward, so please bear with me when I refer to it as simply the shortcuts bar). The difference between the items in the shortcuts bar and the items in the previous list is that these shortcuts appear universally in every category view. Your iPod lets you select which items you want to keep handy in that bar, as described next.

Editing Your Browse Buttons

From the More screen, tap the Edit button to open the Configure screen, as shown in Figure 6–4. This screen allows you to customize your shortcuts bar.

Figure 6–4. *Use the Configure screen to choose which items appear in your shortcuts bar at the bottom of the screen.*

To replace any item on the shortcuts bar, drag an icon from the center of the screen onto the item you want to replace in the bar at the bottom. Say you listen to podcasts and audiobooks more than you listen to music. Drag those two icons onto your bar to replace, for example, Artists and Albums. You'll see your shortcuts bar in every category view. Add whichever icons you use the most. You can also rearrange the icons in the bar by dragging them left or right within the bar.

The bar must always contain four—and only four—icons. You cannot drag icons off the bar, and you cannot set the bar to contain fewer than those four icons. You cannot add more than four shortcuts, and you cannot replace the More button with another item.

Here are the items you can choose from:

Albums: Every album on your iPod, ordered by album name.

Podcasts: A list of audio podcasts that you have chosen to sync to your iPod.

Audiobooks: Every audiobook on your iPod.

Genres: A list of every genre—such as Classical, Rock, Pop, Country, and so on—that appears on your iPod. Each item leads to a list of media that belongs to that genre.

Composers: A list of media sorted by their composers. My iPod contains listings for Bob Dylan, Wolfgang Amadeus Mozart, and more.

Compilations: A list of all media belonging to compilations—that is, albums that have been contributed to by various artists.

Playlists: A list of all the playlists you've chosen to sync to your iPod.

Artists: A list of your media sorted by the artist who recorded them.

Songs: Every song on your iPod, arranged alphabetically by song name.

iTunes U: A list of all your iTunes U lessons and lectures.

When you are finished making changes, tap Done to return to the More screen.

Navigating the Category Screens

All the category screens work in much the same way. The screen displays its members—whether podcasts, artists, or songs—as an alphabetically sorted scrolling list. If the list is long, you'll see an alphabet control on the right side of the screen, as shown in Figure 6–5. Tap a letter or scroll your finger down the alphabet to move to the section you want to view.

> **TIP:** Many category screens offer a Shuffle option as their first item. Tap it to start playing that category in random order.

When the items listed are individual songs or videos, tap any name to play your selection. When the items listed are collections, such as genres or albums, tap to open a screen that displays each item of that collection. For example, you can tap an album to list its tracks and then tap a track name to play it.

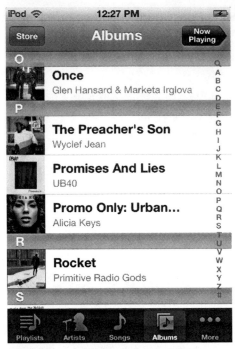

Figure 6–5. *The Albums screen lists albums in alphabetical order. When you've downloaded album art, it appears in the squares marked by the music notes.*

Playing Audio

Figure 6–6 shows the iPod's Now Playing screen. You arrive at this screen whenever you start playing a song. You can also jump to this screen from any category by tapping the Now Playing button at the top-right corner (see Figure 6–5).

Figure 6–6. *The iPod's Now Playing screen provides an interactive screen that controls playback for the currently playing item. From this screen, you can adjust the volume, pause and resume playback, and loop the current track.*

Here are the items you'll find on the Now Playing screen and what they do:

Play indicator: The right-pointing play indicator at the top right of the screen (just left of the battery status) appears universally when you're playing music. This tells you at a glance that music is playing. You'll find this especially helpful when you've removed your earbuds and placed the iPod on a table.

Back button: Tap the Back button at the top-left corner (the arrow pointing left) to return to the most recent album or playlist screen. Tapping Back does not stop playback. Your song continues to play as you browse through your categories or tap Home to do other things on your iPod.

Artist, song, and album: These items appear at the top middle of the screen and are for information only. Tapping them does nothing.

Album View button: This button looks like a three-item bulleted list and appears at the top right of the screen, just below the battery indicator. Tap this to switch between your Now Playing screen and its Album view (discussed in the next section).

Scrubber bar: The scrubber bar appears below the artist, song, and album name. Tap the album cover to make this control appear; tap again to hide it.

> ■ The number at the left of the bar shows the elapsed playback time. The number at the right shows the remaining playback time.

■ Drag the playhead to set the point at which your song plays back. You can do so while the song is playing so you can hear which point you've reached.

■ Look just below the scrubber bar to see which album or playlist track is playing. In Figure 6–6, this is track 5 of 11.

Loop control: This control, which looks like a pair of arrows pointing to each other in a circle, appears when you tap album art.

■ Tap once to loop the currently playing album or playlist. After the last song plays, the first song starts again.

■ Tap a second time to loop just the current song. The number 1 appears on the loop, telling you that the loop applies to just this song.

■ Tap once more to disable looping.

■ A blue loop (both the regular loop and the loop with the number 1) indicates that looping is enabled. A white loop means looping is switched off.

Genius button: This button looks like an atom with electrons swirling around it and lies in the center of the bottom bar. Tapping this creates a Genius playlist based on the song that is currently playing. When you navigate back to the music library, you'll see a playlist labeled "Genius" along with several other options. We'll discuss those options in just a bit.

Shuffle: The shuffle control looks like two arrows making a wavy *X*. It appears to the right of the scrubber bar and, like the loop and scrubber controls, appears only after you tap the album cover.

■ When the shuffle control is off (white), album and playlist songs play back in order.

When the shuffle control is selected (blue), the iPod randomly orders songs for shuffled playback.

Album art: When you've downloaded album art, the cover image appears just below the top bar and occupies most of your screen.

■ Tap the art area to open the gray playback controls that appear just below the artist, song, and album name.

■ Tap again to hide the controls.

■ Double-tapping the album art sends you to the Album view.

■ Swipe to the right to return to the most recent category screen.

Rewind: The Rewind button looks like a vertical line followed by two left-pointing triangles.

- Tap to move back to the beginning of the currently playing song.

- Double-tap to move to the previous song in the album or playlist. If you are already at the start of the song, a single tap moves you back; if you're already at the first song, this works as if you had pressed the Back button—you return to the most recent album or playlist screen.

- Touch and hold to rewind through the current song. You'll hear very short snippets as you move backward through the song. This feature proves especially handy while listening to audiobooks.

Play/Pause: Play looks like a right-pointing triangle. Pause looks like a pair of upright lines. Tap this button to toggle between playback and pause modes.

Forward: The Forward button looks like the Rewind button in a mirror. The line is to the right, and both triangles point right instead of left.

- Tap once to move to the next song in the album or playlist. If you're at the last song, tapping Forward moves you back to the album or playlist.

- Touch and hold to fast-forward through your song.

Volume: Drag along the slider at the bottom of the screen to adjust playback volume. If you've attached an external speaker or remote control, you can use its controls to control the playback volume as well.

Album View

Tapping the Album View button at the top-right corner of the Now Playing screen switches you to an overview of the current album or playlist, as shown in Figure 6–7. This screen shows a track list with item names and durations.

Figure 6–7. *The Album view shows a list of tracks and durations for the current album or playlist.*

Several items on this screen overlap with the Now Playing view and work in the same way. Here's a quick screen rundown:

Return to Now Playing: The icon at the top right (it looks either like a music note or, if you have album art, like a wee version of the album cover) switches you back to the Now Playing screen.

Rate your songs with the rating stars: Use the stars control to rate the current song, from zero to five stars. Drag your finger along the dots to form stars to set your rating. These ratings sync back to your computer, and you can use them when making Smart Playlists. For example, you might choose only your most favorably rated tracks to play. Set up this kind of playlist on your computer using iTunes. When you rate a song, it's personal and does not get sent back to the iTunes Store to be shared with the world.

View the entire track list: Scroll up and down the track list to see all the items on the current playlist or album. Tap any item to start playback.

> **TIP:** When there's empty space on the track list—for example, when you have only one or two tracks—double-tap the empty areas to return to the Now Playing screen. Alternatively, double-tap either side of the rating stars display.

Cover Flow

Tilt your iPod onto its side when browsing or listening to music, and you instantly enter Cover Flow mode. Cover Flow is the iPod feature that allows you to view your media collection as a series of interactive album covers, as shown in Figure 6–8.

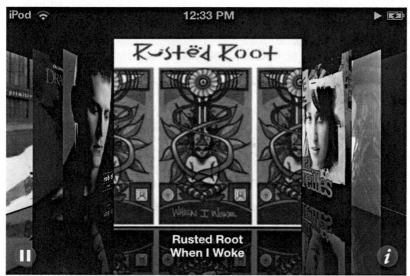

Figure 6–8. *Cover Flow presents your media library as a series of album covers.*

To use Cover Flow, simply flick your way through your collection to the left or right. The iPod provides animated, interactive feedback.

Here's what you can do in Cover Flow mode:

Album selection: Tap any album to bring it to the front. Tap again to enter Album view.

Play/Pause: Tap the small Play/Pause button at the bottom left of the Cover Flow screen to pause or resume the currently playing track.

Album view: To enter the Cover Flow version of Album view, tap the small *i* (Info) button or the album cover. The cover flips and displays a list of tracks.

- Tap a track name to start playback.

- Tap Play/Pause to pause or resume playback.

- Tap anywhere on the screen (other than the Play/Pause button or a track name) to leave Album view.

Turn your iPod back to portrait orientation (with the Home button pointing down) to exit Cover Flow mode. Unless the Home button is down, you'll remain in Cover Flow mode.

Creating Playlists

The Music app on the iPod allows you to create two kinds of playlists, Regular and Genius, right on the iPod itself—no iTunes required. Playlists allow you to build a selection of related songs that you can listen to without interruption, providing you with your own soundtrack throughout the day. You might want an exercise routine playlist or a "I feel depressed and want to hate the world" playlist, depending on your mood, of course. Playlists can be used for feelings, for tasks, for parties, and so on. Think of a playlist as burning your own CD of your favorite songs for a given event.

Creating a Regular Playlist

A regular playlist is simply a collection of songs of your choosing played one after the other. To create a regular playlist on the iPod, tap the Playlist button in the shortcuts bar at the bottom of the screen. Next, tap the Add Playlist... menu item (see Figure 6–9). A New Playlist pop-up appears asking you to name your playlist. Name the playlist whatever you like, and tap Save.

Figure 6–9. *Creating a playlist with the Add Playlist... selection.*

The song list appears next, as shown in Figure 6–10. Navigate through your entire collection, and pick which songs you want to add by tapping the plus sign (+) to the right of each track name. After making your selections, tap Done.

Figure 6–10. *Add songs to your playlist with this Songs selection screen (left). Tap the blue button with the + to the right of each name to add a song. Tap Done to be taken to your new playlist (right).*

Tapping Done sends you to the playlist. From here, you can tap Shuffle to begin a random playback of your playlist songs or tap Playlists to go back to the previous screen. You also have a search field to search by playlist songs if it's a long list. Finally, you can edit the playlist, clear it, or delete it by tapping the buttons above the Shuffle command. Tapping Clear removes all the songs from the playlist but leave the name and empty playlist intact. Tapping Delete deletes the playlist. Your songs still remain on your iPod. You are asked to confirm your Clear and Delete selections before the commands are carried out.

To edit the playlist, tap Edit to add or remove items from your playlist. The playlist Edit mode, shown in Figure 6–11, provides all the tools you need to manage your new playlist:

Figure 6–11. *In Playlist Edit mode, tap – to delete a song or + to add a song. Use the grab bars to the right of each song to change its order in the playlist.*

- Tap the plus sign (+) at the top left to add songs to your playlist.

- Tap Clear Playlist to remove all songs from the playlist. A confirmation dialog box appears. Confirm by tapping the red Clear Playlist option, or tap Cancel to leave your songs unchanged.

- Tap the minus sign (–) in the red circle to the left of any name to begin deletion. Tap Delete to confirm, or tap anywhere else to cancel.

- Drag the move bars (the three parallel gray lines to the right of each track name) to reorder items within your playlist. Grab a move bar, drag it to a new position, and then release.

- Tap Done to leave Edit mode and return to your playlist.

Any playlists created on the iPod will sync back to your iTunes library and appear in the iTunes playlist collection.

Creating a Genius Playlist

Genius is a feature in iTunes that finds songs in your music library that go together. It does this by matching rhythm, beat, artists, genres, and Internet data. A Genius playlist is a list of songs that result when you choose to run the Genius feature on a song you are playing.

Genius playlists can be created in iTunes on your computer or on the iPod touch. However, to enable the Genius feature, you need to enable it through iTunes on your computer first. To do this, launch iTunes on your computer, go to the Store menu, and select Turn on Genius. You'll need to log in with an iTunes Store account (see Chapter 7) or create an iTunes account to access the Genius features. Enter your user name and password, agree to the terms and conditions, and sit back as Apple analyzes your music library.

You can create a Genius playlist by tapping the Genius icon in the center of the bar (see Figure 6–6). The icon looks like an atom surrounded by electrons. The Music app scans all your songs and compiles a new Genius playlist that collects other songs on your iPod that go great with your chosen song.

A new playlist named "Genius" appears on the screen (see Figure 6–12). In its list of songs, you can scroll through to see what Genius has picked out. You then have three options via three buttons at the top of the song list:

New: Tap New if you don't like the Genius playlist compilation. You'll then be presented with a list of your songs to choose a new song from.

Refresh: Tap Refresh if you want to keep the Genius playlist based on the original song you chose but want to get other songs that go well with the original one. This is good when you have listened to a playlist already (for example, Motown) and want to refresh the music that fills it without changing the theme (songs like the Jackson 5's "ABC").

Save: Tap Save once you are satisfied with the Genius playlist. After tapping Save, the Genius playlist labeled "Genius" disappears, and it is replaced by a Genius playlist that is named after the title of the song you chose to create the playlist. This playlist lives on your iPod and even sync back to iTunes on your computer.

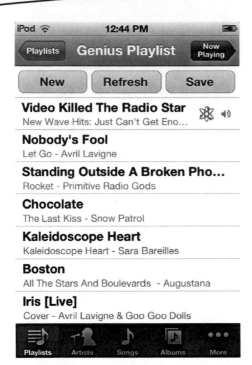

Figure 6–12. *The Genius playlist creation screen. The song with the atom icon is that which the playlist was created from.*

Editing a Genius Playlist

You have three options when editing a Genius playlist. The options appear as buttons above the song list when the Genius playlist is selected (see Figure 6–13).

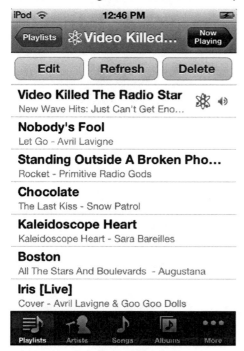

Figure 6–13. *The Genius playlist edit screen*

Edit: Tapping Edit lets you arrange your genius playlist songs in the order you want. You can also remove individual songs from the genius playlist.

Refresh: Tapping Refresh populates the Genius playlist with new songs that go well with the original one. The songs that were previously on the playlist are removed from it (but they'll still remain in the main music library).

Delete: Tapping Delete immediately deletes the saved Genius playlist. Its songs remain on your iPod.

> **NOTE:** Once a Genius playlist is synced back to iTunes on your computer, you will not be able to delete it on your iPod. Your only option will be Refresh. If you want to delete the Genius playlist, you must do so through iTunes on your computer.

Searching

The Music app has a simple yet powerful search feature that enables you to find a song quickly. To begin searching for a song, just scroll all the way up to the top of any category view (playlists, songs, artists, and so on). You'll find a search field at the very top (see Figure 6–14).

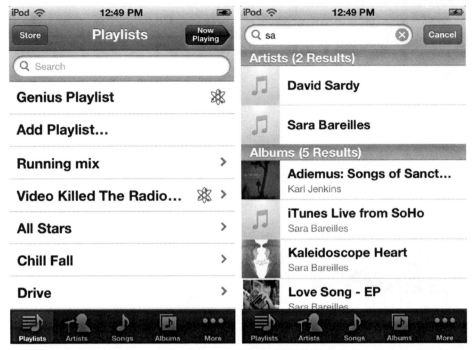

Figure 6–14. *The Music app's search function lies at the top of any category view (left). Results are displayed according to category (right).*

You can scroll through the search results as they are divided into categories by Songs, Artists, Albums, Composers, Podcasts, or Audiobooks. To play a song, simply tap it.

> **TIP:** You can also search for songs without opening the Music app. Use the iPad's Spotlight feature to the left of the Home screen to search for a song, and then tap it to begin playing.

Going Beyond the Music App

As you've seen, the Music app lets you browse through your media and play audio. But you can also work with playback in a couple ways that go beyond the Music application.

Saving Energy

"Sleep" your iPod during music playback to save energy. Press the Sleep/Wake button once. This locks your iPod and turns off the screen but allows your music to keep playing.

To peek at the current album cover during playback, tap Sleep/Wake. When you've loaded album art for the track, the cover appears on your lock screen instead of your normal wallpaper. If your track has no art, you still see the current time and track name. Double-tap the Home button to view your playback controls, as shown in Figure 6–15.

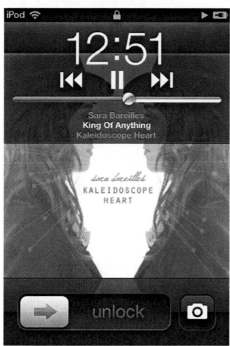

Figure 6–15. *During audio playback, your iPod lock screen displays the currently playing song and, if album art is available, its album cover. The small playing icon just to the left of the battery indicates that audio is playing back.*

Display Music Playback Controls When in Another App

We've already mentioned how your music, podcasts, and audiobooks keep playing even when you leave the Music app. The good news is that you don't need to go back into the iPod app to change tracks. Simply press the iPod's physical Home button twice in quick succession to bring up the iPod's multitasking bar (discussed in detail in Chapter 3). Swipe your finger from left to right until you see the Music controls slide onto the screen (see Figure 6–16). You can access these controls from any app or Home screen; they allow you to quickly play/pause a song, rewind or fast-forward, and skip to the next or previous song. To be taken immediately to the Music app, click the Music app icon.

Figure 6–16. *You can access the Music playback controls from any screen on the iPod by pressing the Home button twice.*

Adding a Sleep Timer

Unlike the Sleep/Wake button, which switches off your iPod screen without interrupting music playback, the Clock application allows you to "sleep" your iPod and tell it to end playback after a set interval. This is handy for those who like to listen to music while falling to sleep.

To set the sleep timer, on the Home screen, tap Clock. Then tap the Timer icon at the bottom right of the Timer screen. Scroll the hours and minutes wheels to select a period of time after which you want the iPod to sleep. Tap When Timer Ends, and choose Sleep iPod from the options list, as shown in Figure 6–17. Tap Set to set your sleep timer, and then tap the big green Start button

Figure 6–17. *The Sleep iPod function automatically ends iPod playback and locks your iPod.*

The iPod begins a timer countdown. When it reaches zero, it automatically stops iPod playback and locks your iPod.

Adjusting Music Settings

Surprisingly, for a feature-rich application like Music, the iPod touch provides just a few settings (see Figure 6–18). You'll find these in **Settings ➤ Music**, and they work as follows:

Shake to Shuffle: When this is set to ON, you can physically shake your iPod to shuffle the current list of playing songs. You should make sure this is switched to OFF if you are going to be moving while listening to music. A friend of mine had his iPod in his pocket while walking around one day, and he couldn't figure out why his songs kept changing!

Sound Check: Say you're listening to a song that was recorded way too low so you crank up the volume during playback. Then when the next song starts playing back, boom!—there go your eardrums. Sound Check prevents this problem. When you enable Sound Check, all your songs play at approximately the same sound level.

> **TIP:** You can also use Sound Check in iTunes. Choose **Edit ➤ Preferences ➤ Playback ➤ Sound Check** (Windows) or **iTunes ➤ Preferences ➤ Playback Sound Check** (Mac).

EQ: The iPod offers a number of equalizer settings that help emphasize the way different kinds of music play. Select **Settings ➤ Music ➤ EQ**, and choose from Acoustic, Dance, Spoken Word, and many other presets. To disable the equalizer, choose Off.

Volume Limit: Face it—personal music players bring your audio up close and very personal. It's so up close, in fact, that your hearing may be in peril. We strongly recommend you take advantage of the iPod's built-in volume limit to protect your ears. Navigate to **Settings ➤ Music ➤ Volume Limit**, and adjust the maximum volume using the slider, as shown in Figure 6–18. All the way to the left is mute—sure, you'll protect your ears, but you won't be able to hear anything. All the way to the right is the normal, unlimited maximum volume. If you're super paranoid or, more usually, if children have access to your iPod, tap Lock Volume Limit to open a screen that allows you to set a volume limit passcode. No one may override your volume settings without the correct passcode.

Lyrics & Podcast Info: Some songs and podcasts have embedded lyrics and text. When this is set to ON, you'll see that embedded text over the cover art in Album view. To disable the text, set this setting to OFF.

Group By Album Artist: With this option set, if a song has multiple artists, the same song appears under both artists when you are navigating your music by Artist in the music app.

For Home Sharing, enter you Apple ID and password here to activate Home Sharing on your iPod touch. Home Sharing allows you to stream music from iTunes on your computer and listen them on your iPod touch. Your iPod touch and computer must be connected to the same wireless network and iTunes must be open on your computer for your iPod to see its music.

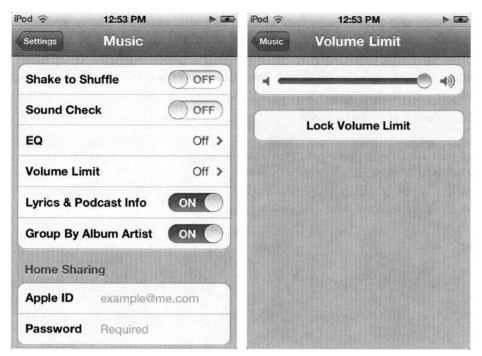

Figure 6–18. *The Music app's settings (left). Set the maximum volume for your iPod (right) by dragging the slider on the Volume Limit settings screen.*

Choosing Headphones

You can use virtually any headphones with your iPod touch, but reviewing every headphone here would fill more pages than *War and Peace*. Just know that you don't need to use the earbuds that came with the iPod touch. You could use any third-party headphone, from the cheap $2 kind you find at Walgreens to the $1,500 Shure noise-canceling earbuds.

You can also use wireless Bluetooth headphones that support A2DP (two-channel stereo audio streaming). Bluetooth headphones are great because you don't have a cord hanging over your body. On the other hand, the great thing about corded headphones is that they don't require power to work. Note that if you do use Bluetooth headphones and are going on a long jog or trip, make sure you have extra batteries or that the headphones are at least fully charged, or you could find yourself cut off from your music mid-song.

Summary

This chapter introduced all the ways you can browse and play media using the Music application. As you've seen, the new music player software is a lot more flexible and intuitive than the old click-wheel approach. With the iPod touch, you can flick through your entire collection and tap your way to the media you want to use. Here are a few points to think about before you move on to the next chapter:

- Cover Flow makes browsing through your media a simple visual pleasure. Tip your iPod on its side to enter Cover Flow mode.

- Don't be afraid to fill your shortcut bar with the items you use the most. It's easy to customize. It's also easy to put it back the way it started.

- Save your ears. Adjust your playback volume using the built-in volume controls and limiters.

- Don't forget about double-tapping the Home button to pull up music controls, regardless of your current application.

Chapter 7

Shopping at the iTunes Store

The iTunes Store realizes the promise of mobile commerce on handheld devices. The program is beautiful to look at and easy to use. It integrates itself seamlessly into your normal iTunes experience. That being said, it is admittedly a contrivance to sell you things. But these are things that you presumably want and can use while on the road. Stuck at an airport or wasting time in a coffee shop? Download some new music to enjoy, catch up on last week's episode or your favorite TV show, or watch that Hollywood blockbuster you never saw in theaters. Yes, the iTunes Store is a point of sale, but it's also a fascinating place to spend some time and an interesting application for your iPod touch.

Connecting to the iTunes Store

The iTunes icon on the button bar at the bottom of your iPod's home screen launches the iTunes Store application. It is purple and shows a white music note with a circle around it (see Figure 7–1).

Figure 7–1. *The iTunes application icon*

When you tap the iTunes icon, the application attempts to connect to Apple's storefront web server. Because of this, you must be located near a Wi-Fi hotspot and be connected to the Internet to use this application.

When your connection is not active or not strong enough to carry a signal, the iTunes Store application displays an error message saying your iPod touch can't connect to the store. To resolve this problem, return to your home screen, and tap **Settings ➤ Wi-Fi**. Make sure your iPod is connected to a wireless network and that the signal registers at the top left of your screen with at least one arc (and preferably three arcs). See Chapter 4 for details on checking your Wi-Fi connection. When your signal is weak, try moving physically closer to the wireless router serving your network.

Unfortunately, sometimes and iTunes Store connection issue is an Apple problem. Sometimes Apple's servers go down for a minute or two. When this happens, your only option is to check back frequently to see whether you can connect.

> **TIP:** It never hurts to ask where the router is. Sometimes the physical layout of a room (such as the large metal furnishings common in diners) may block your Wi-Fi signal in certain locations and not in others.

Signing in to Your iTunes Account

Before you can purchase anything from the iTunes Store, you need to sign in to it. To sign in, scroll to the bottom of any iTunes Store page in the app until you see the Sign In button. Tap it, and you'll be presented with two options, as shown in Figure 7–2: Use Existing Apple ID or Create New Apple ID.

Figure 7–2. *The iTunes Store sign-in screen*

If you are signing in using an existing account, all you have to do is enter your account name (usually your e-mail address) and password. You'll then be logged in and able to purchase songs and videos. If you are creating a new account, the process is quick and easy. Choose what country you are in, agree to the license agreement, and create your user name and password.

> **NOTE:** You may want to think about logging out of the iTunes Store if you have children who might use your iPod and, knowingly or unknowingly, download music or video that costs you money. To log out, scroll to the bottom of a page until you see your account name. Tap it, and then tap Sign Out.

Browsing Through the iTunes Store

Figure 7–3 shows the iTunes Store application screen. At the bottom of the screen you'll see shortcut buttons to different sections of the store. By default you'll see the Music, Videos, Search, Purchased, and More buttons.

> **NOTE:** The description of the iTunes Store is current as of this book's publication; however, the iTunes Store is basically just a web site, and Apple may (and has in the past) decide to tweak its interface whenever it sees fit.

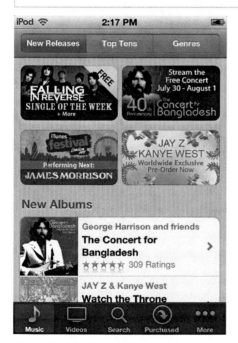

Figure 7–3. *The iTunes Store offers many ways to browse, find, and purchase music.*

If you tap More, you'll be taken to a screen that also links to the Genius, Ping, Ringtones, Podcasts, Audiobooks, and iTunes U sections of the store, as well as your current downloads. On the More screen, tap the Edit button to rearrange icons on the shortcuts bar at the bottom of the screen (Figure 7–4). You can, for example, replace the Videos shortcut button with the Audiobooks shortcut button.

Figure 7–4. *The More screen (left) lets you access other areas of the iTunes Store. You can also rearrange shortcut buttons by pressing the Edit button (right).*

Additionally, when you're in a Starbucks coffee shop, you may see a special option. Tap the Starbucks icon in the button bar to discover which song is currently playing in your location. You can also browse the special Starbucks catalog. These Starbucks features are only available to U.S. iTunes account holders in U.S. Starbucks locations. Now, let's explore the different sections of the iTunes Store.

The Music Store

The Music section of the iTunes Store is the first one you'll see (see Figure 7–3). This section is broken down into three categories: New Releases, Top Tens, and Genres. You'll also see banner ads and album promotions.

Tap any of the buttons at the top of your screen to access the following sections:

New Releases: The New Releases section includes a list of albums with recent release dates. Tap any item to open the album page and find track-by-track listings.

Top Tens: The most popular-selling albums and tracks in more than 20 categories ranging from Alternative to World appear in the Top Tens section. Tap any item to move to its feature page. As you can see in Figure 7–5, Top Tens breaks down the categories into Top Songs or Top Albums.

Genres: Use the Genres list to limit your featured selections to a particular genre, such as Hip-Hop/Rap, Country, or Pop. Choosing a genre opens a screen dedicated to the biggest current hits for that kind of music (see Figure 7–5). Think of the genre sections as mini-stores for your current mood.

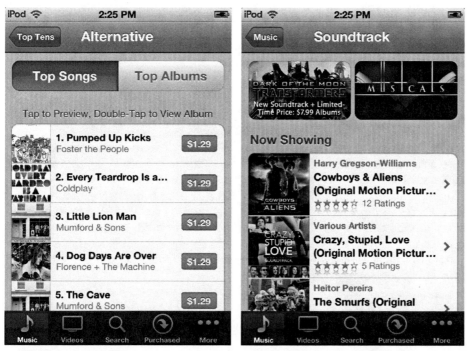

Figure 7–5. *The Top Tens section (left) allows you to view the most popular items by album or songs. This is the top-ten listing for the Alternative genre. The Genres section (right) allows you to view songs and albums in mini-stores according to genre. This is the mini-store for the Soundtrack genre.*

Exploring the Top Tens

The Top Tens section lists the best-selling albums and songs by genre, such as Alternative or Rock. It's also my favorite section and behaves like the rest of the sections in the iTunes Store, so it's a perfect place to get acquainted with. Tap any genre name to open a top-ten listing (see Figure 7–5), and then tap either Top Songs or Top Albums.

Here are a few tips for making the most of the Top Tens section:

■ When viewing songs, tap any song to preview it, or double-tap to open its album.

- When viewing albums, tap the album name to open a track list, and then tap a song to preview. Previews play back for up to 30 seconds.

- View the most popular songs storewide by tapping iTunes instead of a genre. (Figure 7–5 shows the list for the Alternative genre.) It's listed as the first item in the Top Tens section before the actual genres.

- If you do not find your favorite genre on the main Top Tens screen (only Pop, Alternative, Hip-Hop/Rap, Rock, and Country are listed for the U.S. store), scroll down and tap More Top Tens for the complete list. You'll discover Reggae, R&B/Soul, and more.

- What is popular and "top" changes over time. As you navigate through these lists, you may actually see new items as the store downloads updated lists from the iTunes server.

Previewing and Buying Music

Figure 7–6 shows the layout when browsing a typical album. You're shown the cover art, the name of the artist and album, and the option to buy the entire album (in this case, for $9.99). Below the option to buy the entire album, you'll see a Like button and a Post button. Tapping either one of these allows you to "like" or post a link to the album on your Ping wall (I discuss Ping later in this chapter). Below the Like and Post buttons are the average user ratings and reviews. Tap the stars to read through individual reviews. You can also create your own review. Reviews are tied to your iTunes account, so you have to authenticate to leave a review. Apple does this so a single person can't leave multiple negative (or positive) reviews.

Figure 7–6. *Previewing and buying music is fun and easy.*

Tap the name of any song to listen to a preview. You'll see the track number or album image next to the name flip around to show the playback control, as shown in Figure 7–7.

Figure 7–7. *Each song listing allows you to play a 30- to 90-second preview and lists the purchase price for the track.*

Here are a few pointers about previewing music:

■ Previews are 30 to 90 seconds long seconds long, depending on the song, and generally start playback 30 seconds into the song. If a song is shorter than 30 seconds, it plays back for as long as it can. For example, search for Monty Python's "Spam" song. Select it, and its "preview" plays back the entire track.

■ The dark pie wedge shows how much of the preview has played. The wedge grows over time until the preview has finished, and the wedge is a complete dark circle.

■ The Stop button in the center of the control allows you to stop playback.

■ You cannot pause and resume playback. Playback always starts at the same point.

■ When you are previewing a song, you'll have the option to "like" or post a link to that single song on your Ping wall.

To purchase music, tap the price to the right of the track name. The button expands, turns green, and changes from the price to BUY SONG. If you are purchasing an entire album, the price button expands to say BUY ALBUM. Tap a second time to confirm that you really do want to buy the selection. In a delightful animation, your new song jumps directly into the Downloads icon at the bottom of the screen (or the More button if you don't have the Downloads shortcut showing at the bottom of the screen), and a red badge with the number of currently downloading items appears.

If you haven't recently entered your password, the iTunes Store app prompts you to do so by opening a dialog box alert. Type in your password, and tap OK. Pay special care while typing, because you will not be able to see the text. It appears as a series of dots instead to protect your security. Once you've entered the proper password and tapped OK, your download begins.

The Video Store

The great thing about the iTunes Store application is that all sections look and behave in the same manner. As you can see in Figure 7–8, the Video store has the same layout as the music store. The difference between the Music and Video stores are that in addition to purchasing content, in the Video store you can also rent movies and TV shows.

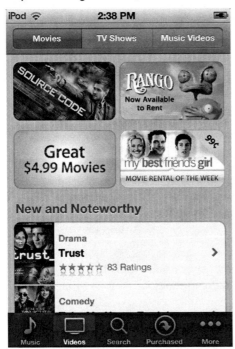

Figure 7–8. *The Video store has a similar look and feel as the other iTunes Stores.*

The video store is divided into three categories along the top: Movies, TV Shows, and Music Videos. All three categories allow you to preview and purchase videos in much the same way. Let's look at your typical movie information page.

In Figure 7–9 we've selected the excellent documentary *The Corporation*. From the *The Corporation* page, you can choose to buy or rent the movie by clicking the respective buttons. Some movies you can only buy, not rent. If you do rent a movie, you have 30 days to begin watching it, but once you begin watching it, you must complete it within 24 hours. After the 30-day and 24-hour time limits are reached, the movie is automatically deleted.

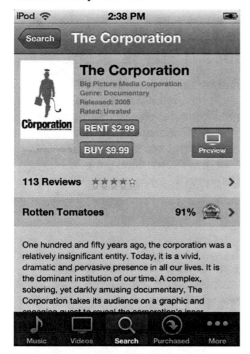

Figure 7–9. *The movie information page*

> **NOTE:** Your iPod is nice enough to remind you about the rental state. You'll be notified when the period is about to expire and when the periods have expired. Let's see Blockbuster do that!

You can view the movie's theatrical trailer by tapping the preview button. The movie preview plays full-screen and automatically returns you to the movie's information page when it is done playing. On the information page you can read user reviews or critic reviews from popular film web site Rotten Tomatoes. Finally, the summary of the movie and a list of major cast and crew are presented.

While the previews for movies are usually the full theatrical trailer, previews for television episodes and music videos run 30 seconds only.

Once you have found a video you want to purchase, tap the Buy button. The button expands, turns green, and changes from the price to BUY MOVIE. Tap a second time to confirm that you really do want to buy the selection. Your new video jumps directly into the Downloads icon at the bottom of the screen (or the More button if you don't have the Downloads shortcut showing at the bottom of the screen), and a red badge with the number of currently downloading items appears.

> **TIP:** Download times can be enormous, especially when you're on the road. Factor slow hotel Wi-Fi into your rental and purchase choices. Want to catch a nice movie on Saturday night? Your download might not finish until Sunday afternoon.

The Podcasts, Audiobooks, and iTunes U Stores

If you understand how to navigate the music and video stores, the remaining Ringtones, Podcasts, Audiobooks, and iTunes U stores will be a breeze, because they are arranged in the same way. One cool difference, however, is that when you preview a podcast or iTunes U lesson, you can actually watch or listen to the entire episode just by streaming it. So, if you are low on available space on your iPod, you don't actually need to download the episode to view it. Also note that you use the iTunes Store app to buy audiobooks only, not regular books. To purchase regular books, you use the iBooks app discussed in Chapter 9.

Searching the iTunes Store

The Search screen, shown in Figure 7–10, allows you to perform a live search with instant feedback. Start typing, and the iTunes Store application shows all the matches to your search string, updating whenever you type a new character.

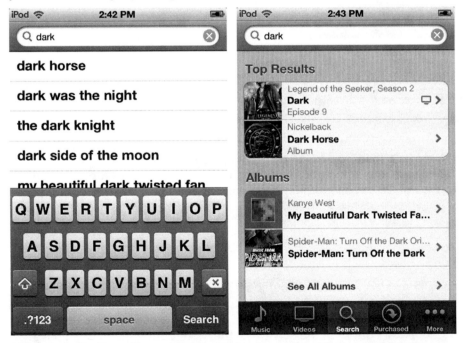

Figure 7–10. The iTunes Store application matches your search string to available tracks as you type (left) and presents your results to you by category (right).

When you locate an item you were searching for, tap its search suggestion. The store moves you to the search results page that lists all the results by categories. Tap the item you are looking for to go to its information page.

Purchased

The Purchased screen allows you to see all the songs, videos, and audiobooks you've ever bought from the iTunes Store. It doesn't matter whether you bought them through iTunes on your computer, through the iTunes Store on your iPod touch, or through the iTunes Store on another iOS device. If you bought any items with the Apple ID you are using on the iTunes Store on your iPod touch, your entire purchase history appears when you tap the Purchased button (Figure 7–11).

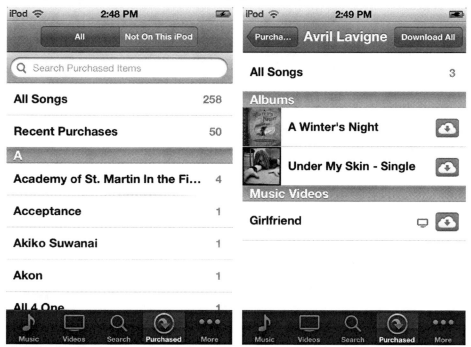

Figure 7–11. *Viewing your purchase history*

You can sort through all your purchase history or just your purchase history for items not currently on your iPod touch by tapping the All or Not on this iPod tab at the top of the Purchased screen (Figure 7–11, left). If you scroll through your Purchased list, you can select any item, an artist, for example, and see all the songs you've bought by that artist (Figure 7–11, right).

To redownload those songs (or videos) for free, tap the button with the downward arrow in a cloud button; to download all the items by that artist, select the Download All button at the top of the screen. You will not be charged again for downloading the items you already bought. This is a great feature if you're away from your computer and find you really want to listen to a song you've purchased but you forgot to sync it to your iPod touch.

Downloads

The Downloads screen (see Figure 7–12) tracks the download progress for your recent purchases. Once you've completely downloaded a track, it disappears from this screen and adds itself to your iPod's library.

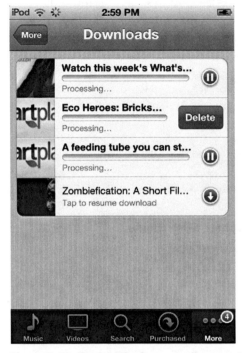

Figure 7–12. *The Downloads screen allows you to track progress as newly purchased tracks arrive on your iPod touch. The red bubble on the More or Downloads button indicates the number of tracks left to download.*

You can interact with currently downloading items in three ways:

Pause a download: Press the blue-and-white pause buttons (the two vertical lines) while a download is in progress. This pauses the download while the next item to be download automatically begins downloading.

Resume a download: Press the blue-and-white arrow button to resume a paused download.

Delete a download: Swipe your finger left to right over the download item, and a Delete button will appear. Tap the button to remove the downloading item.

At times, you may be unable to connect properly from your iPod to the iTunes Store to complete a purchase, at which point your downloads start to back up a bit. This has happened to me numerous times. The tracks collect in the Downloads screen until you get a better connection or until the store resumes regular download service.

Redeeming Codes

You can redeem gift certificates and codes on your iPod touch. On the Music screen, scroll all the way to the bottom of the page until you see a blue Redeem button. Tap the Redeem button; enter your iTunes gift card, gift certificate, or other iTunes code into the text box; and tap Redeem. Your iTunes account updates, and you are able to spend those funds directly in the iPod touch iTunes Store.

Transferring Purchased Items to Your Computer

Transferring something you've purchased on your iPod touch back to your computer is as simple as, well…doing nothing. All music, videos, and podcasts bought on your iPod touch automatically appear in your iTunes library on your computer thanks to the magic of iCloud, Apple's cloud-based storage and syncing solution. Any purchased tracks appear in a special playlist, which appears in the Store section of your iTunes source list. The playlist is called "Purchased on *your iPod touch name*"—in my case, "Purchased on Michael's iPod" (the name of the iPod touch used), as shown in Figure 7–13.

Figure 7–13. *All iPod touch purchases transfer to your computer on your next sync. You'll find all your new songs in the "Purchased on" playlist, which is automatically created during synchronization.*

> **NOTE:** The iTunes Store application is smart enough to know about the Complete My Album feature. If you've already purchased tracks on a given album, you'll be given the option to purchase individual tracks. Bonus content, such as liner notes, becomes available to you when you return to your home computer, but these items do not download to your iPod.

Getting Free Music and Videos

The official iTunes Store for many countries (including the United States, Australia, New Zealand, Canada, France, Japan, the Netherlands, and the United Kingdom) offers a free single of the week each Tuesday. You can download these tracks onto your iPod touch using the iTunes Store application, but you cannot find them easily. They aren't listed separately, and the application does not offer a freebies search.

Likewise with videos, there are many free video clips available on the iTunes Store; it's just rather hard finding them on your iPod touch sometimes. Free videos usually are no longer than a few minutes and are really just commercials for an upcoming TV series or movie. Have a look around, but don't expect to find any truly free full-length movies or TV shows. A caveat to this are free podcast or iTunes U videos.

Getting Social with Ping

You've probably noticed the chat bubble icon labeled *Ping* in some of the images in this chapter (see Figure 7–4). I've saved Ping to talk about until now because, frankly, it's not that cool. Ping is Apple's attempt at social media. Think of it as Facebook for iTunes account holders, except you can't share videos or photos or do most of the other things you can with Facebook.

What Ping allows you to do is follow your favorite artists to see what they're up to: concerts, new albums, and so on. You can also follow your friends to see what kind of music they like at the moment. To use Ping, you first have to sign into it using iTunes on your computer. To do this, open up iTunes 10.0 or newer on your computer, and select Ping from the source bar under the Store heading.

You'll be asked to turn Ping on (see Figure 7–14) and then be asked for your iTunes password. You'll then be taken to your Ping profile home page (Figure 7–15) where you can upload a profile picture, search for friends on Ping, and follow artists.

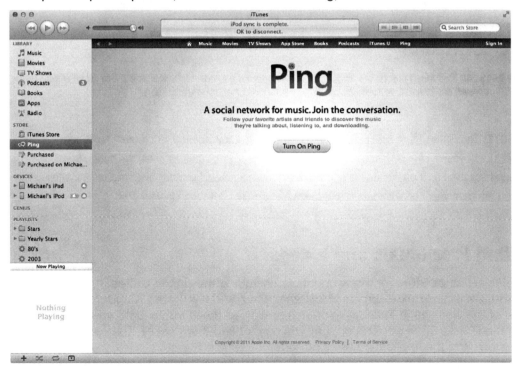

Figure 7–14. *Ping in iTunes 10*

Figure 7–15. *Ping. Meh.*

Once you've set up Ping on iTunes on your computer, you can then go back to the iTunes Store app on your iPod touch (Figure 7–16) and access Ping by tapping the Ping button in the bottom toolbar. From there you can browse through Ping using the three tabs at the top:

Activity: Shows you the latest status updates of the artists you are following.

People: Shows you a list of everyone you follow or who follows you. It also notifies you of any "follow" requests—in other words, people who have friended you.

My Profile: Shows you your Ping profile. It's kind of lame that you can't edit your profile from the app, but again, Ping is kind of lame.

Chances are, unless you are a huge music fan, Ping will not appeal to you. It's a social network for music fans; the rest of us can stick with Facebook.

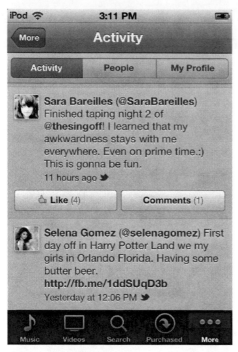

Figure 7–16. *Ping in the iTunes Store app. Still meh, unless it's important to you to know a Disney star had a holiday in Harry Potter Land.*

Summary

Not only does the iPod's iTunes Store application allow you to buy music, videos, podcasts, and audiobooks from iTunes right now, it also shows a great deal of promise as the forerunner of a generation of future mobile points of sale. This chapter has shown you how to use this application to search, select, preview, and purchase music. Here are a few points to take away from this chapter:

- Don't confuse the iTunes Store application with the Music application. The iTunes Store app is for downloading music and videos, and the Music app is for playing your music.

- If you know how to browse through one section of the iTunes Store, you know how to browse through all the sections. Apple has done a good job at making the iTunes Store app easy to navigate.

- Any item purchased on the iTunes Store app automatically syncs back to the iTunes library on your computer. This includes movie rentals! If you started watching a rented movie on your iPod touch and want to finish it on your laptop, sync the iPod to your computer. You can then finish watching the rental on your computer. Just be sure to finish the movie within the 24-hour time window! After that, it is automatically deleted from all your devices.

- Be sure to transfer purchases back to your computer. If you don't and you try to redownload the song or video from the iTunes store on your computer, you will be charged again!

- Play around with Ping, but don't expect to be blown away unless you are a music freak.

Chapter 8

Shopping at the App Store

Perhaps the coolest thing about the iPod touch is the multitude of apps available for it. As of this writing, more than 450,000 apps are available for the iPod touch. These apps range from games to medical programs to reference utilities and more. If there's something you're interested in, there's most likely an app for it. The best news of all is that many apps are totally free, while most others are priced between 99 cents to $2 (though there are some apps that do cost hundreds of dollars). Even long after you've bought it, apps keep your iPod touch fresh and new, and with the App Store on your iPod touch, you can shop for apps wherever you have a Wi-Fi connection.

Connecting to the App Store

The App Store icon on the button bar at the bottom of your iPod's home screen launches the App Store application. It is blue and shows a white *A* made up of a ruler, a pencil, and a brush with a circle around it (see Figure 8–1).

Figure 8–1. *The App Store icon*

When you tap the App Store icon, the application attempts to connect to Apple's storefront web server. Because of this, you must be located near a Wi-Fi hotspot and be connected to the Internet to use this application.

When your connection is not active or not strong enough to carry a signal, the App Store application displays the error message. To resolve this problem, return to your home screen, and tap **Settings ➤ Wi-Fi**. Make sure your iPod is connected to a wireless network and that the signal registers at the top left of your screen with at least one arc (and preferably three arcs). See Chapter 4 for details on checking your Wi-Fi connection.

When your signal is weak, try moving physically closer to the wireless router serving your network.

Signing in to Your App Store Account

Before you can purchase anything from the App Store, you need to sign in to it. To sign in, scroll to the bottom of any App Store page in the app until you see the Sign In button. Tap it, and you'll be presented with three options, as shown in Figure 8–2: Use Existing Apple ID, Create Apple ID, or iForgot.

If you are signing in using an existing account, all you have to do is enter your Apple ID (usually your e-mail address) and password. You'll then be logged in and able to purchase apps. If you are creating a new Apple ID, the process is quick and easy. Choose what country you are in, agree to the license agreement, and create your user name and password. If you've forgotten your Apple ID, tap iForgot, and you'll be taken through a short process to retrieve your existing Apple ID.

Figure 8–2. *The App Store sign-in screen*

Browsing Through the App Store

Figure 8–3 shows the App Store. Because it is dealing only with one thing—apps—and not a multitude of music, videos, podcasts, and audiobooks, and so on, the App Store has a simpler layout than the iTunes Store. At the bottom of the screen, you'll see shortcut buttons to different sections of the store. These buttons are Featured,

Categories, Top 25, Search, and Updates. Let's explore the different sections of the App Store and how to navigate them.

Figure 8–3. *The App Store storefront*

Featured

The Featured section of the App Store is the first one you'll see (see Figure 8–3). This section is broken down into three categories: New, What's Hot, and Genius. You'll also see banner ads for specific apps and collections of apps. For individual apps, tap any listing, and you'll be taken to its information page (discussed later) where you can read more about the app and download it.

Tap any of the tabs at the top of your screen to access the following sections:

New: The New section includes a list of the most recent apps that are available on the App Store.

What's Hot: This section features the most popular free and paid-for apps.

Genius: Genius is a feature Apple originally introduced in iTunes to recommend music you may like based on the music in your existing iTunes library. Apple has extended this Genius capability to its App Store. Tap the Genius tab, and you'll be presented with a list of free and paid apps that Apple thinks you'll like based on your previous app downloads.

In my experience, the Genius recommendations are spotty at best, but give it a try for yourself and see whether the feature works for you. You'll first need to turn on the Genius recommendations feature and agree to send information about the apps you've downloaded to Apple. This is kind of redundant since Apple already knows all the apps you've downloaded. Once you click Turn On Genius (Figure 8–4), you'll see a list of recommendations. You'll see the name of an app you've downloaded above the name of the recommended apps in which the Genius recommendation was based on. If you found an app you are interested in, tap its listing to go to its Info page.

Figure 8–4. *Turning on the Genius feature and the subsequent Genius list of apps*

Not interested in one of the recommendations and never will be? Swipe the app from left to right to reveal a red Remove button. Tap the button to remove the app from the Genius list.

Categories

The second button on the shortcuts bar at the bottom of the screen is the Categories button. This divides the Apps Store into 20 categories (see Figure 8–5). Categories is a great feature when you know you want a certain type of app but are not sure exactly what app that is. Tap any category to be taken to that category screen. On the individual category screens, you'll see three tabs labeled Top Paid, Top Free, and Release Date. The tabs are just different ways of sorting the apps in the category, with the goal of making apps easier for you to find.

Top Paid: Lists the top paid apps people have purchased in that category

Top Free: Lists the top free apps people have downloaded in that category

Release Date: Lists the most recently released apps in that category

Figure 8–5. *The categories screen (left) and a subsequent category view showing lists of Top Paid, Top Free apps, and apps by Release Date*

As you might imagine, the Top Paid, Top Free, and Release Date lists change quite frequently. By default, 25 apps are shown on each tab. At the bottom of the 25th app, you can tap Twenty Five More to add another 25 apps to the list.

> **NOTE:** The Games category has its own category sublist ranging from Action and Arcade games to Trivia and Word games.

Top 25

The third button at the bottom of the App Store is the Top 25 button. Tap this to be taken to a list of the top 25 downloaded apps in the App Store (see Figure 8–6). The Top 25 list takes into account apps from all categories and, as you can image, changes frequently. The Top 25 categories are important because they are probably the single best way to figure out what's worth buying. It's the wisdom of the masses. If an app isn't really good, it probably won't show up in the Top 25 lists.

Figure 8–6. *The Top 25 screen in the App Store*

At the top of the Top 25 screen, you'll see three tabs labeled Top Paid, Top Free, and Top Grossing.

Top Paid: Lists the top paid apps people have purchased in the App Store.

Top Free: Lists the top free apps people have downloaded in the App Store.

Top Grossing: Lists the biggest moneymakers in the App Store. This is a category Apple added in order to help big app developers, such as major game developers, who wanted to port their popular games to the iPhone and iPod touch. Porting major titles to the iPod costs a lot of money, so the developers have to charge more for the games. Top Grossing ensures that costlier apps get eye time with customers and aren't pushed out of the way by all the 99-cent games.

At the bottom of the Top 25 screens, you can tap Show Top 50 to add the next 25 apps to theExploring an App's Information Page

After browsing the App Store, you're sure to come across an app you're interested in. Tap the app's listing on any App Store screen to be taken to its information page (see Figure 8–7). You'll only see parts of the Info page at a time since you have to scroll through it, but in the figure, we show you what the entire Info page for an app looks like for clarity's sake.

Figure 8–7. *The Info page*

The page is basically divided into three parts: the top, the preview images, and the bottom. At the top of the page you'll find the app icon and name, as well as its user ratings. You'll find a blue button either with FREE or with the price of the app in it. Tap the blue button to download the app (we'll talk more about that in a moment). The remainder of the top of the screen is dedicated to a short text description of what the app does. Beneath the price button you'll see the Game Center icon if the app or game offers Game Center support (discussed later in this chapter). Finally, you'll see a section for Top In-App Purchases if the app offers additional add-ons you can buy from within the game.

In the center of the Info screen you'll see a series of pictures. These pictures are screenshots of the app; they show you what the app looks like. Below the screenshots you'll see a series of white dots. Each dot represents a picture. Swipe to the left or right to move through the pictures.

The bottom of the screen is where you'll find a link to user reviews of the app, a Tell a Friend button that allows you to send an e-mail with a link to the app in it, and a Report a Problem button that allows you to send a note to Apple if you find a problem with the app. The remainder of the screen shows general information about the app: who made it, its size, its age rating, its posting date, and its version number.

Keep in mind that ratings aren't always reliable. A developer can easily have a bunch of his friends rate his app five stars. It doesn't happen all the time, but it does happen. As we mentioned earlier, the best way to tell whether an app is really good is if it appears in a Top 25 category. It also never hurts to read an app's reviews.

Buying and Downloading Apps

There are two kinds of apps in the App Store: paid and free. Depending on which the app is, you'll either see a either a blue FREE button or see a blue button with a price in it at the top of an app's Info page. To download the app, tap the blue button. It will turn into a green INSTALL button for free apps or a BUY NOW button for paid apps.

Tap the green button, and a confirmation window will pop up asking you to enter your iTunes account password. Enter it, and tap OK; you will then be taken to your iPod's home screen. On that screen you will see a dimmed icon of the app you just purchased with a blue progress bar signifying the download (see Figure 8–8). Once the bar fills, your app download is complete! Tap the app's icon, and enjoy!

> **NOTE:** If you've already bought an app, you'll see only a blue INSTALL button next to it, and tapping it immediately begins downloading the app to your device. You will not be charged again for redownloading an app you've already bought.

Figure 8–8. *After you buy an app, you are returned to your home screen where the app proceeds to download. The download is signified by the blue progress bar.*

Searching the App Store

Sometimes you may not want to browse the App Store. You may be on a mission to find a specific app or apps related to specific things. That's where the search feature comes in. The Search screen, shown in Figure 8–9, allows you to perform a live search with instant feedback. Start typing, and the App Store shows all the matches to your search string, updating whenever you type a new character.

Figure 8–9. *The App Store search feature matches your search string to available tracks as you type (left) and presents your results to you in a list (right).*

Tap the search button on the keyboard to search for your term, or tap any of the search suggestions that appear above the keyboard. You'll be taken to the search results page that lists all the results that match your query. Tap the item you are looking for to go to its information page.

Downloading Updates and Previously Purchased Apps

Developers are always updating their apps. Updates can include major new features or just subtle performance tweaks. How do you know when there's an update to one of the apps you've downloaded? A red badge with a number appears in the corner of the App Store icon on the iPod home screen (Figure 8–10). The number in the red button tells you how many of your apps have available updates.

Figure 8–10. *The red dot tells you how many apps have an update available. In this case, two apps have an update available.*

To download the updated apps, tap the App Store icon, and then tap the Updates button at the bottom of the App Store (see Figure 8–11). You'll be presented with a list of all the apps on your iPod touch that need updating. Tap Update All to automatically download all app updates. To download just one of many app updates, select the app from the Update list, and tap the blue UPDATE button that appears on the app's Info page.

Figure 8–11. *The App Store's Updates page shows you available updates for apps on your iPod touch.*

> **NOTE:** At this time, if an app shows up in the Updates page, the update is free. You will never be charged again for any apps that appear on the Updates page. This of course can change in the future.

From the Updates section of the App Store, you can also redownload any other apps you have previously download. It doesn't matter if they were free or paid apps. From the Updates screen, tap the Purchased button (Figure 8–11).

The Purchased screen (Figure 8–12) lists all the apps you've ever purchased from the iTunes Store. It doesn't matter if you bought them through iTunes on your computer, through the iTunes Store on your iPod touch, or through the iTunes Store on another iOS device. If you bought any items with the Apple ID you are using on the iTunes Store on your iPod touch, your entire purchase history appears when you tap the Purchased button.

Figure 8–12. *Viewing your purchase history*

You can sort through all your purchase history or just your purchase history for items not currently on your iPod touch by tapping the All or Not on this iPod tab at the top of the Purchased screen (Figure 8–12).

To redownload any of your previously purchased apps for free, tap the button with the downward arrow in a cloud icon. You will not be charged again for downloading the items you already bought. This is a great feature if you're away from your computer and find you really want an app that you had download but you forgot to sync it to your iPod touch. It's also a great way to check through all your apps and locate one you may have forgotten about, like a really good game.

Redeeming Gift Certificates and Codes

You can redeem gift certificates and codes on your iPod touch. On the Featured screen, scroll all the way to the bottom of the page until you see a blue Redeem button. Tap the Redeem button; enter your App Store gift card, gift certificate, or other App Store code into the text box; and tap Redeem. Your App Store account is updated, and you will be able to spend those funds directly in the App Store. Remember to type carefully, or else you might get a "code not valid" error. If you see an error, go back and carefully type in the code again.

Transferring Purchased Items to Your Computer

In the past (iOS 4 and earlier), all apps bought on your iPod touch transferred back to your computer when you synced the next time. Now any apps bought on your iPod touch are automatically downloaded to your iTunes library on your Mac or PC and any other iOS devices you may have, like an iPhone or iPad.

This happens through the magic of Apple's iCloud service, which is essentially a cloud-storage and syncing service. Don't worry about deleting an app from your iPod either. While an app downloaded on any device will download on all other devices, an app deleted from a device will only be deleted on that device and not on the others.

Buying Apps Through iTunes on Your PC

It's important not to forget that you aren't limited to buying apps for your iPod touch on your iPod touch. You can also use the iTunes Store on your computer to browse for and purchase apps. We tend to browse for apps through iTunes more than the App Store app on our iPod because of our large computer screens. As you can see in Figure 8–13, the iTunes Store has a nice wide-screen layout that lets you easily navigate through all the app offerings.

Figure 8–13. *The desktop version of the App Store in iTunes*

Any apps bought in the App Store in iTunes is automatically transferred to your iPod touch on the next sync. See Chapter 2 for more details.

Getting Your Game on in Game Center

Not content at stopping with Ping (see the previous chapter), with iOS 4.1 Apple introduced Game Center, which is a gaming social media application (Figure 8–14). With Game Center, you can play certain games you've downloaded from the App Store against your friends or even complete strangers from around the world. If you are a big iPod touch gamer, then Game Center will appeal to you.

Figure 8–14. *The Game Center icon*

To use Game Center, you'll first need to log in (Figure 8–15). You can do so using your existing Apple ID, or you can create a new ID right inside Game Center. Once logged in, you'll be able to set your online status, see which of your friends are online or invite new friends, view all the Game Center–compatible games you have on your iPod touch, view the leaderboards for those games, and view any pending friend requests.

Figure 8–15. *Log into Game Center (left) to be presented with your personal gaming stats.*

Since its introduction in iOS 4.1, Game Center has become a big hit. Improvements to Game Center in iOS 5 include the ability to add your own profile picture, get game recommendations from within the app, and view overall achievement scores. Needless to say, Game Center caught on as a social media platform where Ping did not.

Summary

The App Store is one of the coolest things about the iPod touch. It's your gateway to hundreds or thousands of apps that constantly turn your device into an amazing new machine. Here are some tips to take away with you:

- You can download apps through the App Store on the iPod touch as well as through the iTunes Store on your desktop or laptop.

- Most apps on the App Store are free or very cheap.

- Use the App Store to check for updates to your apps. All updates will always be free.

- Any item purchased on the App Store app will automatically sync back to your iTunes app library on your computer.

- App Store categories like Top 25 frequently change. Check back often for new apps!

- Use the Genius feature to find new apps you might like based on your current app downloads.

- Game Center brings social media to gaming. If you're a big gamer, it's worth a try. If you're the kind of person who just likes to play Tetris while waiting for the train to work, Game Center is a pass.

Chapter 9

Reading Books and Newspapers with iBooks and Newsstand

Not only is your iPod touch a wonderful device for playing games, surfing the Web, and listening to music, but with iBooks, it's also a powerful e-book reader with a library of more than 30,000 free books at your fingertips as well as thousands more paid books, including many *New York Times* best sellers. But iBooks doesn't stop there! You can add your PDFs to iBooks so you can carry them with you on the iPod touch. This allows you to access all your PDFs from the same library as your books—a great feature for those of you who regularly work with or receive PDF files. In addition to iBooks, Apple has introduced Newsstand in iOS 5. Newsstand lets you view and buy all your magazine and newspaper subscriptions in one easy to access location.

In this chapter, you'll discover how to navigate your iBooks bookshelf and the books themselves. You'll also learn about bookmarking favorite passages from books, creating notes, and even having a book read to you aloud. I'll take you through all the PDF features of iBooks. Finally, I'll explore Newsstand and show you how to shop for and organize all your subscriptions. Let's get started.

iBooks App

The iBooks application does not ship on the iPod touch. To use it, you must download it first for free from the iTunes Store. Once you have done this, the iBooks icon appears on your iPod touch's home screen (see Figure 9–1).

Figure 9–1. *iBooks icon*

Tap the icon to launch the iBooks app. When you do, you'll be presented with your iBooks bookshelf (see Figure 9–2). The bookshelf is populated with any e-books you have added to your books library in iTunes (more on that in a moment).

Figure 9–2. *The iBooks bookshelf*

Syncing Books

Before you can sync books, you need to first get some to sync. We talked about syncing books to your iTunes library in Chapter 2, but we'll touch on it again here. There are a few ways for you to obtain books to sync to your iPod touch.

iBookstore

In the previous chapters, you learned how to buy music, videos, and apps using the separate applications to buy them (such as iTunes for music and movies and the App

Store for apps). With iBooks, Apple has combined both the store and the reader into one app. In the upper-right corner of your bookshelf, you'll see a Store button (see Figure 9–2). Tap this button, and your bookshelf flips around like it's a secret passageway. On the backside of the bookshelf, you are presented with the iBookstore. Here you can buy books, download samples, and navigate best-seller lists. Let's look at the iBookstore more closely now.

As you can see in Figure 9–3, the iBookstore is laid out similarly to the iTunes and App stores. At the top of the store you'll see a Categories button that allows you to select specific sections of the iBookstore like Mystery or Non-Fiction. The Library button on the right flips the store around and brings you back to your iBooks bookshelf. The bottom of the screen is populated with five shortcut buttons that allow you to browse the bookstore in different ways.

Figure 9–3. *The iBooks bookshelf. The Featured page is the first page you'll see.*

Featured: This is the home page of the iBookstore. On it you'll see banner ads for specific books or collections of books. Below the banner ads you'll see individual listing of select books. Tap any listing to be taken to the book's information page. We'll talk more about a book's individual information page a little later.

Charts: This button displays two tabs at the top of the screen: Top Charts and New York Times.

Top Charts shows you the top downloaded paid and free books on the iBookstore in groups of ten. You can tap Ten More Books at the bottom of the listings to show an additional ten books.

The *New York Times* gives you a listing of its fiction and nonfiction best sellers that are available on the iBookstore. Note that only *New York Times* books that are available on the iBookstore appear in the charts. If the iBookstore doesn't sell a particular book that is on the *New York Times* list, it does not appear on the screen.

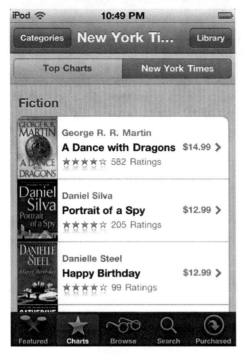

Figure 9–4. *Charts shows you the top iBookstore downloads as well as the New York Times best sellers.*

Browse: This allows you to search through the iBookstore by author (Figure 9–5). Scroll through the list with your finger, or drag your finger along the alphabet on the side to jump to a specific letter. Authors are in alphabetical order by their last names. You can choose to browse by authors of paid or free books by selecting the Top Paid or Top Free tab at the top of the screen. You can further whittle down your authors list by choosing a specific category from the categories button. For example, selecting Romance will show only romance authors.

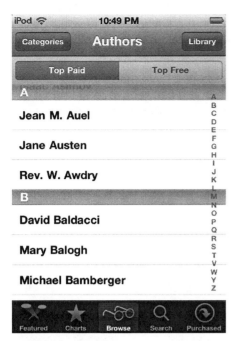

Figure 9–5. *The Browse function lets you search through the iBookstore by author.*

Search: The search function allows you to search for a book by typing in the name of the author or title.

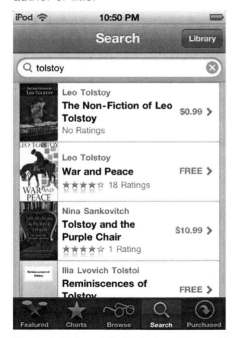

Figure 9–6. *Search for books by author or title.*

After you've entered your query, tap the search button on the keyboard, and you'll be presented with a list of results. Tap any item in the list to be taken to the book's information page.

Purchased: This page allows you to see all the purchases you have made in the iBookstore. Not only can you see all your purchases, but you can redownload them if you've deleted them from your device. Simply tap the button with the downward arrow in a cloud icon. You will not be charged again for downloading book you already bought.

Figure 9–7. *The Purchases screen lets you view and redownload all your iBooks.*

> **NOTE:** You don't need to spend money to enjoy reading books on your iPod touch. The iBookstore offers more than 30,000 free books from the Project Gutenberg book library. Project Guttenberg is a digital collection of books that are in the public domain. The only lame thing about Project Gutenberg titles is that they're given the plain-looking brown covers you see in some of the figures. Though Gutenberg does redeem itself by making plenty of ePub books available with illustrations, there's no need to rely solely on PDFs if you want illustrations in your book.

View a Book's Info Page

Once you have found a book you're interested in, tap it to be taken to its information page. As you can see in Figure 9–8, a book's information page allows you to read a summary of the book (this is equivalent to reading what's on the back of the book in a real bookstore). It also has a link to the author's page where you can read more about the author and his or her other works. You can also view user ratings for the book.

Figure 9–8. An individual book's information page

As you can tell, the information page has a ton of information about the book, but the main features are the two buttons at the top. The first button in Figure 9–8 reads $11.99. This is the price button. If you want to buy the book, tap the price, and it turns into a green Buy Book button. Tap it again to purchase and download the book. You may be asked to enter your iTunes password if you haven't entered it in a while, and then the iBookstore flips around, and the book appears on your bookshelf with a blue progress bar (see Figure 9–9). Once the download is complete, it disappears, and you can begin reading your new book! Note that with free books, the price button will read Free. When you tap it, the button changes to Get Book. Tap it again to download the free book.

The Get Sample button shows on every book listing. It allows you to download a sample of any book on the iBookstore. Simply tap the Get Sample button; the iBookstore flips around, and the book appears on your bookshelf with a blue progress bar. Once the download is complete, the progress bar disappears, and you can begin reading the sample of the book. Samples always start on the first page and usually include the first chapter (or first several chapters if the book has smaller chapters).

Figure 9–9. *Downloading an iBook. Note the blue progress bar on the upper-left book. This means you are downloading the book.*

NOTE: As with the iTunes Store and the App Store, you need to sign into your iTunes account before you can buy or download any book. To sign in, simply scroll to the bottom of the iBookstore home page, and tap the Sign In button. Enter your iTunes user name and password, and you're good to go!

ePub Books

Besides using the iBookstore to read books in the iBooks app, there is a second way to get books on your bookshelf. You can download ePub-formatted books from other web sites and then drag them into your book library in your iTunes source list on your computer. Any ePub books you've added to your iTunes library are automatically synced the next time you connect your iPod touch to your computer.

What Is ePub?

ePub is a universal e-book file format. Any device capable of opening and displaying ePub files can display the book no matter where you bought the e-book. In other words, you don't need to buy your books from the iBookstore only. Several sites sell e-books in the ePub format that are compatible with the iPod touch. ePubbooks (www.epubbooks.com/buy-epub-books) has an excellent list of sites that offer ePub books for sale and for free download. Once you've downloaded an ePub book, simply drag it to your iTunes library, and the book syncs to your iPod touch on the next connection.

> **NOTE:** Amazon's Kindle bookstore is another popular place to buy e-books. However, Kindle books don't use the ePub format. If you buy an e-book from the Kindle store, you'll need to download Amazon's free Kindle book reader app for the iPod touch to read those books. You will not be able to read a Kindle book in the iBooks app. Barnes & Noble's BN eReader for iPod touch is another way to buy e-books on the iPod touch, but the BN eReader app supports the standard ePub format so you can move books back and forth between various ePub readers.

ePub vs. PDF

As you'll see later in this chapter, iBooks can read both ePub books and PDFs. So, if you have a choice between buying a book in ePub format or PDF, which do you choose? Let's look at the pros and cons of each:

ePub pros:

- Selectable and searchable text in iBooks
- Smaller file sizes

ePub cons:

- Requires a dedicated ePub reader if you want to read the book on your Mac or PC. Currently there is no desktop version of iBooks available.

PDF pros:

- Can be read in iBooks or on almost any computer in the world. PDF is one of the most universal document formats.

PDF cons:

- Files sizes can be large. A 300-page book can be more than 100MB in size, taking up valuable room on your iPhone.
- iBooks doesn't offer font adjustment, searchable text, or notes for PDFs.

After looking at the pros and cons, I would say that if you have an option of buying a book in ePub or PDF format, choose ePub, especially if you'll be viewing the book primarily in iBooks. The ePub format offers many more feature-rich options than PDF does.

Navigating Your Bookshelf

OK, you have a bunch of books downloaded and synced. Before you start reading them, let's get a little better acquainted with navigating all your books on your bookshelf. By default, your iBooks bookshelf will look like it does in Figure 9–2. If you swipe you finger down, you'll be presented with a few more options, as shown in Figure 9–10.

Figure 9–10. *From the title bar of the iBooks bookshelf, you can access the iBookstore, navigate between your collections, and access view and edit modes.*

The title bar in the iBooks bookshelf features three buttons with an additional search field and view buttons below it:

Edit: Allows you to rearrange or delete books on your bookshelf as well as sort your books into collections.

> **NOTE:** Deleting a book from the iPod touch does not delete it from the iTunes library on your computer. You are able to resync the book any time you want. You can also immediately redownload the book under the Purchased shortcut button in the iBookstore.

Collections: In Figure 9–10 the collections button is labeled "Books," but the label on the button changes to the name of the collection you are viewing. The collections button displays a list of all your book collections in iBooks. By default you'll see two collections:

Books: When you tap Books, you'll be presented with your bookshelf. This contains all the ebooks you have in the iBooks app.

PDFs: Tapping PDFs takes you to your PDF bookshelf. I'll talk more about the PDF features of iBooks and collections in the second half of this chapter.

Store: As mentioned, tapping this takes you to the iBookstore where you can go shopping to expand your library.

Search: If you have a large collection of books, you can use this search feature to quickly find the book you are looking for. The search feature searches all the titles on your shelf by name or author.

Icon View: This is the default view of your bookshelf. The button with four white squares shows you all your books' covers in large, easy-to-see thumbnails.

List View: This is the button next to the Icon View button. It has three white lines in it. Tap it to display a list view of your iBooks bookshelf (see Figure 9–11).

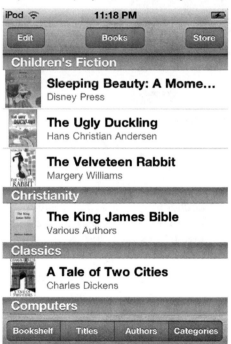

Figure 9–11. *List view with sorting options by bookshelf, title, author, and category*

When you tap the List View button, you'll notice that at the bottom of the screen you have four ways to sort your lists:

Bookshelf: Displays your books in the order that they appear in icon view.

Titles: Displays your books in alphabetical order by title.

Authors: Displays your books in alphabetical order by name of author.

Categories: Displays your books in genre groups. Books are arranged alphabetically in each grouping.

You may notice that some of your books have a blue or red ribbon in their cover's right corner. The red ribbons say Sample, and they signify that the book on your bookshelf is a sample you've downloaded from the iBookstore. Samples stay on your iPod touch until you delete them or buy the full book, but they will not sync back to your iTunes book library.

Blue ribbons say New, and they signify that you have not begun reading the book yet. The New ribbon will appear until you've turned at least one page inside the book (Figure 9–12).

Figure 9–12. *Books with the New and Sample ribbons next to a previously read book*

Rearranging the Order of Your Books

iBooks allows you to rearrange the order of the books in your library. In icon view, tap the Edit button, then tap and hold a book's cover, and finally drag it to a new position on your bookshelf. This is no different from the way you arrange apps on your iPod touch's home screen. In list view in edit mode, you can only rearrange books in the Bookshelf sorting category. Tap and hold the grip bars on the right of the book's genre, and drag to your preferred position.

Deleting Your Books

Deleting books is also easy in iBooks. In icon view, tap the Edit button; you'll notice that a red Delete button appears in the upper-right corner of the screen. Tap the book or books you want to delete so a blue checkmark appears over them (Figure 9–13). Next, tap Delete. A confirmation dialog appears asking whether you're sure you want to delete the book. Tap Delete again to confirm.

In list view in Edit mode, you can delete books from any of the four sort views. Tap the book or books you want to delete so a blue checkmark appears next to them (Figure 9–13). Next, tap Delete. A confirmation dialog appears asking whether you're sure you want to delete the book. Tap Delete again to confirm. You can always redownload any books you've purchased again for free.

Figure 9–13. *Deleting books in icon and list views*

Sorting Your Books into Collections

iBooks does a wonderful job of displaying your books and PDFs on a digital bookshelf. However, there may come a time when your book collection grows so large that seeing all the titles displayed on a single iBooks bookshelf might not make for the easiest browsing experience.

Luckily, Apple has a built-in feature called Collections that allows you to sort your books onto different bookshelves for easier organization. In the center of the iBooks screen you'll see the Collections button. It is labeled according to the name of the selected collection. In Figure 9–10, the collections button is labeled "Books" because that is the currently selected collection. Tap the collections button to reveal a list of book collections in iBooks (Figure 9–14).

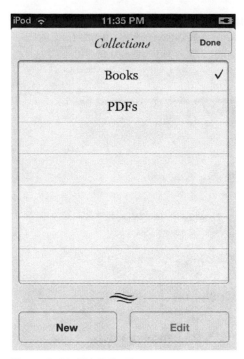

Figure 9–14. *The Collections menu*

Be default you'll see two collections: Books and PDFs. Any ebooks you have appear on their own bookshelf under the Books collection, and any PDFs you have appear on their own bookshelf under the PDFs collection.

Creating New Collections

If you'd like to create new collections to better manage your library, you can do so easily:

1. Tap the Collection button so the collections menu appears.

2. Tap the New button.

3. A new Collections field appears (Figure 9–15). Enter the name of your new collection.

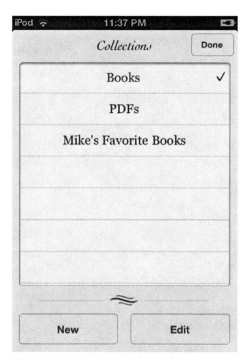

Figure 9–15. *Creating a new collection*

4. When you have entered your collection's name, tap Done, and your new collection is created.

Adding Books and PDFs to Your Collections

Once you've created a new collection, you need to add some books or PDFs to it. To add books or PDFs to a collection, follow these steps:

1. Tap the Edit button in the upper-right corner of an iBooks bookshelf.

2. Tap the book(s) or PDF(s) you want to add to a collection. The selected book or PDF covers fade, and a blue check mark appears in the lower-right corner (Figure 9–16).

Figure 9–16. *Selecting books to move to a collection*

3. Tap the Move button at the top of the iBooks bookshelf. The collections list is displayed (Figure 9–17, left).

4. Choose the collection you want to add the selected books or PDFs to by tapping its name. An animation shows the selected collection sliding on-screen, and you'll be taken to that collections bookshelf where you'll now find your selected books or PDFs (Figure 9–17, right).

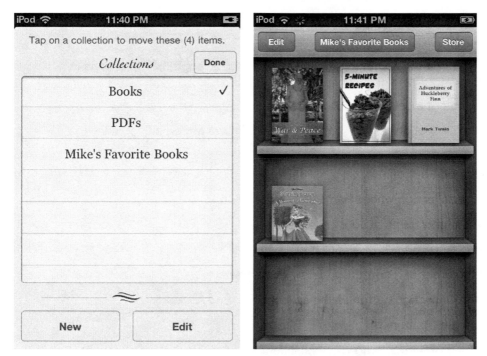

Figure 9–17. *Moving books to your new collection, left, and your new collection, right*

NOTE: You can place the same book or PDF in only one collection at a time. When you add a PDF or book to a collection, it is removed from its previous collection.

Navigating Between Your Collections

iBooks makes it easy to navigate between your collections. As a matter of fact, it gives you two ways to do this:

- Tap the Collections menu and then tap the collection you want to view.

- From any collections bookshelf, drag your finger left or right to swipe to the previous or next collection.

Editing Collections

iBooks lets you edit the names of existing collections, arrange the collections in a specific order, and delete collections.

To edit the name of a collection, follow these steps:

1. Tap the Collection button so the collections menu appears (Figure 9–15).

2. Tap the Edit button.

3. Tap the collection whose name you want to edit.

4. Enter the new name of your collection.

5. Tap the Done button when finished.

To arrange the order of a collection, follow these steps:

1. Tap the Collection button so the collections menu appears.

2. Tap the Edit button.

3. Use the grip bars to drag your collections up or down in the Collections list (Figure 9–18). You can't move the Books or PDFs collections.

4. Tap the Done button when finished.

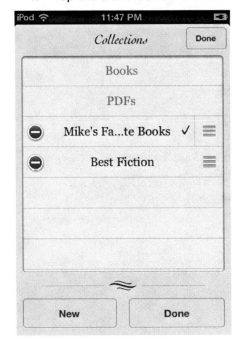

Figure 9–18. *Editing collections*

To delete a collection, follow these steps:

1. Tap the Collection button so the collections menu appears.

2. Tap the Edit button.

3. Tap the red minus sign button (Figure 9–10).

4. A red delete button appears. Tap it to delete the collection. A warning dialog appears asking if you want to remove the collection's items from the device or move them back to their original collections. Tap Remove to remove the items from your iPad, or tap Don't Remove to keep them on the iPad and move them back to their default (Books or PDFs) collection.

Reading Books

The bookshelf displays your books in a gorgeous and easy-to-find layout, but books are meant to be read, not just ogled at on a shelf. Let's get started!

To read a book, simply tap its cover. The book flies forward and opens. If it's the first time you've opened the book, you'll be on the first page. If you have opened the book before, it opens to the last page you were reading.

While reading a book, you can choose between landscape or portrait orientation. As you can see in Figure 9–19, landscape mode shows you about a paragraph of text on average, while portrait mode shows you slightly more text. You can navigate between the two modes by rotating your iPod touch.

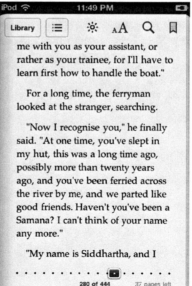
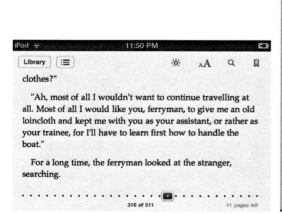

Figure 9–19. *Reading a book in landscape and portrait modes*

At the top of any book's page, no matter what orientation you are in, you'll notice a menu that contains a series of buttons (see Figure 9–20). I'll explain the use of all these features momentarily, but I'll familiarize you with the menu first.

Figure 9–20. *A book's menu buttons*

Library: Tapping this closes the book and takes you back to your bookshelf. The next time you open this book, you'll be taken to the page you were on when you left it.

Table of Contents/Bookmarks: This button is signified by three dots, each with a line after them. Tap this button to go to the book's Table of Contents/Bookmarks page.

Brightness: This is the button that looks like the sun and changes the screen brightness only while you're using the iBooks app.

Font: This button, symbolized by a small and big *A*, allows you to change the font of the book's text as well as the font size. This is helpful for those people who need larger text while reading, such as older people or anyone with sight difficulties. You can also change the background of the book's page to a sepia tone.

Search: The magnifying glass button allows you to search through a book's text.

Bookmark: Tap the bookmark ribbon to lay down a red bookmark in the upper-right corner.

Page scrubber: This is the series of dots that run along the bottom of a book's page (see Figure 9–22). Tap and hold the square button that sits on the dots; then drag it left or right to quickly navigate through the book's pages.

BUY: A Buy button appears when you are reading a sample book. Tap the Buy button to purchase the book. Your sample copy is replaced with the full copy.

While reading, you can tap the center of a book's page to show/hide the menu bar and page scrubber. You'll be left with only the title of the book and name of the author (in landscape view) at the top of the page and the page number at the bottom.

Turning Pages

You have three ways to move through a book's pages:

- Tap and hold the side of a page and then drag your finger across it from right to left. The page curls on the screen (see Figure 9–21), and when you lift your finger, the page turn is complete.

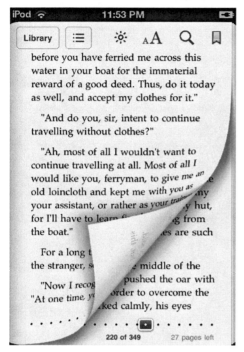

Figure 9–21. *You get cool eye candy when turning a page.*

- Tap the right or left side of the screen to move forward or backward. This accomplishes the same function as the previous one, but with less interactive eye candy.

- Tap and hold the scrubber bar at the bottom of a page (see Figure 9–22); then slide your finger in either direction. The name of the chapter and the page number appear above the scrubber as you slide. When you've found the right page, remove your finger from the scrubber, and the page flips, taking you to the page you've selected. The scrubber lets you go to a specific page number quickly without having to flip through all the pages of the book.

Figure 9–22. *The page scrubber shows the page number and chapter title.*

Adjusting Brightness

Depending on your eyes, you may find it easier to read text with a brighter or darker screen. To adjust the iPod touch's screen brightness while reading a book, tap the Brightness button (the one that looks like a sun) in the menu bar. A drop-down menu appears with a slider on it (see Figure 9–23).

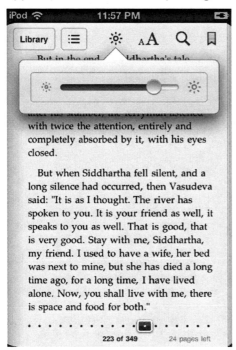

Figure 9–23. *The brightness slider*

Slide to the left to reduce brightness and to the right to increase it. When adjusting the brightness in the iBooks app, the entire screen brightens or dims according to your slider settings, but once you leave the iBooks app, the screen brightness returns to the settings you have specified in the iPod touch's Settings application. This is a great feature because you can instantly switch between brightness levels when you enter or exit the iBooks app without having to reconfigure them each time.

To change your iPod touch's overall brightness levels, go into Settings on the iPod touch's home screen, and choose Brightness. Adjust the slider there to set your preferred brightness.

Adjusting Font, Font Size, and Page Color

Depending on your eyesight, you may want to adjust the font size of the text. Tap the double-A font button to be presented with the font menu (see Figure 9–24). Tap the small A to decrease the font size and the large A to increase it. Increasing or decreasing the font size results in fewer or more words on a page, respectively.

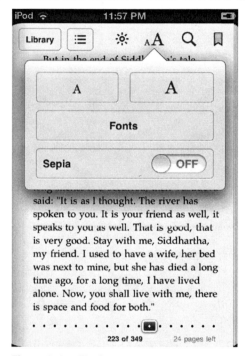

Figure 9–24. *The font panel*

Below the font size controls is a Fonts button. Tap this to select from six font types (see Figure 9–25). Different font types can affect the number of words you see on the screen slightly. Why change the font? Some people have an easier time reading different fonts, especially serif or sans serif fonts. A sans-serif font is like the font of the text of this book; there are no little lines hanging off the letters. A serif font is one like Times New Roman.

Below Fonts is the Sepia button. Tap it to toggle a sepia tone on or off. When set to ON, the entire book takes on a yellow-brown tone, similar to how pages in an old paper book start to turn color after a while. Some people find reading from a sepia screen easier on the eyes since you aren't staring at a bright white background.

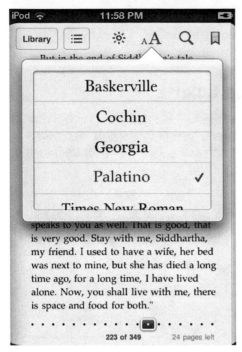

Figure 9–25. *The fonts you can choose from*

Searching Text

You can search for any word or text in the book you are reading by tapping the magnifying glass icon. A search field pops up along with the keyboard. Type any search term you want, and you'll be presented with a list of results, displayed by order of page number (see Figure 9–26). Tap any result to go instantly to that page. On the page, your search term will have a brownish yellow bubble over it.

You can also perform a Google or Wikipedia search for your word or phrase. Below the search results, you'll see a Search Google button and a Search Wikipedia button. Tap either to leave the iBooks app. You'll be taken to Safari where the Google search results or Wikipedia entries are presented.

Figure 9–26. *The search panel lets you perform in-text searches as well as quickly link to Google and Wikipedia searches on the Web.*

Bookmarking a Page

Tapping the bookmark icon causes a red bookmark to appear at the top of the page (see Figure 9–27). Laying down a bookmark adds a shortcut of the page to the Table of Contents/Bookmarks page so you can quickly access the bookmarked page later. Bookmarking in iBooks isn't really like using a bookmark in a physical book. In the iBooks app, the bookmarking feature is more akin to dog-earing a page on a real book, since you aren't limited to one bookmark. You can bookmark as many pages as you want. To unbookmark a page, tap the red bookmark ribbon.

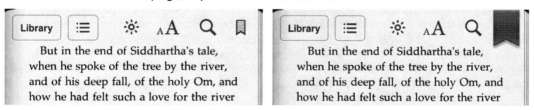

Figure 9–27. *Tap the bookmark button (left) to lay down a bookmark (right).*

Interacting with Text

Your interaction with the book's text isn't limited to search. What we'll show you next is one of the reasons why e-books are superior to traditional paper books. However, paper books still have a leg up on e-books in many ways. See the article about the two formats here: www.tuaw.com/2010/05/08/a-tale-of-two-mediums-despite-the-iPod touch-traditional-books-aren/. Paper books have the advantage over e-books that they are relatively cheap (especially if you buy them used), and you don't need to be afraid to take them to a park or a beach. Sand or dirt isn't going to affect the usability of a paperback like it will an electronic device like the iPod touch. Also, while reading in public, paper books are much less of a theft target than Apple's latest gadget.

While on any page, press and hold your finger to the screen, and a magnifying glass pops up on the page. To move it around, simply drag your finger. Below the magnifying glass, a single word is highlighted in blue. When you've found the word you want, remove your finger from the screen. The magnifying glass disappears, and the word is highlighted with grab bars on either side. Drag the grab bars to select more than one word, such as a sentence or entire paragraph.

With your selection confirmed, you'll be presented with five text-selection tools from the black pop-up menu that appears (see Figure 9–28).

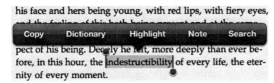

Figure 9–28. *The text selection tools*

Copy: Select to copy the text so you can paste it into another application or the search field.

Dictionary: This is my favorite feature in the iBooks app because it shows off one of the primary advantages—and ease-of-use features—that e-books have over traditional paper books. When you come across a word you don't know in a paperback book, you need to put the book down and grab a dictionary. On the iPod touch, you can select the unfamiliar word and tap the Dictionary button. The first time you tap the dictionary command you'll get a notice that iBooks need to download a dictionary. Tap the download button to download the dictionary. This needs to be done only once. After that, a page appears with the definition of the word (see Figure 9–29). You can then tap Done on the page to close the dictionary window and get back to reading the book.

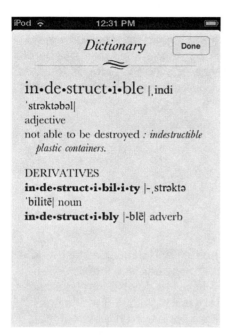

Figure 9–29. *The dictionary panel*

Highlight: Tapping highlight marks the text as if it's been highlighted by a highlighter (see Figure 9–30). Apple has outdone itself here, because the highlighting actually looks the same as it does on physical paper.

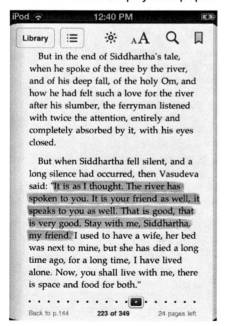

Figure 9–30. *Highlighted text. When you highlight text, it automatically gets added to the bookmarks page.*

If you tap the colored highlight, another pop-up menu appears that allows you to change the color of the highlight, create a note to go along with the highlighted text, or remove the highlight (see Figure 9–31). Color selections are yellow, green, blue, pink, and purple. Any newly selected text you choose to highlight is highlighted with the color of your last choice. Any text you highlight appears in a list on the bookmarks page (which we'll get to in a moment).

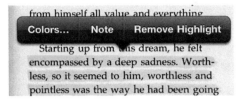

Figure 9–31. *Options for highlighted text*

Note: Tapping Note automatically highlights the selected text and causes a Post-it note to fly forward on the screen and the on-screen keyboard to appear (see Figure 9–32). You can type as much as you want in the note and scroll up and down using your finger. The color of the note is based on the color you chose for your highlight. Tap the note's Done button to close the note. You'll see a small note icon appear on the side of the page (see Figure 9–32). Tap the note's icon to edit the note. Tap the text's highlight, and select Remove Note to delete the note.

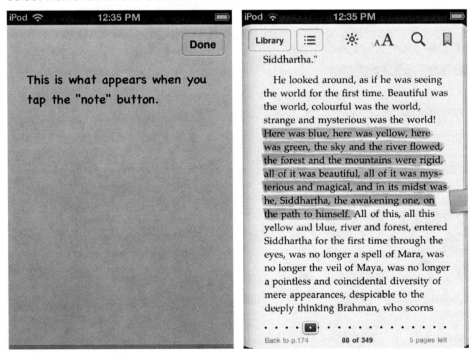

Figure 9–32. *Creating a note and the note icon in the margin of the page after creation. The note is tied to the highlighted text.*

Search: Tapping Search opens the magnifying glass search window in the upper-right corner of the page. The text you selected is automatically filled in as the search query.

Accessing the Table of Contents, Bookmarks, and Notes

Tap the Table of Contents/Bookmarks button (the button that displays three dots followed by three lines; see Figure 9–19) at the top of your page to instantly go to the Table of Contents/Bookmarks page (see Figure 9–33).

The Table of Contents/Bookmarks page is, unsurprisingly, divided into Table of Contents and Bookmarks sections; each has their own tab.

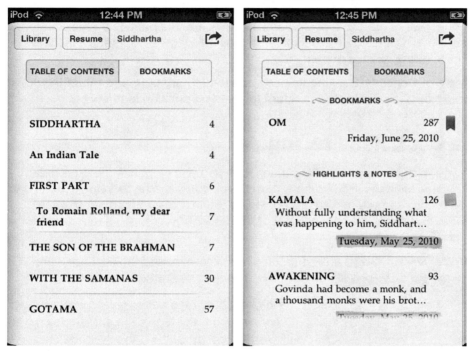

Figure 9–33. *The Table of Contents/Bookmarks page. Switch between the two by tapping the appropriate tab. Return to your last position in the book by tapping the Resume button.*

The Table of Contents tab displays the book's table of contents as a scrollable list. Tap any item in the table of contents to view It immediately.

The Bookmarks tab displays all your bookmarks, highlights, and notes divided into two sections: Bookmarks and Highlights & Notes. Under the Bookmarks heading is a list of chapter names or numbers that hold bookmarks, as well as the page number of the bookmark and the date you bookmarked the page. A red ribbon representing each bookmark lies next to the bookmark's page number. Tap any bookmark to jump to the bookmarked page.

Under the Highlights & Notes heading is a list of all the highlights and notes you've created. For each highlight and note, you'll see the beginning of the first sentence that the highlight or note appears in, as well as the chapter name or number and also the page number and the date you marked the page. The date is highlighted in the color that you chose to highlight the text in. This is a nice feature if you use different colors for different bookmark classifications, such as quotes from the antagonist in blue and from the protagonist in pink.

Remember that whenever you create a note, a highlight is automatically created. You can distinguish between a highlight and a note easily. Any note has a tiny sticky note icon in the right margin. To instantly go to any highlight or note, tap it in the list. To read a note you created without leaving the Table of Contents page, tap the note icon in the margin. The note springs forward on the screen, and you can then tap the note to bring up the on-screen keyboard and edit it. Tap the Done button on the note to close it.

In the top-right corner of the Table of Contents and Bookmarks page is a Share button. Tap it to insert the TOC and your notes into an e-mail message, or print the TOC and your notes to a wireless AirPrint printer.

To exit the Table of Contents/Bookmarks page, tap the Library button to return to your bookshelf, or tap the Resume button to return to your last position in the book.

Having a Book Read to You

Not only can you read books on the iPod touch, but also you can have the iPod touch read books to you. Using the iPod touch's VoiceOver screen reader technology, you can make the iPod touch read any text to you, including the text of an entire novel. I'll talk about VoiceOver in detail in the final chapter of this book, but for now I'll touch on how to activate it for iBook reading.

1. Turn VoiceOver on. Go your iPod touch's home screen, and tap Settings; then choose **General ➤ Accessibility ➤ VoiceOver**. Tap the ON button.

2. Return to your book in iBooks. To have everything on a page read to you, use two fingers held together and flick up. Everything from the top of the screen down will be read aloud. When VoiceOver reaches the bottom of the page, it automatically turns the page for you and continues reading.

3. To stop VolceOver reading, tap anywhere on the screen with one finger. It is also a good idea to return to Settings and turn VoiceOver off, unless you want to continue using VoiceOver gestures.

Now, you might be wondering why you would have VoiceOver's mechanical voice read you a book when you can just buy an audiobook and sync it to the iPod touch. The simple answer is because not all books are in audiobook format. It should also be noted that the iBooks VoiceOver ability isn't a feature intended to appeal to a large number of readers but an accessibility option to help those who are hard of sight read their favorite books.

Syncing PDFs

You have two ways of syncing PDFs to iBooks on your iPod touch -- using iTunes or using the iPod touch's Mail app. To sync PDFs via iTunes, drag any PDFs you want to sync into your iTunes library. They are automatically added to the Books section of your iTunes library. The next time you sync your iPod touch to iTunes, your PDFs are synced as well.

You can also add PDFs to iBooks through the iPod touch's Mail app. To do this, open Mail, and select an e-mail with a PDF attachment. Tap the attachment in the body of the e-mail to see it a full-screen preview of it. While previewing it full-screen, you'll see a Share button in the upper-right corner. Tap this button, and select Open in "iBooks" from the pop-up list (see Figure 9–34). The Mail app closes, and the PDF automatically opens in iBooks and is added to your PDF bookshelf. When you sync your iPod touch with iTunes, any PDFs you have added to iBooks in this manner are added to your iTunes books library.

Figure 9–34. *Opening a PDF in iBooks using Mail*

Navigating the PDF Bookshelf

To see all the PDFs that are in iBooks, launch iBooks, and tap the Collections button in the iBooks menu bar (see Figure 9–10). From the collections menu (Figure 9–14), tap the PDFs collection. Doing so takes you to your PDF bookshelf. As you can see from Figure 9–35, the PDF bookshelf is similar to the regular bookshelf. The PDF bookshelf is populated with any PDFs you have added to iBooks.

Figure 9–35. *The PDF bookshelf is identical to the regular bookshelf. If you know how to navigate one, you know how to navigate the other.*

Just like with the regular bookshelf, you can choose to view your PDFs as icons or in a list. In list view you can sort your PDFs by titles, authors, categories, or bookshelf (the way they are arranged in icon view). List view also presents you with a search field so you can search your PDFs by name or author. The PDF bookshelf works just like the regular bookshelf in editing and deleting items as well. Tap Edit to rearrange or delete PDFs.

Navigating and Reading PDFs

To read a PDF, tap its cover. The PDF flies forward and opens. If it's the first time you've opened the PDF, you'll be on the first page. If you have opened the PDF before, it opens to the last page you viewed.

You can view PDFs in portrait or landscape mode (see Figure 9–36).

Figure 9–36. *Viewing PDFs in iBooks*

At the top of any PDF page, no matter what orientation you are in, is a menu that contains a series of buttons with the name of the PDF document in the center. These buttons should be familiar to you because they are similar to the ones you see while reading an e-book.

Library: Tapping this closes the PDF and takes you back to your PDF bookshelf. The next time you open the PDF, you'll be taken to the page you were on when you left it.

Contact Sheet: This button is signified by three dots, each with a line after them. Tap this button to be presented with a contact sheet—a series of thumbnails of all the pages in a PDF.

Share: Tap this button to email or print the PDF.

Brightness: This is the button that looks like the sun and changes the screen brightness of the iBooks app.

Search: The magnifying glass button allows you to search through the text of a PDF. It also has quick links to search Google and Wikipedia for your selected search term.

Bookmark: Tap the bookmark ribbon to bookmark the current page you are on. Remember that iBooks uses bookmarks differently than traditional bookmarks are used in a paper book. Bookmarking a page in iBooks means you have effectively "dog-eared" the page. You can have multiple bookmarks in the same document. To remove a bookmark, tap the bookmark icon again.

Page scrubber: This is the series of page icons that run along the bottom of a PDF's page. Drag your finger across the thumbnails to quickly navigate through the PDF's pages. You'll see the page number of the page currently selected float overhead. You can also just tap any thumbnail to jump right to that page.

While reading, you can tap the center of a book's page to show/hide the menu bar and page scrubber. While on a page, you can double-tap it to zoom in or, for more control, you can use a pinch gesture to zoom in or out. To navigate the pages of a PDF, swipe your finger to the left or right to move forward or backward one page. You can also tap the margins of a page to move forward or backward, or you can use the page scrubber at the bottom of the page. Alternately, you can scroll through large thumbnails representing all the pages in the PDF document by using the contact sheet.

Using the Contact Sheet

As you can now see, you already know how to use the PDF menu bar because it is so similar to an e-book's menu bar. The only feature that is slightly different is the Table of Contents button, which has been replaced with a contact sheet button (though both icons are identical—three dots, each followed by a line).

Tap the contact sheet button, and all the pages in the PDF document are presented to you in large thumbnails that you can scroll through with a swipe of your finger (Figure 9–37). This is useful when you are dealing with a very large document with lots of diagrams or images, as it allows you to quickly search the PDF by eye. When you find the desired page, tap it, and you'll instantly go to that page in the document.

You'll also notice that some contact sheets might have a little red bookmark in their upper-right corner. This means you've bookmarked that page by tapping the bookmark button in the PDF menu bar (see Figure 9–36). To see only your bookmarked pages, tap the bookmark button in the upper-right corner of the contact sheet menu (see Figure 9–38). Any page without a bookmark is hidden from view.

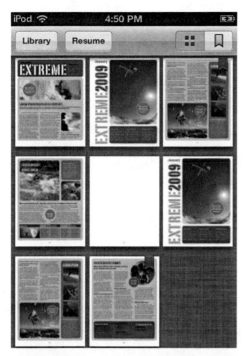

Figure 9–37. *The contact sheet lets you see all the PDF's pages as large thumbnails.*

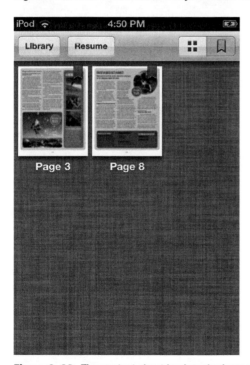

Figure 9–38. *The contact sheet bookmarked pages view*

To leave the contact sheet, you can tap the Library button to return to your PDF bookshelf, you can tap the Resume button to return to the page you were on when you navigated to the contact sheet, or you can tap any page to be taken to that page.

> **TIP:** Want to create a PDF on your computer? On a Mac, if you can print it, you can PDF it. Choose what you want to turn into a PDF, and then choose Print from the File menu of the application you are in (Word or Firefox, and so on). You'll see a PDF button in the lower-left corner of the Print dialog box. Click it, and select Save as PDF from the drop-down menu. Name the PDF, click Save, and then drag it to your iTunes library. On your next sync, your new PDF is transferred to iBooks. If you own a Windows computer, there are several options to turning documents into PDFs. You can find one such solution at `www.primopdf.com`. Google "print to PDF" to find the right solution for you. Apple's Pages for Mac application also lets you output your documents to ePub format, which is perfect for importing into iBooks!

Settings

There are a few external settings for the iBooks app. Navigate to Settings from the iPod touch's home screen, and select iBooks from the Apps header on the left side. You'll see three settings (see Figure 9–39).

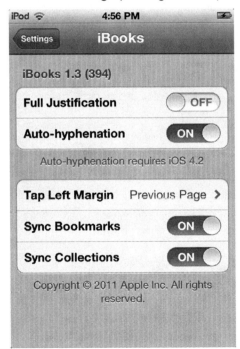

Figure 9–39. *The iBooks app settings*

Full Justification: When this set to ON, the text on a book's page fills the width of the page evenly. When full justification is set to OFF, the text on the right side of the page is ragged (see Figure 9–40).

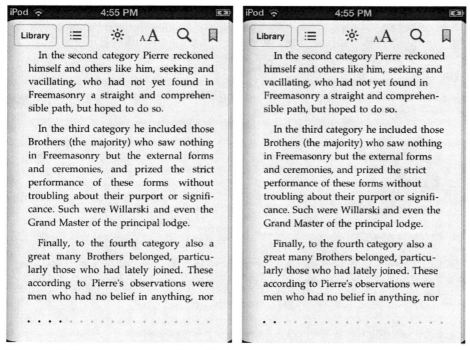

Figure 9–40. *The same page with full justification on (left) and full justification off (right)*

Auto-hypenation: When this is set to ON, iBooks automatically hyphenates words, allowing more words to be displayed on a single page.

Tap Left Margin: You can set this to Previous Page or Next Page. If you set it to Next Page, tapping the left margin of a book advances you to the next page in a book instead of taking you back one page. This setting might be nice while reading a book on the iPod touch at odd angles, like in bed. With Next Page selected, the only way to go back one page in your book is by using the page scrubber bar at the bottom of the page.

Sync Bookmarks: When set to ON, this syncs a book's bookmarks, highlights, and notes between devices. This is nice if you are using iBooks on an iPad and iPhone as well as your iPod touch. When you create a note or bookmark in the book on one device, it appears on the other devices as well.

Sync Collections: When set to ON, this syncs your iBooks collections. When you create or modify a collection on one device, it will appear the same on the other.

Newsstand

Newsstand is a new feature of iOS 5 that allows you to view and manage all your magazine and newspaper subscriptions in one place. We call it a *feature* because Newsstand isn't technically an app. It looks like an app, but it's actually a folder that resides on your home screen and holds all your subscriptions.

You can see the Newsstand icon in Figure 9–41. The icon on the left show you what Newstand looks like with no subscriptions. When you start download subscriptions they appear in the icon (right).

Figure 9–41. *The Newsstand icon*

Unlike books in iBooks, magazines and newspapers in Newsstand aren't actually text epub files. Each magazine or newspaper subscription is its own individual app. What this means is that, unlike with books in iBooks, each magazine you download and view can look and act differently. Again, this is because all subscriptions are just individual apps, they all happen to just be contained in the dedicated Newsstand folder.

To open Newsstand, simply tap it, and your home screen splits to display the Newsstand shelf filled with all of your subscriptions (Figure 9–42).

Figure 9–42. *The Newsstand shelf*

The Newsstand store is part of the App Store, and it's where you'll find all of the magazine and newspaper subscriptions you can buy. To quickly get to the Newsstand section of the App Store from your Newsstand shelf, tap the Store button, and you'll be instantly taken there.

Once you have subscribed to the magazines or newspapers of your choice, the newest issues are automatically downloaded as they become available and are placed in your Newsstand. The cover of the most recent issue or the front page of the most recent newspaper is displayed at the top of that periodicals subscription stack on your Newsstand shelf.

To read an issue, tap it, and that periodical's app will open as a normal app would.

Summary

In addition to doing so many other things, the iPod touch is also a breakthrough e-book and PDF reader. iBooks, the all-in-one application that lets you buy books and read, search, and mark them up, is an elegant yet powerful tool for discovering new titles and taking your entire book library with you, and Newsstand allows you to subscribe to and automatically download the latest issues of your favorite magazines and newspapers. Here are a few key tips for you to carry away with you:

- You aren't limited to buying books from the iBookstore. Many web sites sell books in the ePub format that you can download and sync to the iPod touch. A great place to start is www.gutenberg.org. Also, Googling *free e-books* returns a host of results of sites that let you download e-books for free.

- iBooks has a powerful dictionary-lookup feature that gives you the definition of a word right on the screen.

- iBooks bookshelf has many views and a search function to help you navigate your books library.

- No audiobook? No problem. You can use the iPod touch's built-in VoiceOver technology to read any book out loud to you.

- Choose different colors for your notes and highlighting. Maybe use blue for passages you like and green for something you want to reference later. See all your bookmarks, notes, and highlights in one easy place (the Bookmarks page, of course!), and tap any one to instantly jump to it in the book.

- iBooks isn't limited to reading e-books. It's also a PDF reader. Now you can organize, view, and easily navigate all your PDFs—even while on the go!

- Newsstand automatically downloads your latest subscriptions in the background, so when you wake up in the morning, the day's paper will be ready and waiting for you.

Chapter 10

Setting Up and Using Mail

Unlike many other MP3 players, your iPod touch can send, receive, and browse e-mail without getting weighed down with compromise. The iPod doesn't settle for cramped, odd presentations the way you have to deal with on some lesser "smartphones." Your e-mail looks the way it should—the way it would if you were reading it on your home computer. That's because the iPod provides an HTML-compatible rich-text client. Mail looks better because the client is better. It's made to work right.

Getting Started with iPod Mail

As you can see in Figure 10–1, the Mail icon looks like a white envelope floating in a pleasant blue sky. The iPod's Mail app is surprisingly compatible. It works with most major e-mail providers, including Yahoo!, Gmail, AOL, Hotmail, and of course Apple's own iCloud mail services. This high level of provider support is because of the iPod's protocol support. The iPod understands the most popular e-mail standards: POP, IMAP, SMTP, and even Microsoft Exchange. If you're not already familiar with these types of e-mail, you can read a brief overview of them in the "Kinds of E-mail" section later in this chapter.

Figure 10–1. *The Mail icon*

Adding Mail Accounts to Your iPod touch

You can add accounts to your iPod in two ways. First, you can synchronize with iTunes. The first time you connect your iPod to your computer and sync, iTunes searches your computer for mail accounts and adds them to your unit. Second, you can add accounts directly on your iPod using Mail settings. It takes a few more steps than using iTunes, but it's not at all complicated. Let's look at both ways to add accounts.

Adding Accounts with iTunes

iTunes takes most of the work out of setting up your iPod with your existing mail accounts. It looks through your computer at programs like Outlook Express and Apple Mail, finds account information, and offers to synchronize those account settings with your iPod (see Figure 10–2). This makes it really easy to get your iPod up to speed. A single sync puts these account details on your iPod, and you're pretty much ready to get going.

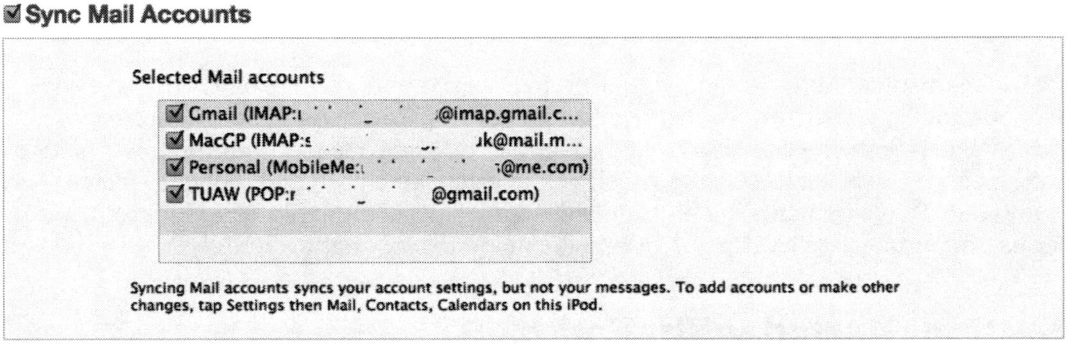

☑ **Sync Mail Accounts**

Selected Mail accounts

☑ Gmail (IMAP: ⠀ ⠀ ⠀ .@imap.gmail.c...
☑ MacGP (IMAP:s ⠀ ⠀ ık@mail.m...
☑ Personal (MobileMe: ⠀ ⠀ ;@me.com)
☑ TUAW (POP:r ⠀ ⠀ @gmail.com)

Syncing Mail accounts syncs your account settings, but not your messages. To add accounts or make other changes, tap Settings then Mail, Contacts, Calendars on this iPod.

Figure 10–2. *The iPod Mail Accounts settings appear on the Info tab in iTunes.*

To select which accounts to add, launch iTunes and connect your iPod. Select your iPod from the source list (the column at the left of the iTunes window; your iPod appears under the Devices heading). The iTunes window updates and displays a summary of your iPod, including its name, the software version, and so forth. Click the Info tab at the top of this window. Scroll down the Info tab to the Sync Mail Accounts section. Here, you can choose whether to synchronize your mail accounts to your iPod. Check the "Selected Mail accounts" check box, and pick the accounts you want to use. In Figure 10–2 you can see I've selected to sync four accounts.

Next, scroll down on the Info tab, below the Mail Accounts and Other sections, to the Advanced section (see Figure 10–3). As a rule, your iPod won't add new accounts until you force things. Unlike normal syncs that just update data, when you select to replace your mail accounts on your iPod using the Advanced settings, iTunes updates your iPod with all the accounts you just selected in the Mail Accounts settings.

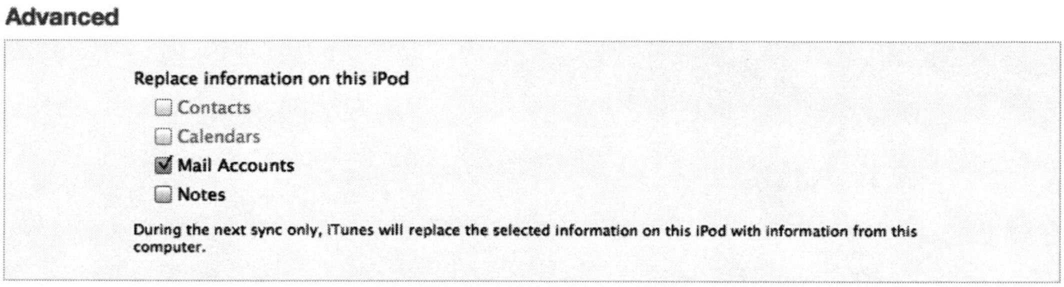

Advanced

Replace information on this iPod
☐ Contacts
☐ Calendars
☑ Mail Accounts
☐ Notes

During the next sync only, iTunes will replace the selected information on this iPod with information from this computer.

Figure 10–3. *Use Advanced settings to replace mail accounts during the next sync. You can also choose to update your contacts, calendars, and bookmarks from this settings section.*

Replacing mail accounts isn't something you do all the time. You'll want to do this account replacement with new iPods that you want to initialize, when you've moved your iPod's home to a new computer, or after you've restored your iPod's firmware to factory settings. If you just want to add a new e-mail account, add it directly on your iPod rather than using iTunes. It's easier.

Adding a Preferred Provider Account from Your iPod

1. Adding a new mail account to your iPod is especially easy when you use one of the preferred providers: Microsoft Exchange, MobileMe, Gmail, Yahoo!, or America Online (AOL). Your iPod already knows how to contact the mail servers and which protocols they use. Here are the steps to take to add a preferred provider account:

2. From the home screen, tap Settings, and navigate to **Settings ➤ Mail, Contacts, Calendars ➤ Add** account.

3. The Add Account screen appears, as shown in Figure 10–4.

Figure 10–4. *When you use a preferred provider, the e-mail setup process is vastly simplified to entering a few items of information. Tap Other to set up e-mail with another provider. You will see this Add Account screen the first time you run the Mail application if you haven't already set up your accounts.*

4. Select the kind of account you will use.

5. For Name, enter the name you want to appear in your From line, usually your full personal name.

6. For Address, enter your full e-mail address (such as, *yourname*@yahoo.com).

7. In the Password field, enter your password. Make sure to type carefully and slowly, and look at the key confirmations as you type. You will *not* see the password itself as you type it. Try not to make mistakes. If you mistype your password, your e-mail account will not show up in Mail.

8. Finish by entering an account description. Your iPod uses the text you type in the Description field as a label in the Accounts list, so enter something meaningful, like "Work Yahoo! Account" or "Home AOL."

9. Tap Next, and wait as the iPod verifies your account information. You can then choose whether to sync just your e-mail for the account or your calendars and notes as well (if your e-mail provider offers those features). Tap Save, and you will then return to the Mail settings screen, and you are finished setting up your account.

Adding an Other Provider Account from Your iPod

Adding accounts from other providers, such as Comcast or EarthLink, requires a few more steps. Here's how to add such an account:

1. From the home screen, tap Settings, and navigate to **Settings ä Mail, Contacts, Calendars**.

2. Tap Add Account.

3. On the New Account screen (see Figure 10–4), tap Other. The Other screen appears, as shown in Figure 10–5.

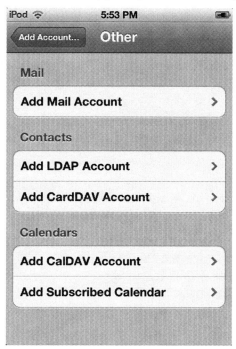

Figure 10–5. *The Other screen*

4. Tap Add Mail Account. The New Account screen appears (see Figure 10–6).

Figure 10–6. *The New Account screen*

5. Enter the name, address, password, and a description, such as "work," "home," and so on, of the account. Tap Next.

6. Tap the button that describes the kind of e-mail account you'll use, either IMAP or POP (Figure 10–7). If you're unsure which account type to use, contact your Internet service provider (ISP) or your organization's information technology (IT) support group to get the information you need to work through these steps.

Figure 10–7. *Choose IMAP or POP.*

7. Determine the incoming and outgoing e-mail servers for your provider. You'll need this information to set up your account. Most providers, including ISPs and IT departments, offer web pages with this information, or you can call their technical support line. For example, my personal EarthLink account uses pop.mindspring.com for incoming mail and smtpauth.earthlink.net:587 for outgoing mail. Notice the colon and the number, which refers to the port used by the mail server. Make sure you get a full host address, which may or may not include a port number.

> **NOTE:** If you find that setting up your iPod touch e-mail account with these steps exceeds your tech comfort zone, I strongly encourage you to physically bring the iPod to your in-house IT department. This can save you a lot of grief and headaches.

8. Enter the name you want to appear in your From line, usually your full personal name, in the Name field. This name appears in all your outgoing messages. For Address, enter your full e-mail address (such as *yourname*@earthlink.net). Enter an account description. Your iPod uses the text you type in the Description field as a label in the Accounts list, so enter something meaningful, like "Work EarthLink Account" or "Comcast from Home."

9. In the Incoming Mail Server section, type the incoming mail server host address in the Host Name field. Enter your account address (such as *yourname*@comcast.net) in the User Name field. Type your password in the Password field. Make sure to type carefully and slowly, and look at the key confirmations as you type. You will *not* see the password as you type it.

10. Repeat the previous step for the Outgoing Mail Server section, entering the outgoing host address in the Host Name field. For outgoing mail, the User Name and Password fields are optional. You'll need them if your mail server uses authorized SMTP.

11. Tap Save, and wait as the iPod verifies your account information. You automatically return to the Mail settings screen, and you are finished setting up your account.

> **NOTE:** By default, the iPod attempts to connect to a password-protected account using the Secure Sockets Layer (SSL) protocol. If this fails during the verification process, the iPod prompts you to confirm whether it should try again without SSL. Feel free to agree.

Removing and Disabling Accounts from the iPod

To remove an account from your iPod, go to Settings ➤ Mail, Contacts, Calendars, and tap one of the items in your Accounts list. Scroll all the way down to the bottom of the account screen, and tap Delete Account. The iPod prompts you to confirm the account deletion (Figure 10–8). Tap Delete Account one more time to remove the account, or tap Cancel to keep the account.

At times, you may want to disable an account without removing it from your iPod. To do this, go to Settings ➤ Mail, Contacts, Calendars. Locate and select the account you want to disable, and switch the Mail button to OFF (Figure 10–8). This disables the account. Switch it back to ON to reenable it.

Figure 10–8. *Deleting or disabling Mail accounts. The Notes button allows you to sync notes with your e-mail account if your e-mail provider has a notes function.*

Choosing E-mail Check Intervals and Other Settings

You're ready to start using Mail, but I suggest that you check your application settings before diving in. Navigate to **Settings ➤ Mail, Contacts, Calendars**, and scroll down to the Fetch New Data. The Fetch New Data settings (Figure 10–9) allow you to choose between push e-mail and fetch e-mail.

Push: When this is turned on, any new e-mails you receive are automatically sent to your iPod immediately. Push is like someone telling you that you have a letter waiting the moment it arrives.

Fetch: If your e-mail account doesn't support push (or even if it does, but you don't want to use it), fetch gives you several options as to the intervals that the Mail app will check to see whether you have new messages. You can set Fetch to check for new mail every 15 or 30 minutes, on every hour, or manually. When you set fetch to manually, you'll have to open the Mail app to check to see whether you've gotten any new e-mails. When your Mail is set to Push or Fetch (excluding Manually), you'll see a red badge over the Mail icon (see Figure 10–10) on your iPod home screen that shows the number of new messages you have received.

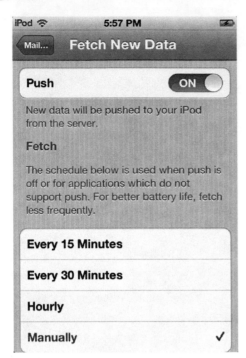

Figure 10–9. *The Fetch New Data settings*

Figure 10–10. *A red badge with a number in it means that's how many new e-mail messages you have waiting for you.*

Mail has many other options besides Fetch and Push. Navigate to **Settings ➤ Mail, Contacts, Calendars**, and scroll down to the Mail section (see Figure 10–11). Here, you'll find preferences that control the way your iPod displays e-mail. You'll find that Mail works far more smoothly and predictably when you customize these settings *before* using your new accounts.

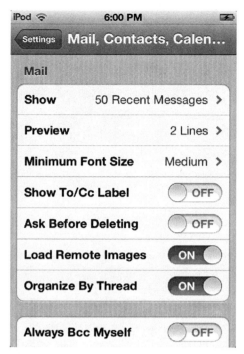

Figure 10–11. *The Mail settings screen contains many basic settings you'll want to configure before using your e-mail accounts.*

Here is a rundown of the Mail settings you'll want to look over:

Show: How many messages should the iPod download and display at once? Choose from 50,100, 200, 500, and 1,000 recent messages.

Preview: Your inbox displays information about each message. It shows who sent the message, the time it was sent, the message subject, and, depending on your setting here, a brief preview of the message itself. For the preview, you can choose how many lines to show: None (no message preview), 1, 2, 3, 4, or 5. The example in Figure 10–12 shows two lines per message.

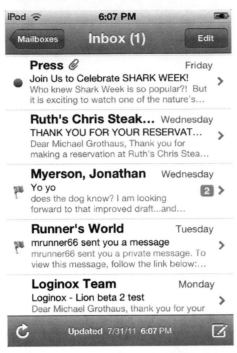

Figure 10–12. *Each message in the inbox shows the recipient, the subject, the date or time the message was sent, and a message preview. You can control how many lines of text are shown for each message preview in Settings ➤ Mail, Contacts, Calendars ➤ Messages ➤ Preview. Blue dots indicate unread mail on this screen. Red flags indicate messages you have flagged.*

Minimum Font Size: My eyes are pretty bad. Fortunately, the iPod has a choice for minimum font size, so I can make sure that the text displays in a size that I can read. Choose from Small, Medium, Large, Extra Large, and Giant. I use Large.

Show To/Cc Label: By default, your iPod does not show the To or Cc lines from e-mail. The iPod normally hides them to save screen space. If you want to override this behavior for your mail, switch this option from OFF to ON.

> **TIP:** You can view the To and Cc lines even if you haven't enabled the option to show them on the Mail settings screen. From the e-mail message screen, tap Details to reveal the lines. Tap Hide to hide them again.

Ask Before Deleting: You might think that asking for confirmation before allowing the iPod to delete a message is a great idea. When working your way through 100 messages in your inbox, this idea quickly becomes less attractive. The iPod allows you to delete e-mail without confirmation by default. If you want to add an extra layer of protection, switch this option to ON.

Load Remote Images: Sometimes e-mails have HTML images embedded in them. If load remote images is set to OFF, those images are not displayed when viewing your e-mail.

Organize By Thread: When this is set to ON, related messages appear in their own threads. Related messages are e-mails in which the subject is the same. So if you've been having a back-and-forth e-mail conversation about your birthday, all the e-mails related to that thread are grouped together. A small, gray, boxed number next to the e-mail message denotes threads. The number signifies how many e-mails are in that thread.

Always Bcc Myself: Some mail services, such as Gmail and Yahoo!, always create copies of sent mail. Others do not. Enable this option to send a blind carbon copy (Bcc) to yourself when writing letters. The "blind" part of carbon copy means that you won't be visibly added to the recipient list. When correspondents "reply to all," you won't (necessarily) receive multiple copies of those e-mail messages.

Increase Quote Level: When ON, a level of indentation is added when you forward or reply to a message.

Signature: By default, the iPod adds "Sent from my iPod" to all outgoing e-mail. To remove this tag, erase the text in the Signature line here. You can also customize this message or replace it entirely. Perhaps you might want to add contact information or a favorite quote. To do this, tap the current signature. A keyboard appears. Use it to edit the text. After making your edits, tap Mail to return to the **Settings ➤ Mail, Contacts, Calendars** screen.

Default Account: Choose the default account you want to use for sending mail. This applies only to non-Mail iPod applications such as Safari or Photos. When you pass along a bookmark or a picture you've snapped, this option sets the account used to send that message.

Working with Mailboxes

When you enter Mail for the first time (and after reboots), you're greeted by the Mailboxes screen (Figure 10–13). The Mailboxes screen is divided into two sections: Inboxes and Accounts.

Inboxes: This section lists two or more inboxes, depending on how many e-mail accounts you have set up. All Inboxes will take you to a unified inbox. A unified inbox shows you all your messages across all your e-mail accounts. This is handy if you frequently work with more than one e-mail account. It allows you to check one place for all of your newest messages. Below All Inboxes you'll see the inboxes listed for all your other e-mail accounts. In Figure 10–13 you can see I have two e-mail accounts set up, Personal, and TUAW. You can tap on either of those to only see the inbox from that single account.

Accounts: Under this heading you'll see all the e-mail accounts you've set up. Clicking any e-mail account under the Accounts heading will take you to a screen that lets you navigate further to that account's inbox, drafts, sent messages, trash, and any other subfolders you have for that e-mail account (see Figure 10–14).

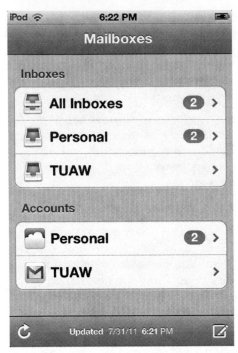

Figure 10–13. *The Mailboxes screen lets you quickly jump to a unified inbox and also lets you explore your e-mail on a per-account basis.*

Tap an account name to open any of the individual account screens. Return to the Mailboxes screen by tapping the Mailboxes button at the top-left corner of that screen.

Each account screen presents one or more mailboxes and folders, as shown in the example in Figure 10–14. When a mailbox contains unread mail, a blue number appears to the right of that box. Tap a mailbox to open it and display the messages stored inside.

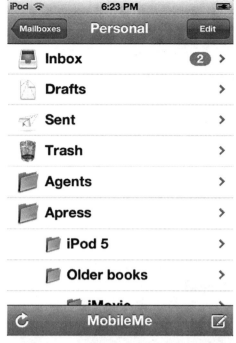

Figure 10–14. *Each mail account uses one or more mailboxes and folders. The account screen lists these, allowing you to access each with a single tap. Mailbox types may include Inbox, Drafts, and Trash, as well as others. Blue numbers indicate the number of unread messages in that mailbox.*

Each account may include some or many of the following standard mailboxes and folders:

Inbox: All new messages load into your inbox. You have an inbox for each account.

Drafts: Messages that are written but not yet sent get saved to Drafts.

Sent: When your mail account saves copies of outgoing mail, they're placed in a Sent folder.

Trash: The iPod stores deleted mail in Trash folders. To permanently delete messages from the trash, select your Trash folder, tap the edit button, and then tap the Delete All button at the bottom of the screen.

Additional folders (or *mailboxes*, as Apple calls them), such as the Agents folder shown in Figure 10–14, were created in the Mail app itself.

To create a new folder/mailbox, follow these steps:

1. Tap the Edit button at the top of the screen in your chosen Mail account (Figure 10–14).

2. Tap the New Mailbox button that appears at the bottom of the screen (Figure 10–15).

3. Enter the name of the folder you want to create (Figure 10–15); then tap the Mailbox Location field, and choose where you want to place the folder. Tap Done.

Figure 10–15. *Creating mailbox folders inside the Mail app*

You can open a mailbox or folder and view the messages stored inside by tapping its name. For example, tap Inbox to see the list of messages stored in that mailbox (see Figure 10–12). From here, you can choose messages to display and manage your mailbox. Here are the actions you can take from this screen:

View a message: Tap an e-mail to open it for viewing.

Refresh mail: Tap the icon that looks like a semicircular arrow, at the bottom-left side of the screen, to have your iPod contact your mail provider and request new mail.

Compose a new message: Tap the icon that shows a square with a pencil through it, at the bottom-right side of the screen, to start writing a new message.

Edit a message: Tap Edit to enter edit mode (see Figure 10–16). In edit mode, you can tap the red circle next to any message to delete it. Confirm by tapping Delete, or tap anywhere else to cancel. You can also move messages to other folders using the edit button. Tap the circle next to the message you want to move and tap the move button. A screen appears listing all the folders you have in your e-mail accounts. Tap the folder you want to move the message to, and you'll see a little animation of an envelope dropping into the folder. You can also move messages between e-mail accounts by tapping the Accounts arrow in the folder list. Finally, you can mark e-mail messages in Edit mode. Marking an e-mail allows you to flag it or change the status of an e-mail to unread. Flagging an e-mail places a red flag next to it, and marking an e-mail as unread places a blue unread dot next to it (Figure 10–12 shows an example of both).

Tap Done to leave edit mode.

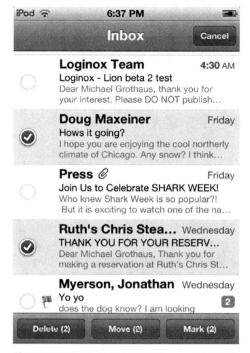

Figure 10–16. *Edit mode allows you to delete or move a single or multiple e-mails at once as well as flag and mark messages as unread.*

> **TIP:** You don't need to be in edit mode to delete mail. Just swipe your finger through any message to instantly bring up the Delete button; or, when displaying a message, tap the trash can icon at the bottom of the screen. Some people have trouble mastering the swipe at first—they open their messages instead of deleting them. Keep trying. The swipe becomes second nature after a while.

Return to the mailbox list: Tap the button at the top-left side of the screen to return from this mailbox to your account screen. The button name varies, but it's always shaped like a pentagon on its side, with the point facing left.

Reading Your Mail

If you're used to reading e-mail on another portable device, the iPod's mail-viewing capabilities come as a welcome relief. It's not watered-down, odd-looking e-mail. It's fully loaded e-mail that behaves the way it should. Sure, there are some missing features. Save for copying and pasting a photo into the body of an e-mail, you cannot add other kinds of attachments such as documents. Still, when it comes to mail viewing, the iPod performs to a much higher standard than any other pocket-sized gadget I've used.

> **TIP:** You can scroll up and down your message—flicking if needed to move more quickly—and zoom in and out using all the standard pinching and tapping tricks described in Chapter 2.

Figure 10–17 shows you the typical e-mail message screen. I'll break it down in parts.

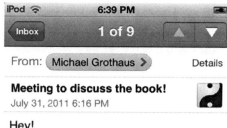

Figure 10–17. *The message-display screen offers many unlabeled icons for your mail-management pleasure.*

Starting with the icons at the bottom of the message-display screen, from left to right, are as follows:

Mail Refresh: As on other account screens, tap the semicircular arrow icon to request new mail from your provider.

File This Message: Tap the icon that shows a folder with a small down arrow to move messages from one mailbox to another. The iPod prompts you to "Move this message to a new mailbox." Select the mailbox to which you want to transfer the message, and the iPod rewards you with one of its most adorable animations. The message flies from one mailbox to the other. If you would rather not transfer the message, tap Cancel instead.

Garbage Can: Tap the small garbage can in the bottom center to delete the currently displayed message. The lid flips up, and your animated message moves down into the can. It's visually delightful. Your message moves from the Inbox folder (or whatever folder you're displaying) to the Trash folder.

> **TIP:** To undelete a message, navigate to the Trash folder (tap Back, Back, Trash), select the deleted message, and tap the File This Message button to return it to the original mailbox.

Reply/Forward: Tap the icon that looks like a backward-pointing arrow, just to the right of the garbage can icon, to reply to or forward a message. From the menu that appears, select Reply to reply to the currently displayed message, or tap Forward to pass it along to a new recipient.

Compose: As on other account screens, tap the icon that looks like a square with a pencil on it to compose a new message.

The icons at the top of the message display screen, from left to right, are as follows:

Back: Tap the button in the top-left corner to return from the message display to the mailbox screen. The button looks like a pentagon on its side, pointing left. The text inside the button varies according to the name of the mailbox.

Message number display: The iPod displays the number of the current message at the top of the screen (for example, 1 of 9).

Next Message/Previous Message: Tap the up triangle to move to the previous message in the current mailbox, and tap the down triangle to move to the next.

Details/Hide: This button appears just below the Next Message arrow. Tap Display to reveal your message's To and Cc lines. Tap Hide to hide them again.

Mark as Unread/Flag: Appearing to the right of the date and time when you've tapped the Details button, the Mark as Unread button allows you to do exactly what the name implies. It restores the little blue dot to the message and updates the unread message count to include this message. You can also choose to flag your message.

Following Embedded Data Detectors

The iPod's Mail app supports embedded data detectors within a message. Data detectors are text or images with hyperlinks, phone numbers, addresses, e-mail addresses, calendar events, and package tracking numbers.

Hyperlinks: When someone sends you an embedded URL in a text or image link, you can tap it to open it in Safari (see Chapter 3 for details on using Safari). If you aren't sure where the link goes, tap and hold it for a second or two. A menu pops up showing a preview of where that URL leads—convenient when you don't know (or trust) the party who sent you the message. To continue to Safari and open the URL, tap Open. You can also copy the URL by pressing the Copy button. To cancel and stay in the Mail app, tap Cancel.

Phone numbers: Mail makes phone numbers into clickable links. Tap any phone number to bring up a pop-up menu that allows you to create a new contact based on the phone number or add the number to an existing contact.

Addresses: If someone sends you an address in an e-mail, tap the address to be taking to the Maps app. A drop pin appears on the map showing you where the address is located. In Chapter 11 I go into more detail about the Maps app.

E-mail addresses: You can click an e-mail address in the body of a message to create a new e-mail with that address in the To field. Alternatively, if you click and hold the e-mail address, a pop-up menu appears allowing you to create a new message (the same action as if you just tapped the e-mail address), create a new contact, add the e-mail to an existing contact, or copy the e-mail address to the clipboard.

Calendar events: If someone sends you an e-mail with a date and time mentioned in the body of the message, you can tap the date and time to create an event in the iPod's Calendar app. There's more on Calendar in Chapter 11.

Tracking numbers: If you have an e-mail with a package tracking number in it, tap the tracking number to open the carrier's tracking web page in Safari to see where you package is. Right now, this feature works only in the United States.

Viewing Attachments

The iPod touch supports many e-mail attachment file formats including Word files (.doc and .docx), Excel spreadsheets (.xls and .xlsx), and PDF files. When a message arrives with an attachment, the iPod shows you that the attachment is available (see Figure 10–18).To view it, tap the attachment and wait for it to load in a new screen. Tap Message to return to the message from the attachment viewer.

> **NOTE:** At the time of this writing, Apple supports these attachment file formats: .c, .cpp, .diff, .doc, .docx, .h, .hpp, .htm, .html, .key, .m, .mm, .numbers, .pages, .patch, .pdf, .ppt, .pptx,.rtf, .txt, .vcf, .xls, and .xlsx.

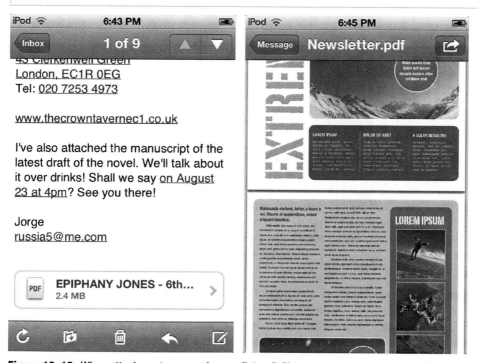

Figure 10–18. *When attachments appear in e-mail, tap (left) to open them in a separate viewer (right).*

Writing an E-mail Message

To write an e-mail message, tap the icon showing a square with a pencil at the bottom-right corner of the screen. You'll see the New Message screen, as shown in Figure 10–19.

Start by tapping either the To or Cc line on the New Message screen. The iPod opens a keyboard so you can enter text. As you type, the iPod searches its contacts list to match what you're typing to the contacts in its list. Tap in a few letters until you see the name of the contact you want to use. Tap that contact, and the iPod automatically adds it to the field (To or Cc) you selected.

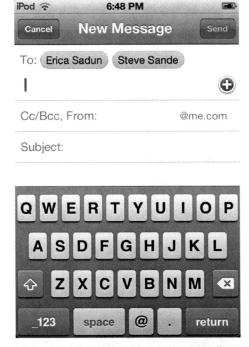

Figure 10–19. *The New Message screen allows you to address and personalize your e-mail.*

You do not need to use an address from your contacts list. You can type in the full e-mail address (the iPod helpfully provides you with the @ sign on the main keyboard for e-mail) and address your e-mail by hand. Also, it remembers the e-mail addresses you use. So, the second time you type "alex@nowhere.nomail.org," the proper address pops up by the time you type *a* and *l*. Just tap that e-mail address to add it to the To or Cc field.

To remove a recipient from the message, select one of the blue recipient bubbles—they're labeled with a name or e-mail address—and tap the Backspace key on the keyboard. You can also drag the e-mail addresses between the To, Cc, and Bcc fields. To do so, touch and hold an e-mail until is expands a little and then drag it to the appropriate field.

Tap the Subject line to move the cursor to that field. Use the keyboard to enter a meaningful subject for your message.

Tap in the message area to begin writing your message. A blinking cursor indicates where the keyboard will enter text. Use the typing skills covered in Chapter 2 to type your message. Remember to use the magnifying glass trick to move the cursor if you need to back up and make corrections.

Mail gives you a few extra formatting options that you won't find in other text entry apps on your iPod. In Mail, you can format text using bold, italics, and underlining. To format your text, follow these steps (See Figure 10–20):

1. Select the text you want to format.

2. In the Cut/Copy/Paste contextual menu, tap the right-facing arrow.

3. In the next contextual menu, tap the B/U button.

4. The format contextual menu appears. Tap the buttons of the formatting you want to apply.

Figure 10–20. *Formatting text in Mail*

> **TIP:** To remove an attached photo from e-mail, position the cursor right after the picture and tap Backspace.

You can also increase the quote level, or indentation, of text in a Mail message. To do so, follow these steps:

1. Move the cursor to the beginning of the text you want to indent.

2. In the Cut/Copy/Paste contextual menu, tap the right-facing arrow.

3. In the next contextual menu, tap the Quote Level button.

4. The Quote Level contextual menu appears. Tap Decrease or Increase to adjust the level of indentation.

Saving a Draft

At any time, you can take a break from composing a message and return to it later by saving it as a draft. This is one of my pet peeves about the Mail app. Saving a message as a draft isn't exactly the most intuitive thing to do because there is no visible Save as Draft button. Instead, you need to tap the Cancel button at the top left of the New Message screen. A pop-up menu appears. Tap Save Draft to save the message for later, Delete Draft to abandon the message, or Cancel to return to the message without doing either. When you choose Save Draft, the iPod creates a copy of your message in the Drafts folder for your default account. Return to that folder when it's convenient to continue composing the message and/or to send it.

> **TIP:** You can set the default names for the Drafts, Sent, and Deleted folders in **Settings ➤ Mail, Contacts, Calendars ➤** *account name* **➤ Account ➤ Advanced ➤ Advanced** .

Sending E-mail

When you are finished addressing and composing your letter, you can send it on its way by tapping Send. If you haven't disabled the feature, the iPod alerts you with a whoosh sound to indicate that the message has been sent to the outgoing mail server.

Searching Your E-mail

Mail allows you to search for an e-mail by sender, receiver, subject, or the body of the message. To search, scroll to the top of the screen in any e-mail inbox or folder (see Figure 10–21). Tap the search field, and select one of the buttons labeled From, To, Subject, or All (All searches From, To, Subject, and the body of the e-mail message). You can also search messages on the server with MobileMe, Exchange, and some IMAP e-mail accounts.

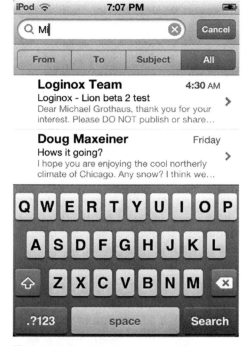

Figure 10–21. *Searching your e-mail*

Kinds of E-mail

For your reference, here's a quick roundup of the various kinds of e-mail services that can be used with your iPod. If you need to contact your personal e-mail provider, this section should help you get up to speed so you recognize the important terms.

POP

POP (sometimes POP3) stands for Post Office Protocol. It's probably the most common e-mail retrieval protocol in use today. It allows mail clients to connect to a server such as Gmail or AOL, retrieve messages, and disconnect afterward. This usually happens on a set schedule, such as every ten minutes or every hour. You do not receive mail until your client connects to the server and requests that new mail.

> **NOTE:** The 3 in POP3 indicates the third version of the protocol standard. POP1 and POP2 are obsolete.

POP works by checking in with a server, downloading your e-mail, and optionally leaving the original copies of your e-mail on the server. This leave-on-server option works well with the iPod, because when you're on the go, you probably want to check your mail on the iPod and retrieve it again later, when you get back to the office or return home.

POP also has its downsides. Unlike the newer and improved IMAP protocol, POP downloads entire messages all once, so it's a bit of a space hog on portable devices.

SMTP

Mail clients use one protocol for receiving mail and another for sending mail. Your iPod uses SMTP to send outgoing messages. SMTP stands for Simple Mail Transfer Protocol. SMTP contacts a mail server and transmits whatever messages you've written, along with any attachments (text files, photos, and so forth). A common kind of SMTP, called SMTP-AUTH (AUTH stands for authorization), allows you to send secure, authorized mail. You provide your account name and a password. Your mail client authenticates itself to the server, and your e-mail gets sent on its way.

The iPod makes sending authenticated e-mail easy. Enter your account name and password into the Mail settings screen. Once you've done this, just use outgoing mail to send a note or share a web page's URL. The iPod takes care of all the protocol issues.

IMAP

IMAP stands for Internet Message Access Protocol. Like POP, it allows you to receive e-mail on the iPod. It's a newer and more flexible protocol. As the name suggests, IMAP was built around the Internet. It introduces advanced ways to connect to the mail server and use limited bandwidth in the most efficient way.

Yahoo! offers free IMAP accounts for iPod users. To sign up for an account, point your browser to http://mail.yahoo.com.

> **NOTE:** The Yahoo! iPod IMAP service runs off http://imap.apple.mail.yahoo.com. You can connect with a normal web browser, but the web site brushes you off with a "do you yahoo?" message. In other words, move along—nothing to see here if you're not using an iPod or iPhone.

The key to understanding IMAP is to recognize that messages are meant to live on the server rather than go through a retrieve-and-delete cycle. You manage your mail on the IMAP server. You read your mail on a client, like the iPod.

When you download mail with POP, you download entire messages. When you download mail with IMAP, you download headers instead, at least initially. *Headers* are the bits that tell you who the mail is from and what it's about. You don't download the main body of the message until you explicitly request it from the server. Since the header occupies only a fraction of the space of the message, you can download IMAP data a lot faster than you download POP data. The rest of the message stays on the server until you're ready to read it.

The same thing goes for attachments. Say that someone sends you a 10MB video. It doesn't get downloaded to your iPod. It stays on the server until you're ready to watch it on your home computer. If you downloaded the message with POP instead, the entire video would be transferred with the message. With IMAP, you get to read the message that came along with the video without needing to download the video file itself.

> **NOTE:** IMAP also offers a feature that's called *push e-mail*. Geeks will tell you that technically speaking, IMAP is not exactly the same thing as push e-mail. True push e-mail reaches out and tells your e-mail client whenever new mail arrives in the system. Instead, your iPod IMAP client connects to and gently tickles the server until new mail arrives. This kind of always-on connection allows the iPod to receive mail as soon as it arrives—or nearly as soon. In practice, there's better intention there with push-style mail than actual results.

Microsoft Exchange

Microsoft Exchange provides e-mail along with other enterprise-level services intended to support Outlook on the Web, personal computers, and mobile devices. With iOS 4, the iPod fully supports Exchange accounts.

What else can you do to access your Exchange mail? If your IT department has enabled Outlook Web Access (OWA), you can access your Exchange mail in iPod Safari. Limitations aside, this works almost as well as running Outlook on Windows. The most important thing about setting up Exchange accounts is getting instructions and details from a system administrator at your workplace. Doing so will guarantee you'll get your Exchange account up and running fully on your iPod touch.

Summary

Using Mail on your iPod is just as user-friendly and powerful as using a desktop e-mail client. After you play around with it for a week, you'll find yourself using your iPod to check your e-mail more and more. Here are some things to take away with you from this chapter:

- Although Mail attachments introduce occasional difficulties, the rest of the time they work really well. Make sure to use your full iPod interaction vocabulary of touches, pinches, and so forth, to get the most out of viewing attachments.

- It's really easy to add preexisting mail accounts using iTunes, but it's not difficult to add new ones directly in your iPod.

- Remember and use the URL-preview trick. Make sure that e-mail links really take you where you think you're going. This is a good way to avoid "phishing" Internet scams.

- You can change the "Sent from my iPod" signature in the Mail settings.

▇   Mail in iOS 4 supports a unified inbox so you can see all the message from your various e-mail account inboxes all in one place.

▇   Don't forget, there is no Save as Draft button. You need to tap Cancel and then Save Draft.

Chapter 11

Staying on Time and Getting There with Clock, Calendar, and Maps

The iPod touch was never meant to be a major player in the organizer/PDA world, but that's what it has become. It plays music and video. It lets you send and receive e-mails, read books, takes photos, and play games. Given all that, it should be no surprise that the iPod touch offers several very nice utilities that allow you to manage your time, keep track of your appointments, and set alarms. This chapter introduces you to the Clock, Calendar, and Maps applications and shows you how to get the most from them.

Using the Clock Tools

Your iPod comes with a Clock application. This application is far more flexible and useful than you might first imagine. Although you may think that it would show only a clock face and maybe set a timer, it actually provides *four* separate and useful time tools.

To launch the application, tap the white clock face icon on the black background, as shown in Figure 11–1.

Figure 11–1. *The Clock icon*

Along the button bar at the bottom of the Clock application screen are icons for each of the four utilities (see Figure 11–2).

Figure 11–2. *The four Clock utilities appear in a button bar at the bottom of the application screen.*

World Clock: Use this application to monitor the time for multiple clocks around the world.

Alarm: Set your alarms, both one-time and repeating, with this utility.

Stopwatch: Time events with the iPod touch's built-in stopwatch.

Timer: Set a timer to go off after a specific interval with this utility.

NOTE: All clock utilities continue in the background, even if you're not in the Clock application itself. You can start an alarm, a timer, or the stopwatch and go off to other iPod applications. The utility keeps ticking away as you work on other things.

World Clock

The iPod World Clock utility keeps track of time zones around the world. It's really handy if, for example, you regularly travel or make phone calls across time zones. The iPod touch's World Clock can instantly tell you the time in another city. Load it with your favorite cities, and you have an at-a-glance reference that keeps track of the times and time zones for you.

This utility is smart enough to take into account daylight saving time and other quirks, such as New Delhi being 30 minutes off standard. As Figure 11–3 shows, white clock faces indicate daytime, and black clock faces indicate night.

Figure 11–3. *The iPod World Clock utility monitors time around the world.*

Adding Cities

Tap the + at the top right of the screen to add new cities to the World Clock. A search field pops up, prompting you to search for a city. Tap a few letters of the city name. As you type, a list of matching cities appears below the search field. When you find the city you want to add, tap it. Your new clock appears at the bottom of the World Clock screen.

> **NOTE:** World Clock uses a limited database of cities. You may not find a specific city, town, or village. Instead, look for the nearest large city. For example, if you are interested in the time in Massapequa, Long Island, you'll need to use New York City instead.

Reordering Cities

If the cities do not appear in the order you prefer, tap the Edit button at the top left of the World Clock screen. Grab handles (three parallel gray bars) appear to the right of each clock. Drag these handles to reorder your clocks into any position you like. Tap Done when finished. The World Clock screen updates to reflect your new ordering.

Removing Cities

You can easily remove any or all city clocks from your World Clock screen. Tap Edit (again, at the top left of the screen) to reveal the red remove controls to the left of each city name. Tap any red circle. A Delete button appears to the right of the selected clock. Tap Delete to confirm removal, or tap anywhere else on the screen to cancel the action. Tap Done to leave edit mode and return to the normal World Clock screen.

Alarm

The Alarm utility allows your iPod to alert you at a specified time. Use alarms to wake up in the morning or remember business meetings. Unfortunately, the external speaker for the iPod touch is extremely limited. It's tinny and not very loud, and the set of alarms is minimal. Keep in mind that the alarm works better in quiet locations than in loud ones, and avoid using it for mission-critical events.

Creating Alarms

Create alarms by tapping the + on the Alarm screen. This opens the Add Alarm screen shown in Figure 11–4. From this screen, you can set your alarms as follows.

Figure 11–4. *Create custom alarms that play sounds at a given time.*

Set a time: Spin the wheels to specify the time for the alarm to sound. Drag your finger up and down, and the wheel spins with you. Flick your finger, and the wheel continues spinning, even after your finger leaves the screen. If you like, you can also tap a number rather than spin to it.

Make an alarm repeat: Alarms are day-specific. You must choose days of the week for repeating events. For a daily alarm, select every day from Monday through Sunday. For a weekday alarm, use Monday through Friday instead. I use a weekday-only alarm to remind me ten minutes before I need to pick up my kids at the bus stop.

Select a sound: Choose any of the built-in sounds. They are all quiet. They are all tinny. You'll hear them better if your iPod is plugged into an external speaker system.

Allow snooze: The Snooze button, as you might expect, allows you to delay an alarm and repeat it ten minutes later. To enable this, set the Snooze option to ON. To disable snoozing, set it to OFF.

Label an alarm: Give your alarm a custom label by tapping its name and entering text with the keyboard. This helps you differentiate your alarms at a glance. So, you know which one is "Pick Up Kids at Bus Stop" and which one is "Leave for Dental Appointment."

Save an alarm: Tap Save to store your new alarm, or tap Cancel to exit the Add Alarm screen without saving the alarm.

Managing Alarms

The main Alarm screen lists all the alarms you've added to your iPod. To manage your alarms, you can do the following:

Activate alarms: Use the ON/OFF toggles to activate or deactivate each alarm.

Remove alarms: To remove an alarm, tap Edit, tap the red button to the left of the alarm name, and then tap Delete. This permanently removes the alarm from your iPod. Tap Done to return to the main alarm screen.

Edit alarms: To edit an alarm, tap Edit, and then tap the gray reveal button (>) to the right of each name. The Edit Alarm screen opens. It looks similar to the Add Alarm screen (Figure 11–4). Make your edits, and tap Save.

Stopwatch

The iPod Stopwatch utility (see Figure 11–5) allows you to time events. On the Stopwatch screen, tap Start to begin the timer, and tap Lap to mark the latest lap time. The laps appear as a scrolling list at the bottom of the screen. Tap Stop to pause. Tapping Reset returns the timer to 00:00.0.

Figure 11–5. *The Stopwatch application allows you to keep track of lap times in a scrolling list at the bottom of the screen. Tap Start to start, Stop to stop, Lap to end a lap, and Reset to return the time to zero and erase the lap times.*

Timer

The iPod Timer utility (Figure 11–6) plays a sound after a set period of time. Unlike alarms, timers are not tied to a particular time of day. Use alarms for appointments; use timers for cooking eggs. On the Timer screen, set the amount of time you want to pass (three minutes, ten minutes, one hour, and so on), and then tap Start. After the timer counts down, it plays one of the standard alert tones you've selected.

> **TIP:** During the timer countdown, you can select a different alarm tone or cancel the timer before it finishes.

Figure 11–6. *Use the Timer application to play an alarm after a set period.*

Working with the Calendar

The iPod touch Calendar application allows you to keep track of your appointments while on the go. With it, you can view your existing events and add new ones.

Launch Calendar by tapping the white-and-red icon that looks like a page from an old-fashioned, tear-off calendar (see Figure 11–7). The day and date are current and update every day.

Figure 11–7. *The Calendar icon appears on the top row of your iPod touch home screen and shows the current date.*

Switching Calendar Views

The Calendar application offers four views: List, Day, Week, and Month. Each of these helps you locate and review your appointments.

List View

The List view does exactly what the name suggests. It displays your calendar events as a scrolling list. The list is ordered by day and time, as shown in Figure 11–8. The easy-to-follow formatting groups all events on a single day together. All events are listed, providing a powerful overview of all upcoming happenings.

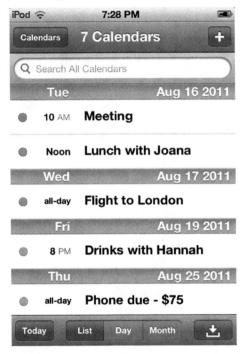

Figure 11–8. *Use the List view to see your appointments as a scrolling list.*

Here are a couple of points about the List view:

- ■ Tap any event to view it in more detail.
- ■ As you scroll, the currently displayed date "sticks" at the top of the screen, even as you scroll through it. It's a very cool but subtle effect.

Day View

Calendar's Day view shows your day's events in day-planner style (see Figure 11–9). Each event occupies a certain amount of space on the layout and is marked with the event and location.

Figure 11–9. *View a day at a time with the Day display.*

Here are some things you need to know about Day view:

- Tap the previous and next arrows to scroll through your calendar a day at a time.

- The day starts and ends at 12 a.m. So if you schedule your New Year's Eve party from 11 p.m. on December 31 until 2 a.m. on January 1, the Calendar application splits it into two Day views, even though it's a single event.

- Tap an event to open its detail view.

Week View

When you rotate your iPod touch to a landscape position, Calendar's Week view appears (see Figure 11–10). You must rotate your iPod to see the Week view. There is no button in the Calendar app that activates it.

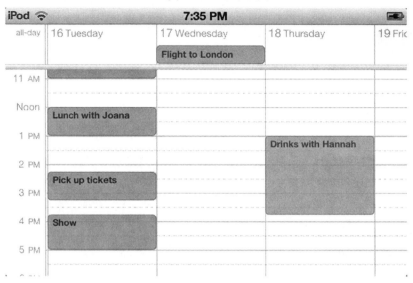

Figure 11–10. *View a week at a time with the Week display.*

Here are some things you need to know about Day view:

- Swipe left or right to move through the week.
- Swipe up and down to move through the hours of the day.
- Tap an event to open its detail view.

Month View

The month-at-a-time view highlights all days with appointments (see Figure 11–11). A small dot appears below all days containing appointments. Tap any marked day to view a scrolling list of events at the bottom of the screen. As with the other views, tap those events to view their details.

Figure 11–11. *The Month view marks a dot under all dates that contain events.*

Here are some things you need to know about Day view:

- The darkened, recessed square represents the current date.
- A blue square represents the date you have selected.
- Tap an event to open its detail view.

The Today Button

Clicking the Today button in any view automatically jumps you back to the display for the current day but preserves whichever view you are using. So, you'll see the current month for Month view or recenter the list in List view.

The Calendars Button

The Calendars button at the top left of the screen allows you to choose which calendars you want to show (see Figure 11–12). A calendar with a check mark displays events in any of the calendar views. To hide a certain calendar, tap it to uncheck it.

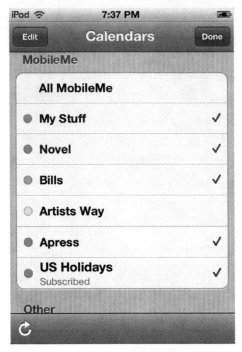

Figure 11–12. *The Calendars button screen allows you to choose which calendars you want to show.*

You can create new calendars right on your iPod touch. To do so, tap the Edit button in the Calendars window (Figure 11–12). Next, tap Add Calendar and then enter the name of the new calendar and the color you want to use for it. You can also delete and rename any calendar from the same calendar edit screen. Tap Done when finished.

Adding Events

Your iPod touch allows you to add calendar events on the go. This lets you adjust and update your schedule when you are away from your computer. You have two ways to add events. In Day or Week view, you can simply tap and hold on the screen, and a new event bubble appears (Figure 11–13). Drag the grab circles to adjust the times that the event covers. In Week view, you can also drag an event from one day to another.

Figure 11–13. *Creating new events by touch*

If you are in the List, Day, or Month view, you can also add a new event by tapping the + button at the top right of the screen. The Add Event screen opens, as shown in Figure 11–14.

Start by entering a title and location for the event. Tap in either field, and use the keyboard to enter a name and place. To finish naming your event, tap Done, or tap Cancel to leave the screen without adding a new event.

Once you have named your event and tapped Done, you are returned to the Add Event screen. Here, you can update the event name and/or location and specify when the event starts and ends, its time zone, whether it repeats, when to play an alert to notify you about the event, and what calendar the event should appear on (Work, Bills, and so on). You can also add a URL and note to the event. Customize any or all of these options, as described in the following sections, and then tap Done to finish adding the event. Tap Cancel if you want to return to the List, Day, Week, or Month view without adding that event.

Figure 11–14. *Add new events directly on your iPod touch.*

Updating an Event Name or Location

Tap the name and location line (just below the Add Event title) to open an editor that allows you to update the event's name and location text. After making your changes, tap Done to save your changes, or tap Cancel to return to the Add Event screen without applying those changes.

Setting the Event Start and End Times

Tap the Starts/Ends field to open the screen that allows you to set these times. You enter the time by way of a scroll control. This control contains date, hour, minute, and a.m./p.m. wheels. You set the start and end time by scrolling your way to the proper combination.

Tap either Starts or Ends to switch between the two times (when the event begins and when it ends) and make your adjustments as needed.

The basic scroller is great for relatively near-term appointments. It is not so great when you're scrolling six months into the future for your next tooth cleaning or your child's commencement schedule. It can take an awful lot of scrolling to get to the date you want. For quicker access to future dates or for all-day events (such as when you go on vacation or will be out of town on a business trip), set the All-day indicator from OFF to ON. The scroll wheel updates, replacing the date/hour/minute wheels with month/day/year wheels. You can schedule appointments this way, all the way up to December 31, 2067. (Don't count on me to be there. I have a tooth-cleaning appointment that afternoon.) You can also set the time zone for the event on this screen.

Tap Done to confirm your settings, or tap Cancel to return to the Add Event screen without changing the start and end times.

Setting a Repeating Event

When your event repeats, you can select from a standard list that defines how often: Every Day, Every Week, Every Two Weeks, Every Month, or Every Year. To make this happen, tap the Repeat field on the Add Event screen, select a repetition interval, and tap Done. To return to the Add Event screen without adding a repeated event, tap Cancel. To disable repeats, tap None, and then tap Done.

Adding Alerts

Add event alerts to notify you when an event is coming due. For example, you may want a one-hour notice for those dental appointments and a two-day notice for your anniversary. The iPod provides a nice selection of options. These include five, fifteen, and thirty minutes before the event; one or two hours before the event; one or two days before the event; and on the date of the event itself.

Tap the Alert field to set an event alert. After selecting an event alert time, tap Done. To cancel without setting the alert time, tap Cancel. To remove event alerts, tap None and then Done.

Once you've saved your first alert, the iPod offers you the option to add a second one. This allows you to remind yourself both a day before an event and a few minutes before you need to leave. This is a particularly useful feature for people who need extra reminders.

> **NOTE:** Unfortunately, there are no "snooze" options for calendar events.

Assigning Event to a Specific Calendar

You can select which calendar the event is assigned to by tapping Calendar and then selecting which calendar the event belongs on from the checklist.

Adding URLs

If there is a web site associated with the event, you can type its web address (URL) into the URL field.

Avenue, Washington, DC") or search for contacts ("Bill Smith"), landmarks ("Golden Gate Bridge"), or even pizza places in your local zip code ("Pizza 11746").

Bookmarks button: This blue book-looking button lies within the search field. Tap it to select addresses from your bookmarked locations, your recent locations, or your contact list.

Map: The map itself appears in the center of your screen. It's fully interactive. You can scroll by dragging your finger along the map, or zoom in and out using pinches and double-taps. (Use a single-fingered double-tap to zoom in and a double-fingered tap to zoom out.)

Red pushpins: The red pushpins indicate locations found by the application after a search. For example, Figure 11–17 shows a café called Curved Angel Café. Tap a pushpin to view a location summary, and then tap the blue > icon for more details and options. These options include directions to and from that location, bookmarking the location, and assigning the location to contacts. Tap the orange-and-white icon with a man in it to enter Street View.

Purple pushpins: The purple pushpins show where you've dropped pins onto the map to add your own user-defined locations.

Locate Me button: Tap the arrowhead button at the lower-left side of the screen to contact Google and search for your location. Google uses a kind of pseudo-GPS position based on your Wi-Fi signal. Some local Wi-Fi networks can return approximate locations within about a half mile and help you determine your location. Other times, Maps thinks you're in Cleveland when you're actually in Arizona. So, don't count on this service; your results will vary.

Search/Directions buttons: The two buttons at the bottom of the screen switch between normal mode and directions mode. Tap Directions to enter start and end locations for your trip or scroll through the stages of your current trip. The directions appear at the top of the screen, along with Previous and Next buttons. When viewing directions, tap the curvy arrow to switch your start and end points and get reverse directions.

Options button: Marked with a page curl icon, this button reveals options hiding below your map. (The map actually bends back to reveal the options.) The list includes the following options:

- Switch between the standard map, satellite, and hybrid imagery or show your directions as a text list, such as "Go west for 5.4 miles."

- The drop pin feature lets you include additional feature points without needing to enter an address. This is perfect for when you need to remember where you parked the car or saw a cool product in a shop window while walking.

- Choose Show Traffic to request traffic conditions along your route. This feature is limited to certain regions, mostly major metropolitan areas.

- Tap the Print button to print your map and directions to an AirPrint printer.

Figure 11–17. *The Maps application (left) allows you to interactively view and search standard and satellite maps. The red pushpins show the locations found by your search. Tap the page curl icon in the lower-right corner to be presented with your Maps options (right).*

Navigating Maps

The Maps app makes it so you can explore the world from the comfort of your hands. Like any other app, you navigate the map using gestures. You can also view the map in different modes.

Gestures

On maps you use gestures to zoom in, zoom out, pan, and scroll.

Zoom in: You have two ways of zooming in. Either pinch the map with two fingers, or use one finger and double-tap the location on the map that you want to zoom in on. Double-tap again to zoom in even closer.

Zoom out: You can zoom out in two ways. Either reverse-pinch the map with two fingers, or use two fingers double-tap the map. Double-tap with two fingers again to zoom even farther out.

Panning and scrolling: Touch and drag the map up, down, left, or right to move the map around and view another location.

Changing Map Views

The default map view is Google's classic road map with orange, yellow, and white streets. But the Maps application also allows you to view the map in four additional views as well as with traffic overlay.

To access these features, tap or tap and drag the page curl at the bottom of the maps screen. The map curls up, and you are presented with the Map settings page (see Figure 11–17). Your settings include map views, overlays, and a special feature called "Drop Pin," which places, or "drops," a pin anywhere on the map. These dropped pins let you easily mark a business, street corner, beach, or any other kind of location on a map.

Standard: This is the classic default map view. It uses Google's standard road map.

Satellite: This view shows you the world using satellite imagery. It's perhaps the coolest maps view because you can zoom in on streets and see little blips of people walking the day the satellite imagery was taken. No labels appear in satellite view.

Hybrid: This view combines Classic and Satellite. You see the map in satellite imagery, but it has labels, roads, and borders overlaid on it.

List: This view shows you your location or direction using a list.

> **TIP:** The standard map view uses orange, yellow, and white to color streets. Orange indicates interstate highways. Yellow indicates state highways and county parkways. White indicates local and private streets.

Show Traffic: Tap to turn Traffic ON. While on, the current traffic conditions are overlaid on the map. To see current traffic conditions, you must be connected to a Wi-Fi network. I'll talk more about traffic later in this chapter.

Drop Pin: Tapping this button causes the page to uncurl and drops a location pin in the center of the map. Use a dropped pin to easily mark a business, street corner, beach, or any other kind of location on a map. You can also drop a pin by touching and holding anywhere on the map. I'll talk more about dropping pins later in this chapter.

You'll notice I said that the Maps app allows you to view the map in standard map view as well as four additional views, so there are five views total. The fifth view is called Street View, and you access it from a search results or dropped pin. I'll talk more about Street View later in this chapter.

Finding Locations

The Maps app provides multiple ways to find locations. You can search for locations using the search field, automatically find your current location using the iPod's Skyhook location services, or even just zoom in and browse the map like a bird flying overhead.

Depending what you are looking for, some types of search are better than others. For example, if you are looking for your favorite spot on a beach, chances are it doesn't have an address or name, so your best bet is to navigate to the beach and then zoom in and scroll around in satellite view until you find that favorite spot.

Search

You'll find most of your locations through the search field at the top of your screen (see Figure 11–17). Tap the search field, and a keyboard appears. There are many ways to search for a location.

Enter your search query and one or more red pins fall onto the map. Imagine you're taking a trip next week to Chicago. As you'll see in Figure 11–18, I searched for "Pizza Chicago." Several red pins populate the map, all representing pizza places.

Figure 11–18. *Search result pins on the map*

When you touch one of the red pins, you get the pin's information bar (see Figure 11–19). The information bar tells you the name of the establishment (a pizzeria, in this case) and displays an icon on either side. Those icons represent the Information window and Street View.

Figure 11–19. *A search result pin's information bar shows the name of the establishment with a Street View icon on the left and an Information icon on the right.*

Information Window

Tap the white-and-blue > on the pin's information bar to make the Info window slide open. The Info window (see Figure 11–20) displays information for the establishment, such as its phone number, web page, and physical address and gives you several options on how you can use this location further on your iPod touch.

Figure 11–20. *The Info window*

Phone: The establishment's phone number. Touch and hold to copy the number to the clipboard.

Home page: The establishment's web address. Tap it to close Maps and open the web address in Safari.

Address: The establishment's address. Touch and hold to copy the address to the clipboard.

Directions To Here: Tap here to be taken to the directions toolbar. The address of the establishment is populated in the second (end destination) directions field. I'll talk more about directions later in this chapter.

Directions From Here: Tap here to be taken to the directions toolbar. The address of the establishment is populated in the first (origin destination) directions field.

Add to Contacts: Tapping this button adds the name of the establishment, the phone number, the web address, and the physical address to a contact. You have the options Create New Contact or Add to Existing Contact.

If you choose Create New Contact, a new contact window slides up (see Figure 12-12) in the Info window populating contact fields with information and also allowing you to add more information to the contact. Tap Done to save the new contact.

If you choose Add to Existing Contact, a list of all your contacts from your address book slides up in the Info window. Tap the contact you want to add the information to. The information is added, and the contacts list disappears from view.

Share Location: Tapping this button allows you to e-mail a link of the establishment's name, Google Maps link, and attach a vcard (a virtual business card the receiver can choose to add to his address book).

Add to Bookmarks: Tapping this button allows you to save the location to your Maps bookmarks. You'll be able to name the bookmark, so you can change "Pizano's Pizza & Pasta" to "My favorite pizza joint." I'll talk more about bookmarks in a moment.

Tap Map to close the information window and return to the map.

Street View

Street View uses Google technology to display 360° panoramic views of the location you are looking at. To enter Street View, tap the white-and-orange Street View icon in the pin's information bar (see Figure 11–19). Your map zooms in on the pin and then tilts up to present you with a street-level panoramic view (see Figure 11–21).

Figure 11–21. *Street View fills the entire screen. Tap the white arrow on the road to move forward down the street. Tap the map navigation icon to return to map view.*

Google has had Street View available on the Web for some time, but using it on the iPod touch brings it to a whole different level. The fact that you can touch and drag and pinch and zoom around the street gives Street View an immediacy it's never had on a desktop or laptop.

While in Street View, drag your finger around to experience the 360° panoramic views. Pinch or double-tap the screen to zoom in. Reverse-pinch to zoom back out. To "walk" down the street, find the big white arrows at the end of a street label and tap them. You'll then move that direction.

The small circular navigation icon at the bottom right of a Street View map shows you the direction you are looking in. Tap the icon to return to your last map view location.

Street View isn't available in all cities yet, but it is in most major North American and European ones. Street View is a wonderful tool because it lets you check out what a place or area looks like in advance. Thinking of moving to a new area of town? You can virtually scroll down the street in Street View to see whether you like the looks of it before you take the time and trouble to start searching for houses in the neighborhood.

Current Location

Curious about where you are in the world? The Maps app allows you to find your current location with a tap of a button. The current location button is located in the bottom left of the screen (see Figure 11–22). It looks like an arrowhead. Tap it to jump to your current location on the map.

Current Location works by using the iPod's built-in positioning tool called Skyhook Wi-Fi positioning to locate you. Skyhook Wi-Fi positioning uses known wireless hotspot locations to triangulate your current position with an accuracy of 60 to 100 feet (20 to 30 meters).

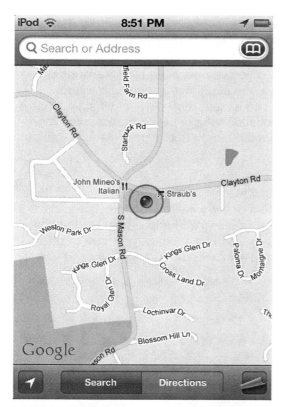

Figure 11–22. *The blue dot surrounded by the circle represents your approximate location.*

Your current location is signified by a blue dot, as in Figure 11–22. If the Maps app can't determine your exact location, a blue circle appears around the dot. The circle can range in size depending on how precisely your location can be determined. What the circle means is you are somewhere in that location. The smaller the circle, the more precise the current location marker.

> **NOTE:** Location Services must be turned on for your iPod to find your current location. To turn on Location Services, go to **Settings ➤ Location Services ➤ ON**.

When you are in Current Location mode, the current location icon in the toolbar turns blue. If you've found your current location and then drag the map around, you can tap the current location button again to have the map center back on it.

You can tap the blue current location dot on the map to bring up Current Location information bar. The address of the current location is displayed. Tap the > button to get the information window for the location, including the ability to get directions to/from the location, bookmark it, add it to contacts, or e-mail the location; or tap the Street View button to enter Street View (if available in the area).

Bookmarking and Viewing Saved Locations

There are two ways you can bookmark locations you've navigated to in Maps: dropping a pin or tapping the Add to Bookmarks button in the location's information window. Dropping a pin allows you to mark any location on a map, regardless of whether it has a physical address; you can then add the pin's location to your saved bookmarks. Once you've saved locations, you can view them all in the handy Bookmarks menu.

Dropping a Pin

Navigate to a point of interest on the map without doing a search for something. In the example in Figure 11–23, we found a location by Chicago's Shedd Aquarium that has beautiful views of the sunrise over Lake Michigan. To drop a pin, all you have to do is press and hold your finger on the map where you want to drop it. After a second or two, a purple pin appears and sticks in the map.

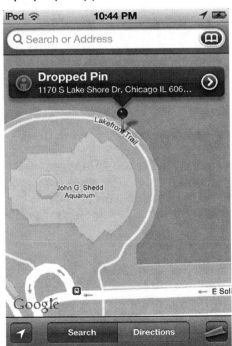

Figure 11–23. *A dropped pin and its information bar with the approximate address*

The pin's information bar appears with the approximate address of the pin as well as the usual icons for Street View and the information window. If the pin's location isn't exactly where you want it, you can tap and hold the purple pin's head and drag it to the location you want. Remove your finger to sink the pin into the map.

Tap the > button to view the information window for the pin's location, including the ability to get directions to/from the location, bookmark it, add it to contacts, or e-mail the location; or tap the Street View button to enter Street View (if available in the area).

You can also drop a pin in the center of the map by accessing the Maps settings page behind the page curl in the lower-right corner. Tap the page curl at the bottom of the maps screen and tap the Drop Pin button. The settings page uncurls, and a pin drops in the center of the map. You can then tap and drag the pin to move it to anywhere you want on the map.

Dropping pins might seem like a nice but unnecessary feature at first. Why, if you can search maps with the apps powerful search features, would you manually add locations? Again, dropped pins are great because it allows you to mark locations that do not have a fixed address, such as a good trail in the mountains, the sight of your first kiss (for the romantic among you), or even the location of your favorite bench in Central Park.

Bookmarking

So far in this chapter we've shown you several ways to bookmark locations, whether it be by a dropped pin or the information windows of a business, friend, or address you looked up. But where are all those bookmarks you've saved? In the bookmarks window, of course!

Tap the bookmarks icon that's located in the search field (see Figure 11–17). It looks like a book folded open. The bookmarks window appears and presents three views: Bookmarks, Recents, and Contacts (see Figure 11–24).

Bookmarks: This lists all the bookmarks you've saved in the Maps app. Tap any bookmark to jump to it on the map. Tap the Edit button to delete a bookmark, move it up or down the bookmarks list, or change the name of the bookmark.

Recents: This lists all the resent search queries, driving directions, and dropped pins you've made. Tap any item on the list to jump to it on the map. Press the Clear button to remove all items from the list. Remember, clearing your Recents list ensures that people who use your iPod can't spy on locations you've searched for. Be aware, however, that doing so also clears your direction routes. Routes can't be bookmarked, so the only way to quickly access them is through the Recents window. If you clear the window, you'll need to perform your route searches from scratch.

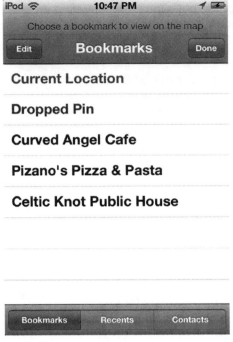

Figure 11–24. *The bookmarks window displays your bookmarked locations, recent locations, and contact's locations.*

Contacts: This list shows you all the contacts who you have addresses for. Tap any contact on the list to jump to their address on the map. If a contact has more than one address, you'll be asked to choose which address to navigate to. Tap the Groups button to navigate through your contact groups.

Directions and Traffic

The iPod Maps app lets you search for directions and view current traffic conditions. Like the Maps app itself, directions and traffic require an Internet connection. Since the iPod only has a Wi-Fi connection, you'll need to look up the directions before you leave home.

Directions

To get directions, tap the Directions tab in the Maps bottom toolbar (see Figure 11–17). You'll notice that the search field becomes a double field to enter your start and end locations (see Figure 11–25). The Maps app will put your current location, if available, as the starting location. If you don't want to use your current location as the starting address, tap in the first search field, and press the *X* to remove it and type in whatever address you want.

Figure 11–25. *The Maps search field changed to directions input when you tap the directions button.*

NOTE: You can also begin a directions search from any pin's information window.

To enter an address from one of your contacts, tap the bookmarks icon, and then choose a contact. You'll be asked to choose whether you want Directions to Here or Directions From Here. Choose, and the contact's address is populated in the appropriate directions field. To reverse the start end points, tap the curvy, sideways S-arrow to switch the points (and get reverse directions). The reverse directions feature is nice because sometimes the route you came isn't the quickest route back. Reverse directions shows you whether another route home is quicker.

When you have selected both a start point and an end point, one or more blue lines appear on the map showing you suggested routes you can take (see Figure 11–26). Tap the route label (Route 1, Route 2, and so on) to select a route. A green pin represents your starting location on the map, and a red pin indicates your end location. You'll also notice a blue directions bar has appeared at the top of the screen. The directions bar lets you choose between driving (car icon), public transit (bus icon), or walking (person icon) directions. These different modes of transportation may give you different direction routes on the map between the exact same two locations. This is because people aren't allowed to walk on highways and cars aren't allowed to drive on pedestrian malls and on certain bus routes, depending on the city you live in.

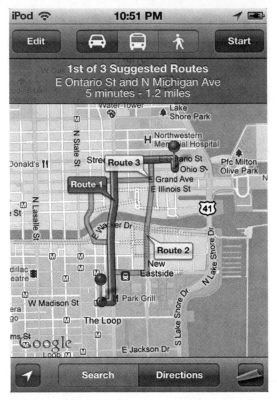

Figure 11–26. *The map with the car route showing three possible routes*

Driving or Walking Directions

Tap either the driving or walking icon. You'll see the length of the route and the estimated time it takes to get to your destination. If traffic data is available, the estimated journey time adjusts accordingly.

To navigate through the directions step-by-step, tap the blue Start button in the upper-right corner. The directions bar changes to the one in Figure 11–27.

If you'd like to navigate through the directions step-by-step in the map, tap the right-pointing arrow on the bar. Each subsequent tap brings you forward one step in the route. To move back a step, tap the left arrow.

Figure 11–27. *Tap the left or right arrow to move through the directions step-by-step.*

Public Transit Directions

Tap the public transit button. In the blue directions bar you'll see the estimated time it takes to get to your destination. If traffic data is available, the estimated journey time is adjusted accordingly.

Tap the clock icon to display a list of departure times and schedules (see Figure 11–28). Tap Depart to choose a date and time. The Depart field defaults to the current date and time unless you change it. Below the depart time is a list of alternate schedules. Select one, and then tap the Done button.

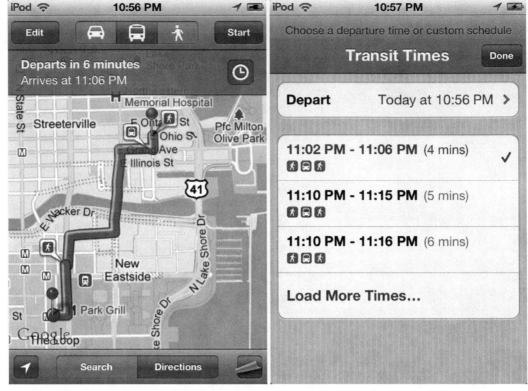

Figure 11–28. *The directions bar shows public transit routes (left). The clock icon allows you to select between different transit schedules (right).*

To navigate through the directions step-by-step, tap the blue Start button. If you'd like to navigate through the directions step-by-step in the map, tap the right-pointing arrow on the bar. Each subsequent tap will bring you forward one step in the route. To move back a step, tap the left arrow.

> **NOTE:** We've mentioned it before, but unfortunately, you can't bookmark routes. That's a pity because it would be nice to be able to quickly pull up traffic conditions on your favorite routes. Ideally Apple will add this feature in the future.

Traffic

The Maps app can display traffic conditions that help you when planning an immediate journey. To turn on traffic conditions, tap the page curl at the bottom of the maps screen, and then tap Show Traffic to ON (see Figure 11–17). Back on the map you'll notice that green, yellow, and red lines have appeared over some of the roads (see Figure 11–29).

Just how on Earth does the Maps app know what the current traffic conditions are? Most major U.S. cities have sensors embedded in the highways and major roads. These sensors feed data back, in real time, to the Department of Transportation (DOT). The DOT uses this information to update digital traffic signs that report local traffic conditions (like those bright Broadway-like signs that hang from overpasses on major metro highways that tell you how long it will take to get to a certain exit). The DOT also shares this data, which Google collects and uses to display near real-time traffic maps.

Figure 11–29. *Traffic overlays on the map*

Green lines indicate traffic is flowing at least 50 mph. Yellow ones mean that traffic is flowing between 25 and 50 mph. Red highways mean that traffic is moving slower than 25 mph. A gray route indicates that traffic data is not available for that street or highway.

The traffic feature is limited to certain regions, mostly major metropolitan areas in the United States, France, Britain, Australia, and Canada, but new cities and new countries are frequently added. If you don't see traffic conditions, try zooming out on the map. If you still don't see any, they aren't available in your area yet.

Maps Tips

Here are some tips for using Google Maps on your iPod:

- When a person or business is in your contacts list, save yourself some time. Don't type in the entire address. Just enter a few letters of the name, and select the contact.

- URLs that link to Google Maps automatically open in the Maps application, whether they are tapped in Safari or Mail.

- Tap individual items on the directions list to jump to that part of your route.

- The Recents screen (in Bookmarks) shows both recent locations *and* recent directions.

Find a Lost iPod touch

Have you lever lost your iPod? Horrible, right? Don't worry! Now Apple has created a free app called Find My iPhone (Figure 11–30) and you can use it should you ever lose your iPod touch again. Yes, it says "iPhone" but it works for iPads, iPod touches, and Macs as well. Using this app, you can locate all your iDevices from any iPhone, iPad, or iPod touch, or by logging into your iCloud account at www.icloud.com.

Figure 11–30. *The Find My iPhone icon.*

Before you can find a lost iPod, you need to make sure you've installed and set up the Find My iPhone app on the device. Therefore, it's best to do that as soon as you get your iPod. Once you've set up Find My iPhone to work with your iPod and other iOS devices, launch the app and sign in. You'll then be presented with the screen shown in Figure 11–31.

Figure 11–31. *The Find My iPhone app lists all your devices. Select one to see its location on a map.*

You can choose what Mac or iOS device you want to see the location of. Select a device and it will be located on a map. An iPod touch will be represented by a tiny iPod touch icon. Tap the icon to see the name of the device, then tap the blue Info button to display a window that shows you the various actions you can perform with the device:

- *Play Sound or Send Message*: This lets you display a text message on your iPod touch or play a sound at full volume for two minutes (even if the iPod is muted). The sound feature is great if you don't know where in the house you have left your iPod or iPhone.

- *Remote Lock*: Use this to set up a remote passcode lock on your device or initiate your current passcode lock. This will keep anyone out of the device who doesn't know the passcode.

- *Remote Wipe*: This is a worst-case scenario feature. If your iPod touch has been stolen and you don't want to play detective and track it to the perpetrator's house, you can remote wipe your iPod. Remote wiping your iPod will permanently erase all your personal data on it, ensuring that whoever has or finds your iPod can't commit identity theft against you.

It's important to note that all the Find My iPhone features as they relate to an iPod touch require that the iPod be connected to the Internet to work.

Find a Friend

Your iPod touch is so amaing that not only can it help you find other iOS devices and Macs you own, it can help you find friends as well! Well, not "find friends" as in make new ones, but it can help you find the frineds you already know. It does this through an app (and iCloud service) called Find My Friends (Figure 11–32).

Figure 11–32. *The Find My Friends icon.*

Using Find My Friends, you can instantly see the location of any of your friends who have iPhones, iPod touches, or iPads. That is, you can see where they are as long as they've given you presmission. The Find My Friends app allows you to also share your location. It's a great way to see where you are in location to your friends. Perhaps you're out shopping and you're thinking of grabbing a coffee. Just open Find My Friends and looks for any buddiess that are near you to meet up for a quick drink.

As you can see in Figure 14-33, all your friends who have allowed you to know their location show up in a list. Tap the friend's name to get the address of where they are and also view their location on a map.

Figure 11–33. *The Find My Friends app shows you a list of the locations of all your friends.*

And for those of you concerned about privacy know that Apple has built in a great many of privacy options into the app. For instance, you can choose to only share your location for a certain period of time, like three hours; or a certain time of day, like from noon to five pm. You can also revoke all location invitations at any time, which will disable any of your friends from following you.

The Find My Friends app is a great new social netowrking app that's a free download in the App Store. The only requirement is that you have a free iCloud account. Get one at www.icloud.com.

Summary

As you can now see, the iPod touch offers you tools to stay on time and get to places you need to be! Its Clock and Calendar applications certainly complement the other onboard applications and expand usability in a vague time-management way. Maps is the world in your pocket. With it, you can now find directions to your favorite pizza joint, get an instant fix on your current location, or check out what the tops of the Pyramids of Giza look like without leaving your living room. You've learned how to use maps to find public transport times and routes, view current traffic conditions, or just virtually stroll down the street of a neighborhood.

Before we move on to the next chapter, here are a few key points to keep in mind:

■ The sound levels for the iPod touch's built-in speaker are pretty good. Still, if you are going to rely on your iPod touch as your only alarm, you may want to buy an iPod speaker system with built-in dock. You'll get much louder sounds, and your iPod is charged while it is plugged into the dock!

■ Calendar has four views: List, Day, Week, and Month. Get used to them all because they all provide unique ways of planning and viewing your events.

■ You don't have to pop over to Google every time you want to check the current time in London. Set up the World Clock utility and have that information just a couple of taps away.

■ Street View is not only fun; it's useful if you want to explore an area of your city—or almost any major city in the world—you've never been to.

■ Using your iPod touches built-in positioning features, an iCloud account, and the free Find My iPhone and Find My Friends apps from the App Store, you can now find your missing iOS devices, Macs, and friends all right from the iPod touch!

Chapter 12

Using Your Desk Set: Contacts, Calculator, Notes, Weather, Stocks, Voice Memos, and Reminders

The iPod touch is your digital gateway to more tools and apps than you could ever imagine. Chapter 8 taught you how to navigate and download apps from the App Store; this chapter shows you how to use many of the productivity apps that come preinstalled on the iPod touch, namely, Contacts, Calculator, Notes, Weather, Stocks, Voice Memos, and Reminders.

Synchronizing Your Address Book with Your Computer

Before you even get to the iPod, start thinking about your contacts while you're at your computer. In iTunes, the Info tab controls how and when your iPod touch syncs its contacts with those stored on your computer. You can sync your iPod with contact information from Windows Address Book or Microsoft Outlook (Windows) or Address Book, Microsoft Entourage or Microsoft Outlook (Mac).

Choosing Sync Options

In Chapter 2, I already told you how to sync your contacts from your computer with your iPod, but let's quickly look at it again. In iTunes, click the Info tab, and locate the Contacts section—it's near the top of the screen, as shown in Figure 12–1. To synchronize your address book, you must select the "Sync contacts" check box. Then all the grayed-out options turn dark black, and you can select your settings.

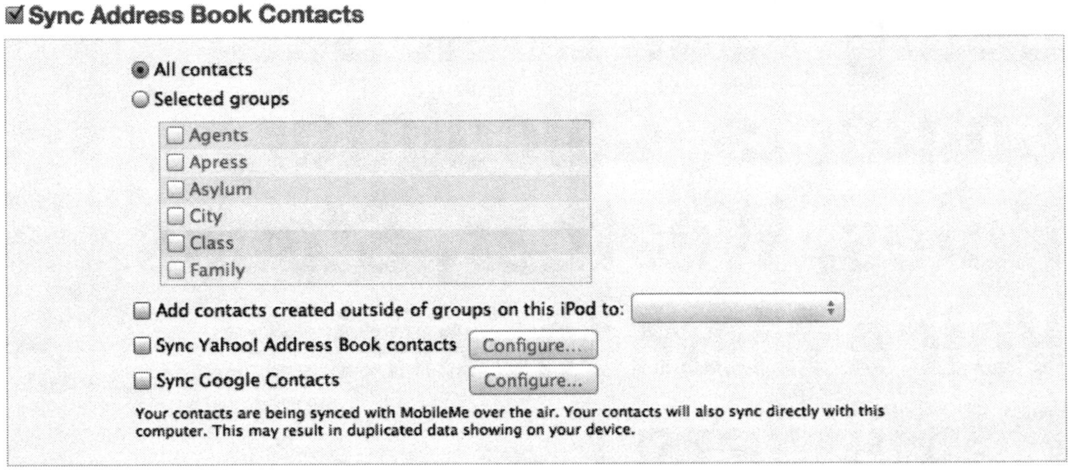

☑ **Sync Address Book Contacts**

◉ All contacts
○ Selected groups

☐ Agents
☐ Apress
☐ Asylum
☐ City
☐ Class
☐ Family

☐ Add contacts created outside of groups on this iPod to: [_____ ⬍]

☐ Sync Yahoo! Address Book contacts [Configure...]

☐ Sync Google Contacts [Configure...]

Your contacts are being synced with MobileMe over the air. Your contacts will also sync directly with this computer. This may result in duplicated data showing on your device.

Figure 12–1. *Unless you check the "Sync contacts" check box, your contacts will not copy over to your iPod touch.*

Choose where to sync your contacts from (and, for that matter, to). iTunes looks for address books on your system and lists those available in a drop-down list. The list varies by system and by your installed software.

Next, determine whether you want to use all contacts or select a group like Home or Work to sync. If you do not divide your contacts into groups, just leave the default option, "All contacts." You can also sync contacts from your online Yahoo! or Google contacts. Select either box, and then enter your Yahoo! or Google ID and password.

After making your choices, tap Apply to save your changes. The button is located at the bottom right of the iTunes screen.

> **NOTE:** If you are syncing your contacts through iCloud (see Chapter 2), you don't need to worry about any of these steps.

Replacing Contacts

At times, you may want to replace the information on your iPod entirely with the contact information from a computer. For example, you may be restoring your iPod after upgrading your system to a new machine, or you might be reassigning the iPod from one employee to another.

Start by locating the Advanced Info options for your iPod, at the very bottom of the Info tab. Scroll all the way down using the scroller at the right side of the iTunes window. In that section, select the Contacts box under "Replace information on this iPod," and then click Apply.

During the next sync—and the next sync only—iTunes completely wipes the contact information off your iPod and replaces it with the information found on the computer.

Working with the Contacts Application

The Contacts application appears on the top row of your iPod touch home screen. It looks like a brown, spiral-bound address book with tabs (see Figure 12–2). Tap this icon to open the Contacts application.

Figure 12–2. *Use the Contacts application as a palm-top address book. You can search for existing contact information and add new contacts directly from your iPod.*

Finding Contacts

When you launch the Contacts app the first time, you'll be presented either with the Groups screen, which lists all your contacts by groups, or with the All Contacts screen, which lists all your contacts alphabetically. Which screen you see depends on whether you have contact groups set up. If you do not, then you are presented with the All Contacts screen. As Figure 12–3 shows, both the Groups and All Contacts screens are quite basic. The Groups screen consists of an alphabetical listing on all your groups, while the All Contacts screen consists of a scrolling list of names, an alphabetic index, and an Add button. You can scroll, drag, or flick up and down the screen to move through your entire groups or contacts collections. On the contacts screen you can also tap a letter to move instantly to that part of the address book or drag your finger up and down the alphabet to jump through the names. Tap the Refresh button in the upper-left corner to make sure you've synced the latest contacts.

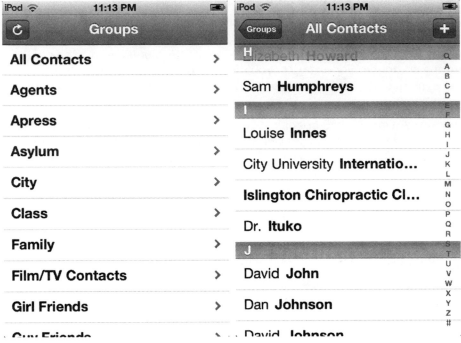

Figure 12–3. *The Groups (left) and Contacts (right) application screens*

Ordering Your List

You can choose how Contacts orders your contacts list: by first name and then last, or by last name and then first. How you set this up depends on whether you want to search for your friends and business acquaintances informally or formally or whether your country uses a non-English ordering method, as in Japan or China.

To change your settings, navigate to Settings ➤ Mail, Contacts, Calendars, and choose an ordering method for sorting and for displaying.

Viewing Contact Details

Tap any contact name to view its information screen. Figure 12–4 shows a contact information screen for Apple's mythical John Appleseed. The level of detail and the amount of information shown depends on how much information you've entered into the address book. A contact may include a physical address, a web site URL, e-mail address, phone numbers, and more.

Figure 12–4. *The Info screens contains as much or as little contact information as you have set.*

A contact's info screen isn't just to be looked at; it's interactive. Tap and hold a phone number to copy it to the clipboard. Tap an e-mail address to be taken to a new compose mail message screen with the e-mail address filled in the To field. Tap a web link to open the Safari browser to that web address. Tap a physical address to open the address in the Maps app. Tap and hold other information on the page to copy its text to the clipboard. Finally, tap Share Contact to compose an e-mail with the contact's information attached as a VCF (virtual business card file) to the body of the e-mail. The recipient of the e-mail can then add the card to their address book.

Adding Contacts

One of my favorite iPod touch features is its ability to add contacts on the go. When I'm talking with another parent and trying to set up a play date or when I'm in a business meeting, I can pull out my iPod touch and enter contact information right where I am. When I return to my computer or sync to iCloud, I sync that information into my main computer-based address book.

Contacts you create or edit on your iPod touch sync back to your computer and update the information there. If you've set the Sync contacts option in iTunes, all changes made on your touch synchronize to your computer and reflect your updates.

Tap the (+) button at the top right of the screen to create a new contact. A detail screen opens, as shown in Figure 12–5. Here, you can enter all the information for your new contact. Fill in the fields, as described in the following sections, and then tap Done to add your new contact to the list.

> **TIP:** Once you've added a field to your contact, the green + next to each defined field turns into a red –. Erase any field by tapping the red button and then tapping Delete.

Figure 12–5. *Use the New Contact screen to add information about your new contact.*

Adding a Contact Name

As you can see, adding a contact name is straightforward. Type in the contact's first name, and then touch the last name field to enter their last name. One caveat is when you are entering a business name. Here you have a choice. You can enter a name and a company ID, just one, or just the other. For example, you might add a contact for your favorite pizza parlor using just its company name, without adding a contact name for that establishment.

After entering the new information, tap Done. This returns you to the New Contact screen.

> **NOTE:** The iPod expects you to separate a contact's first and last names into separate fields so that it can properly alphabetize the results.

Adding a Contact Photo

The Contacts application can take advantage of any photos you have synchronized to your iPod. Tap the Add Photo box at the top left of the New Contact screen, and then tap Choose Photo from the pop-up menu that appears to assign a photo to your new contact. The Photo Albums screen opens. From there, navigate to a photo thumbnail, and tap it to display it. Move and scale that photo as desired, and then tap Set Photo. The iPod saves the picture and adds it to your contact.

You can also take a photo of the contact if you happen to be with them. Tap the Add Photo box at the top left of the New Contact screen, and then tap Take Photo from the pop-up menu that appears. Snap your pic, move and scale it, and then tap Use Photo to assign the photo to your new contact.

Adding Phone Numbers

The Contacts application supports not one or two but *eight* different kinds of phone numbers. And on top of that, it also offers a free-form phone number label. You can enter almost unlimited quantities of phone numbers and assign them to standard types, including mobile, home, work, pager, and more.

Tap the Phone field, and the iPod opens an Edit Phone screen. Enter a phone number. You can then tap the current label of that phone number (such as "mobile" or "iPhone") to get a pop-up list of labels you can choose from. The label defines the kind of number you're using, such as "work" for work numbers and "home" for home numbers. In addition to the standard labels (mobile, home, work, main, home fax, work fax, and page), you can also add custom labels to your heart's content. See the upcoming section on managing custom labels to learn more about adding and editing labels.

Tap Done to save your new phone number for the contact, or tap Cancel to go back to the New Contact screen without adding that number.

Adding E-mail Addresses and URLs

The E-mail and URL fields allow you to add Internet addresses for your contacts. Tap either option, enter the e-mail or web address desired, and tap Done. As with phone numbers, you can set standard labels for these items or enter custom ones as needed.

Adding Addresses

The address fields refer to a contact's physical location, including street address and city. As with all the other contact information, you can add more than one address to a contact and label these items as home or work or with a custom label.

The Contacts application is smart enough to adjust the address fields based on the country you pick. So for Australian addresses, you're prompted for suburb, state, and postal code. Japanese addresses include postal code, prefecture, and county/city.

Adding Other Fields

In addition to the standard name, phone, and address fields, you can add a number of other predefined fields to a contact's information. Tap Add Field, and choose from Prefix, Middle, Suffix, Phonetic First Name, Phonetic Last Name, Nickname, Job Title, Department, Birthday, Date, and Note. The Note field allows you to enter a free-form note and can prove very handy.

Adding Outside Data to an Existing Contact

If someone who is already in your contacts list sends you an e-mail with their address or phone number or if you find contact information on the Web for someone you already have in your address book, tap and hold that information, be it a phone number or address, and wait for the Add to Existing Contact menu pops up. Tap Add to Existing Contact, and then choose your contact from your address book. When their address card opens, the new phone number or address populates the respective field. Add more information if you like, and then press the Done button.

Managing Custom Labels

There's a big world out there that goes beyond "home fax" and "work address." The Contacts application allows you to add custom labels to your phone numbers, e-mail addresses, URLs, and physical addresses. Manage these labels using any of the label-selection screens, each of which contains an Edit button. Tap this Edit button—it is at the top-right corner of the screen—to switch to edit mode, as shown in Figure 12–6.

In edit mode, you can perform the following actions to add and remove custom fields to and from your iPod:

Add a field: Tap the green + button at the bottom of the edit list to add a new custom field. A Custom Label screen opens. Here, you can type in the name for the new label. Tap Save to add the label.

Remove a field: Tap the red button next to any custom field you want to remove. A Delete button appears at the field's right. Tap Delete to confirm deletion, or tap anywhere else on the screen to cancel. Once removed, all phone numbers, e-mail addresses, and other items that have been labeled with that custom field are renamed to the generic "label." You will not lose phone numbers and other data items you've entered.

To finish making your edits, tap Done.

Figure 12–6. *Contacts allows you to interactively manage your custom fields.*

Editing and Removing Contacts

To edit a contact, first select it in the contacts list, and tap it to open its Info tab. There, tap the Edit button in the top-right corner. This sends you to an edit screen that is functionally nearly identical to the New Contact screen (Figure 12–5). Make your changes, and then tap Done to finish and save them.

A Delete Contact button appears at the bottom of the edit screen. To remove a contact from your address book, scroll down to the red button, and tap it. A confirmation dialog box appears. Tap Delete Contact again, and Contacts removes the item from your address book. Tap Cancel to retain the contact.

As you can see, Contacts are a big part of the iPhone experience. Not only does the app help you manage all your contacts, it's fully integrated into iOS itself. You contacts appear in other Apple and third-party iOS apps such as Maps, Messages, Calendars, Facebook, and more. Get used to adding and organizing your contacts because the payoff in user experience is huge! Now, let's move on to some other desk set apps, which will help you in your everyday tasks.

Using the Calculator

iPod touch's Calculator app provides a thorough interactive calculator with a simple memory. The icon on your home screen looks like four calculator buttons. By default it appears on the second row of the home screen, the second icon in. You can see this icon in Figure 12–7.

Figure 12–7. *The Calculator icon*

When you launch the Calculator app, you'll see a simple calculator that allows you to add, subtract, multiply, and divide (Figure 12–8). When you tap an operation button, a white circle appears around the button to let you know which operation will be carried out. But remember, many apps have multiple views depending on which way you are holding your iPod. Rotate the iPod into landscape mode to reveal the built-in scientific calculator!

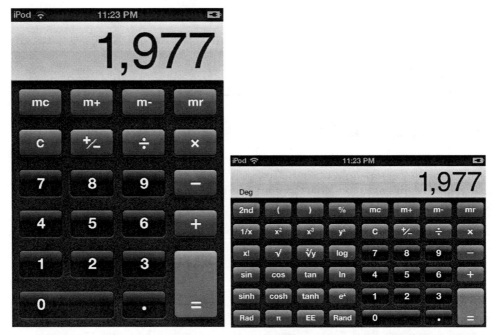

Figure 12–8. *The iPod touch Calculator application allows you to use your iPod as a calculator (left) when you're on the go. Rotate the iPod vertically to reveal the scientific calculator (right).*

The Calculator application allows you to add, subtract, multiply, and divide (and much more if you're in scientific mode). When you tap an operation button, a white circle appears around the button to let you know which operation will be carried out.

Use the memory buttons to add to the stored number (m+) or subtract (m–). Once a number is stored in memory, the button highlights with a white circle. Tap mr to recall the stored number. Tap mc to clear the number from memory.

TIP: If you're more interested in splitting a restaurant bill with friends than doing advanced math, you may want to use one of the many free online tip and bill-splitter calculators instead when visiting restaurants. Search the App Store for *tip calculator*.

Taking Notes

The iPod Notes application allows you to jot down quick notes on the go. This application isn't meant to be a full-powered word processor. It just provides a simple way to create notes and bring them with you.

To launch Notes, tap the yellow notepad-styled icon on your home screen (Figure 12–9).

Figure 12–9. *The Notes icon*

Figure 12–10 shows the Notes screen. From this screen, you can add and manage notes as follows.

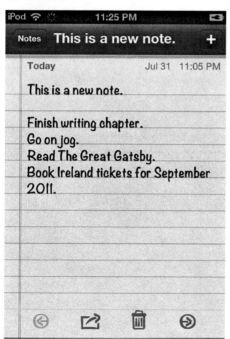

Figure 12–10. *Use the Notes screen to write quick notes. You can e-mail your notes to others.*

Create new notes: Tap the + button to add a new note.

Enter and edit text: Tapping in the text area summons the keyboard. Type your note, make any changes, and then tap Done to dismiss the keyboard.

Delete a note: Tap the garbage can icon, and then tap Delete Note.

Navigate between notes: Use the left and right arrows to move between notes, or tap Notes in the upper-left corner and select the note you want to view from the list.

E-mail notes: Tap the envelope, enter an address, and tap Send. The text from the note is pasted into the body of an e-mail.

In Chapter 2, I talk about setting up a Bluetooth keyboard. If you are using Notes a lot, you might want to think about investing in one.

Syncing Notes

If you like, you can sync notes between your iPod and your computer. To sync notes, you'll need to be using Mail.app, Entourage 2008, or Outlook 2011 on a Mac or Microsoft Outlook 2003 or newer on a Windows computer. Again, if you are using iCloud, your Notes will sync over the air automatically. You can also sync notes with various e-mail providers such as Gmail, Yahoo!, and AOL. To sync notes with those e-mail accounts, navigate to **Settings ➤ Mail, Contacts, Calendars,** and choose your e-mail account. Where you see the Notes icon, tap the switch to ON. Syncing notes allows your notes to be viewed and edited in Mac OS X's Mail app or Windows Outlook.

If you are using multiple note accounts, you'll see the option of viewing all notes together or just notes from a certain account on the Accounts screen (Figure 12–11).

Here are some tips on using the Notes application:

■ Although your Notes files are backed up, you cannot sync your notes to text files on your personal computer. Use e-mail to send yourself your notes if you want to sync them to your computer.

■ To search through your notes, navigate to a notes list screen (the second image in Figure 12–11), and swipe down to reveal the search field at the top. The results screen populates with any notes that match your search criteria.

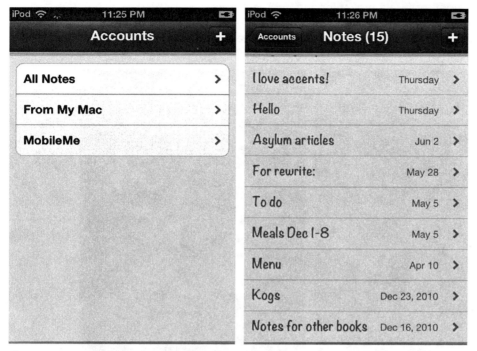

Figure 12–11. *Use the Accounts screen (left) to view all your notes together (right) or on a per-account basis.*

Checking the Weather

The iPod Weather application allows you to view the current temperature and six-day forecast for each of your favorite cities. Weather uses forecast data from Yahoo! and the Weather Channel to provide up-to-the-minute data on your iPod. To launch Weather, tap the blue icon with the sun on your home screen (Figure 12–12).

Figure 12–12. *The Weather icon*

Viewing Weather Info

Figure 12–13 shows a typical Weather screen. From here, you can flick left and right to scroll between your cities. The bright dot at the bottom of the screen shows which item you're viewing. The dim dots show the other cities you've added to the Weather app. The arrowhead in front of the line of dots is the current location weather. This screen displays the weather for whatever location you are currently located in. Cities that are experiencing daylight have a blue background, and cities where it is already dark have a purple background. Tap any weather screen to see an hourly forecast for the selected city.

Figure 12–13. *The iPod Weather application provides six-day forecasts for your favorite cities and your current location. Tap the weather screen to see an hourly forecast.*

When you're ready to specify your cities, tap the small *i* at the bottom right of any Weather screen. This flips from the forecast to the city-management screen. From this screen, you can customize your cities:

Local Weather: Toggle this ON or OFF to show the current location weather screen.

Add a city: Tap the + button, enter the city name, tap Search, and then tap the city you want to add. You cannot find every city. Only those supported by Yahoo! and the Weather Channel are available.

Remove a city: Tap the red – button next to any city name, and then tap Delete.

Reorder cities: Use the grab controls to the right of each name to drag your cities into a new order.

Switch between Fahrenheit and Celsius: Tap °F or °C.

Tap Done to return to the forecast screen.

Weather Tips

Here are some tips for using the Weather application:

- As Figure 12–13 shows, the dots at the bottom represent how many cities you've added. The first "dot" is an arrowhead, which denotes the weather for your current location..

- Tap the Y! icon to visit Yahoo Weather in Safari.

- You don't need to keep the Cupertino forecast. Although the iPod offers Cupertino as its default forecast, feel free to add your own city and remove Cupertino from the list. Apple will never know.

Monitoring Stocks

You can use your iPod to keep track of the stock market so you could see how much you've made (or lost!) that day. The Stocks icon looks like a blue-and-gray stock ticker (Figure 12–14). Tap it to go to the application that monitors your favorite stocks using 20-minute delayed data from Yahoo!

Figure 12–14. *The Stocks icon*

The Stocks screen, shown in Figure 12–15, consists of a list of stocks above a historic graph. Current prices appear to the right of each name, with the changes listed in green (positive) or red (negative). From this screen, you can view and customize stock information as follows.

Figure 12–15. *Yahoo! Finance powers the iPod Stocks application using 20-minute-delayed data.*

View a stock: Tap any stock to load its associated graph.

Choose the history length: Choose the length of time over which you want to view a stock's history. Pick from one day (1d), one week (1w), one month (1m), three months (3m), six months (6m), one year (1y), and two years (2y).

Customize: You can add or remove stocks from your list by tapping the *i* icon at the bottom right of your screen. This opens the customization screen (Figure 12–16).

Figure 12–16. *Customizing the stocks app*

- To add a stock, tap the + button and either search for a company name or enter the stock symbol directly.

- To remove a stock, tap the red – button, and then tap Delete.

- Reorder stocks by using the drag controls to the right of each stock name.

- The %, Price, and Mkt Cap buttons switch between the percentage gained or lost, the current price, and the market cap of the stocks.

- Tap Done to return to the main Stocks screen.

Notice the three dots below the chart in the stocks app (see Figure 12–15)? If you swipe left or right, you can also view the summary and news headlines for a specific stock (Figure 12–17). When viewing the news headlines, scroll up or down to see more. Tapping a headline displays the news article in the Safari browser.

Figure 12–17. *You can view the summary (left), chart, or news (right) for a particular stock by swiping left or right.*

The Stocks app also support landscape mode. Turn your iPod on its side to be presented with an interactive chart of a particular stock (Figure 12–18).

Figure 12–18. *Rotate the iPod to landscape mode to see the interactive chart.*

Use the time buttons (1 day, 3 months, and so on) to show a specific time frame. Drag your finger across the chart to see the precise stock price for any given time. Drag two fingers along the chart (Figure 12–19) to show the price difference between any two different points in time. Finally, swipe left or right to switch to another stock's chart.

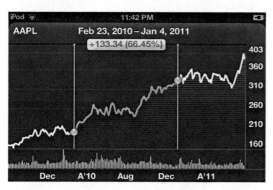

Figure 12–19. *Place and drag two fingers on the chart to see the price difference between any two points.*

Here are some tips for using the Stocks application:

- Tap Yahoo! Finance at the bottom of the customization screen to jump directly to the Yahoo! Finance web site. You can also tap Y! at the bottom left of the main Stocks screen to get to this web site.

- Stock quotes are delayed according to the rules of the stock exchange. This provides an advantage to on-floor traders and allows vendors to charge for premium real-time quotes.

- You don't need to press the customization button to switch between percentage, price, and market cap views; you can just tap the value column (red and green squares) to switch between views.

I am sure there's a limit to how many stocks you can add to your list, but I have yet to personally encounter that limit.

Dictating Voice Memos

When Apple decided to include the Voice Memos app (Figure 12–20) on the iPod touch, I thought I would never use it. Now, however, it's one of the apps I turn to most. With voice memos, you can quickly record ideas or entire classes or meetings with the tap of a button.

To use the Voice Memo app, your iPod touch will need a microphone. If you have the fourth-generation iPod touch or later, it has a mic built-in. The second- and third-generation iPod touches didn't have built-in mics, but they did ship with earbuds with a built-in mic. If you don't have those original earbuds, you'll need to grab them or something similar. iPod-compatible mics can be purchased at http://store.apple.com.

Figure 12–20. *The Voice Memos icon*

Tap the Voice Memos icon to launch that app. You'll be presented with a screen that shows a large, old-fashioned radio mic from the 1930s. The radio mic is just for show. You interact with the Voice Memos app using the two buttons, situated on either side of the audio level meter (Figure 12–21).

Figure 12–21. *The Voice Memos app*

To record a memo, tap the red-and-silver record button on the left of the screen. A red bar will appear at the top of the screen with the word *Recording* in it followed by the recording time that has elapsed (Figure 12–22). You'll also notice that the record button has changed to a pause button. Tap it to pause the current recording. Tap it again to resume recording. To stop a recording, tap the silver-and-black stop button on the right side of the screen.

Figure 12–22. *Recording a memo*

To view and listen to all your recordings, tap the Memos button. The Memos button has three horizontal lines and rests in the lower-right corner in Figure 12–21. The Voice Memos screen will appear (Figure 12–23).

From the Voice Memos screen, you can play back any memo you've recorded.

Play a Memo: Tap the memo you want to play so it is highlighted in blue. Then tap the memo again to play it.

Scrub through a memo: Use the slider at the bottom of the screen to scrub through your memos. This is particularly helpful for long recordings.

Share a memo: Select a memo, and then tap the Share button. A pop-up menu will appear asking you whether you want to share your memo using e-mail or in a message. Tap E-mail, and a new e-mail compose screen will appear with the recording attached to the body of the e-mail. Tap Message, and a new message compose screen will appear with the recording attached to the body of the message. I discuss the Messages app in Chapter 14.

Deleting a memo: Select a memo, and then tap the Delete button. Tap the Delete Voice Memo pop-up that appears to confirm your deletion.

Figure 12–23. *The Voice Memos screen lists all your memos.*

You can also label and edit voice memos by navigating to their information screen. To do this, tap the blue-and-white > button next to a voice memo. You'll be taken to that voice memo's information page (Figure 12–24).

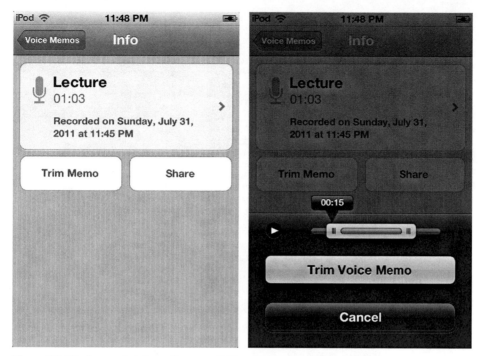

Figure 12–24. *A memo's information page (left) and trimming options (right)*

From this page you can do the following:

Label the voice memo: Tap the field with the microphone icon in it (next to the time stamps) to be taken to the labels screen. From this screen you can select from the following labels: Podcast, Interview, Lecture, Idea, Meeting, or Memo. You can also name your memo anything you want by tapping the Custom button and entering a name. To keep length of time of the memo as its name, select None as the label.

Trim the voice memo: You can actually edit your voice memos right on the iPod. Tap Trim Memo, and a black-and-yellow trim menu appears (Figure 12–25). Adjust the beginning and end times by using the yellow and blue slider, and tap Trim Voice Memo to trim the selection. The trim feature is a great way to cut out the usual dead air times at the beginning or ending of a recording. However, you cannot edit out snippets of the recording piecemeal. You can only trim its edges. Also, note that edits you make *cannot* be undone.

Share: This button functions the same as the Share button on the main information page. Tap Share, and then tap E-mail, and a new message compose screen appears with the recording attached to the body of the e-mail.

iTunes automatically syncs any voice memos you have created the next time you connect your iPod touch to your computer. The memos are stored under a playlist that is created called Voice Memos (see Figure 12–25).

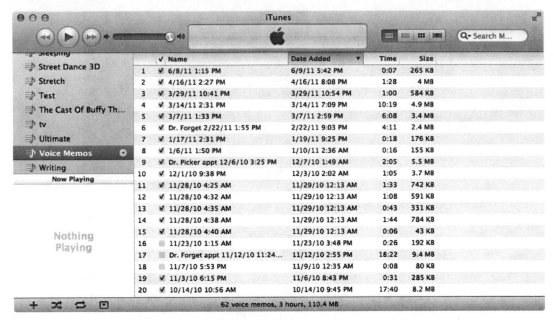

Figure 12–25. *iTunes automatically creates a playlist called Voice Memos when it detects a voice memo on your iPod touch.*

When you sync voice memos to iTunes, they still remain on the iPod touch until you delete them. Deleting them on the IPod touch does not delete them from iTunes; however, deleting a voice memo from iTunes also deletes it from the iPod touch on the next sync.

Setting Reminders

Reminder is a new app included on every iPod touch. It's a to-do app that lets you create lists and set reminders so you never forget anything again. To launch Reminders, tap its icon on your home screen (Figure 12–26).

Figure 12–26. *The Reminders icon*

When you launch the app, you'll first see a loose-leaf piece of paper with the title "Reminders" at the top. This is your main reminders list (Figure 12–27). To create a reminder, tap the + button and enter a name or description for the reminder. Tap Done when you have finished naming the reminder. In Figure 12–27, one of our reminders is to "Buy flowers."

Figure 12–27. *The Reminders app*

But Reminder isn't just an app that helps you create lists. It's called "Reminders" for a reason. You can set a number of ways to be reminded to do something on your list. Reminder reminds you of your to-do list items via the Notification Center, and you can set reminders to notify you based on date and time.

To set details and notifications for your reminders, tap an item from your reminders list. On the details screen that appears (Figure 12–28), you can set the time and date for your reminder, the time and date the item is due, whether the item on your list is a one-time or repeating event (such as weekly), when to end the repeating reminders, the priority of the to-do item (None, Low, Medium, High), and even add notes to the reminder to give it more details.

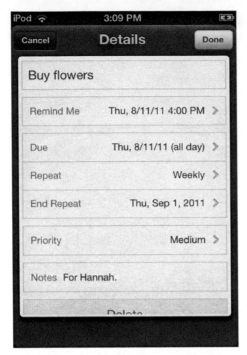

Figure 12–28. *Setting the details of a Reminder event*

When you are done entering details about a reminder event, tap the Done button. To delete a reminder, tap the red delete button that appears at the bottom of the Details screen.

Besides viewing your reminders as a list, you can also view them by date. Tap the Date button at the top of the screen (Figure 12–27), and you'll be taken to the date view (Figure 12–29). In date view you can swipe left and right between days, or tap the calendar button in the top-left corner to view monthly calendars. Tap any date on the calendar to be taken to its date page.

Figure 12–29. *Browsing Reminders by date. Day view, left; calendar view, right.*

When you complete an event in your reminders list, tap the box to mark it off (Figure 12–27). The event is removed from your Reminders list and added to your Completed list (Figure 12–30). To view your Completed list, swipe right on the reminders screen or tap the lists button.

Figure 12–30. *The Completed list*

The lists button appears at the top-left corner of the screen and has three lines on it. Tap it to reveal all your lists (Figure 12–31). Tap a list to jump right to that list. To create a new list, tap the edit button on the list screen and then tap Create New List. Multiple lists can be very handy. You can create one for work, one for groceries, one for your personal life, and so on.

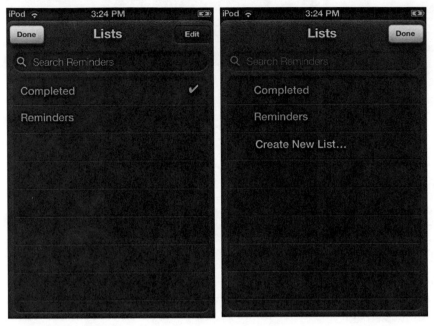

Figure 12–31. *The lists screen shows you all your lists (left). Add new lists by tapping the Create New List button, right.*

Summary

As you can now see, the iPod touch includes several useful tools for the user, whether they are a business professional or a student. The Notes, Voice Memos, and Reminders applications provide helpful on-hand references for when you need a quick jog to your memory in written or audio form. The Contacts app also lets you expand your address book while on the go and synchronize it to your home computer. The Calculator is always there to get you out of a jam when you realize you didn't pay attention in Algebra 101 and Stocks and Weather lets you check both your current and future financial and climate forecasts.

Here are a few last thoughts:

- Although the iPod touch does not have an onboard phone, it's easy enough to look up numbers on the iPod and type them into your cell phone.

■   It's *really* nice to have all your numbers and addresses in one place. Because our iPods sync to our computers, you don't have to keep a half dozen separate address books, each on a separate device. You can rely on the iPod's version instead.

■   The iPod's calculator is a lifesaver when you realize math isn't your strong suit.

■   The Stocks and Weather applications provide great ways to keep up with real-time information using classic Apple design.

■   Although the Notes application is limited, it offers a convenient way to jot down notes in a central and easy-to-remember location.

■   How many times have you been in a class or meeting and wish you had a voice recorder with you? With your iPod touch, now you do.

■   Reminders is a wonderful app that can help those of us with poor memories remember when things need to get done.

Chapter 13

Photographing and Recording the World Around You

The iPod touch features two cameras—one in the front and one in the rear. These cameras allow for the most significant features of the iPod touch: the ability to capture photos and high-definition video, as well as make FaceTime video calls.

Are you lucky enough to have one of the latest iPods? If not, this chapter is really not for you, at least until you're ready to upgrade. But if you've been able to purchase one of the newest-generation iPods, then here are some great ways to take photos and record video.

The Camera Hardware

As mentioned, the newest iPod touch's features two cameras—one front and one rear—with which to take photos and record video. The cameras aren't created equal, however. As you'll see, each one has been designed for different uses.

Front Camera

The front iPod touch camera is located at the top of the iPod, directly in the center of the iPod's upper bezel. If you shine a light directly on your iPod, you can make out a tiny opaque dot about the size of a pencil tip. Behind this dot lies the front-facing camera.

You'll be using this front-facing camera primarily for FaceTime video calls (see Chapter 14), but you can also take photos and record video with it. The front-facing camera particularly makes a great tool for taking self-snapshots for profile pictures for your Facebook account. No more shooting your picture in a bathroom mirror or turning the camera around and hoping you get yourself in the shot! With the front camera, you can see and compose the shot as you take it.

It's important to note that the front-facing camera isn't as powerful as the rear camera. The front-facing camera does not record high-definition (HD) video. High-definition video is defined as video that has at least 720 lines of resolution. The more lines of resolution, the sharper the picture. Although the front camera can record video, its resolution is limited to standard-definition (SD) video. SD video has a resolution of 640x480.

Why didn't Apple use an HD camera in the front? Well, it would be unnecessary. The front camera was designed for FaceTime video calling, not recording video. The image quality while video calling on a small device like the iPod touch is more than good enough using an SD camera and requires less bandwidth for transmission.

Rear Camera

The rear camera is the primary one used to take photos and record video. If you flip your iPod touch over, you'll see the rear camera in the top-left corner of the device.

The rear camera records video in 720p HD resolution at 30 frames a second; that's 1280 horizontal pixels x 720 vertical pixels. Although its still-camera capabilities are better than the front-facing camera, the rear-facing camera is still limited to taking still pictures in 960x720 resolution. If that doesn't sound like a lot, it's because it isn't. 960x720 resolution isn't even equivalent to a 1-megapixel camera; or, if you want to get specific, the iPod touch's still capabilities record photos in 0.69 megapixels.

The less than 1-megapixel resolution is fine for simple snapshots for e-mailing or posting to Facebook, but if you are at an important event like a wedding or a child's birthday and want to take some good-quality pictures suitable for framing, leave the iPod touch at home and bring your digital camera.

> **NOTE:** What's the "p" stand for in 720p, you ask? P means progressive. When HD video is displayed on a screen, it shows either all 720 lines of resolution at a time or just half of them. If it only shows half of them, this is known as *interlaced video* and is denoted with an *i*. Simply put, progressive video generally looks sharper because it shows you all the data (or lines of resolution) in a single frame at a time, and interlaced shows you only half the data at a time (followed quickly by the other half). Interlaced video used to be the norm when bandwidth issues were more of a factor, but as bandwidth increased, progressive video slowly took over.

Real-World Use

In real-world use, the iPod touch does a great job at recording HD video in good lighting conditions. While developing this chapter for the book, all the video I shot outdoors in the daytime or inside with good lighting looked gorgeous when I played it back on my HDTV. The iPod touch uses a light-sensitive sensor, which can be used in a wide range of lighting situations. This sensor allows for the best video quality the hardware can record. Because of this sensor, the video quality was still very good even in low-light conditions.

As for taking still images, the iPod touch is great to have when you're out and about and might not necessarily have your digital camera on you. However, because of its 0.69-megapixel images and lack of a camera flash, the iPod touch is in no way a replacement for your standard digital point-and-shoot camera. That being said, Apple didn't set out to design the best camera possible; Apple set out to design the best iPod possible at the best possible price—and at that, Apple excelled. The iPod isn't about taking great art; it's about social use. So, it's a trade-off. If you want a really good camera, then buy a camera or an iPhone or wait for a newer-generation iPod touch with a better camera when these components prices go down.

Navigating the Camera App

To launch the Camera application, tap the Camera icon. It looks like a gray button with a camera lens on it (see Figure 13–1). The camera can be used in either portrait or landscape mode. Simply rotate your iPod to switch between the two orientations.

Figure 13–1. *The Camera app*

Figure 13–2 shows the standard layout of the Camera app. With the exception of the Switch Camera and Options button at the top of the screen, all the camera controls reside in the gray bar at the bottom of the screen in portrait orientation. When you rotate into landscape orientation, the Switch Camera and Options buttons remain at the top of the screen, but the camera control bar shifts to the left (or right) of the screen. The icons on the control bar rotate to match your iPod's orientation.

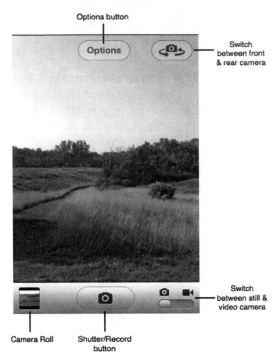

Figure 13–2. *The camera controls*

The camera controls are as follows:

Switch between still and video camera mode: Tap the slider that lies below icons of a still and video camera in the right of the control bar. The slider button is beneath either the still or the video camera, and the position of the slider indicates the camera that it currently in use (in Figure 13–2, the slider is below the still camera, so you know that you are in still-camera mode).

Switch between cameras: Tap the Switch Camera icon in the top right of the screen to switch between the front and rear cameras. The icon looks like a traditional still camera with swirling arrows on either side. You'll see a 2D animation of the screen flipping between cameras.

Options: This button allows you to access the camera gridline overlay (discussed later).

Shutter button: Tap the oval button with the icon of a traditional still camera in the center of the control bar to take a still photograph. This button changes to show a red dot in the center when you are in video camera mode. Tap the button to record video, and then tap again to stop recording. If you have your finger on the Shutter/Record button but then change your mind about photographing or recording your subject, you can slide your finger off the button and no image or video is captured.

Access the Camera Roll: Tap the square button on the left of the control bar. The square is filled with an icon of the last image or video recorded. Once tapped, your Camera Roll slides up on the screen. This is a great feature for reviewing your last photo or video. It saves you a lot of time since you don't have to leave the Camera app to check out your Camera Roll in the Photos app.

Taking Still Pictures

Taking a still photograph couldn't be easier. Point your camera at what you want to take a picture of, and tap the shutter button. You can also press the topmost volume button on the side of your iPod. While in camera mode, the topmost volume button acts as a shutter button. You'll hear a shutter click sound effect and see a cool animation of a lens's iris quickly closing and then opening. After that, the still image you just took jumps down into the Camera Roll icon.

> **NOTE:** Some people find that tapping the on-screen shutter button to take a still photo causes their composition to get messed up. A neat trick Apple included to counteract any accidental nudging when you tap the shutter button is this: tap and hold the shutter button and *then* compose your shot. When you are ready to take the photo, simply remove your finger from the shutter button, and the shot is recorded.

Autofocus and Exposure

You can set the exposure of the camera by tapping anywhere on the screen. You'll see a white box with crosshairs quickly appear. The iPod's camera reads the exposure setting of the part of the image inside the box and adjusts the image accordingly.

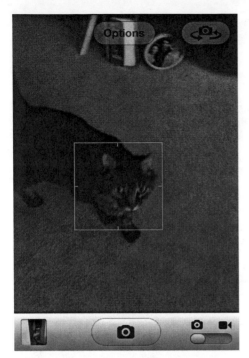

Figure 13–3. *Tap the screen to autofocus and set the exposure.*

Setting the exposure helps when you are shooting an image of a cloudy sky, for example. If you want the sky to appear other than blinding white, tap the area of the image on your iPods screen, and the exposure adjusts accordingly. When you tap any portion of the image, the camera also autofocuses on that part of the image.

Composing Shots with Gridlines

There's a tenet in photography called the "rule of thirds." Basically it states that if you divide your shot into nine imaginary grids by placing three horizontal and three vertical lines "over" the image and keep the subjects of your shots sequestered to one of those lines, preferably the outer ones, it makes for a much more interesting shot. This sequestering, or composition, can be helped when you can see a grid on your screen.

With this in mind, Apple built gridlines into the Camera app. To turn on gridlines, tap the Options button (Figure 13–2), and set Grid to ON (Figure 13–4). Gridlines appear on your screen, dividing it into nine squares. Tap Done to exit the options menu. To turn off gridlines, go back into options and set Grid to OFF. While gridlines appear on your iPod touchscreen, they do not appear in your photographs.

Figure 13–4. *Turning on gridlines can help you compose your shots.*

Pinch to Zoom In and Out

To zoom in or out, simply pinch the screen with two fingers. The zoom slider appears. (Figure 13–5). This zoom bar allows you to adjust the digital zoom settings of the photograph; it lets you zoom in and out on your subject. Slide your finger along the bar to zoom in or out. You can also tap the + or – button to zoom in or out in increments or simply continue pinching in or out.

Figure 13–5. *The zoom controls appear above the control bar while tapping the screen in still-camera mode.*

NOTE: You can only zoom on while in still camera mode using the rear camera. You cannot zoom using the front-facing camera or while in video camera mode.

Recording Video

To record video, set the slider in the control bar to video camera mode. The camera's shutter button is replaced with a recording button (see Figure 13–6). Tap the record button to begin recording your video. The red dot on the record button begins to pulse, and a time code stamp appears in the upper right of the screen showing the hours, minutes, and seconds that have elapsed since recording began. To stop recording, tap the record button again. Before or during recording, double-tap the screen to enter a 16:9 wide-screen aspect ratio.

Just how much video can you record on your iPod touch? That depends on the size of your iPod touch and how much space you have available. If you have a 32GB iPod touch but only have 10GB of free space on it, you'll be able to record only 10GB of video.

720p/30fps video takes up about 120MB per minute. If you think in terms of gigabytes, one hour of 720p/30fps video will take about 7GB of space on your iPod. One hour of video is a lot, but so is 7GB of storage space. If you are going to be recording a lot of video, it's helpful to be close to your computer or have your laptop with you so you can easily dump your video onto your computer's hard drive and then wipe it from your iPod touch, freeing up space for more video.

Figure 13–6. *The video-recording screen shows the time elapsed while recording. Double-tap the screen to enter a 16:9 aspect ratio.*

> **TIP:** If you are going to be using the recorded video in a movie or be viewing it on your TV, you might want to make sure you are recording in landscape mode. You can record in portrait mode, but portrait mode is a weird aspect ratio to view videos in.

Changing the Autofocus and Exposure

As with still images, you can set the autofocus and exposure of recorded video. You'll see a white box with crosshairs quickly appear. The iPod's camera reads the exposure setting of the part of the image inside the box and adjusts the video's exposure settings accordingly. When you tap any portion of the image, the camera autofocuses on that part of the image.

Accessing Your Camera from the Lock Screen

An amazing new feature of iOS 5 is the ability to quickly access your camera from your iPod touch's lock screen. This feature eliminates precious time wasted from having to unlock your iPod, swipe to the camera app, and then tap its icon to open it. Now you can access the camera from the lock screen and get that spontaneous shot.

To access your camera from the lock screen, double-press the home button on your iPod touch. Doing so brings up audio playback controls on the lock screen and a shortened slider bar. As you can see in Figure 13–7, there's also a camera icon next to the slider bar. Tap it to be immediately taken to your camera.

Figure 13–7. *Accessing the camera from your iPod touch's lock screen*

Viewing Your Camera Roll

To view all the photos and videos you have captured, tap the Camera Roll icon in the left of the control bar. The last image or video you recorded appears on the screen. Tap the Camera Roll arrow to be taken to the Camera Roll (Figure 13–8).

18 Photos, 4 Videos

Figure 13–8. *The Camera Roll contains all the photos and videos you have taken with the iPod's camera.*

As you can see in Figure 13–8, the Camera Roll allows you to sort through your recordings in three ways:

All: Displays all of your photographs and videos

Photos: Shows just the photos you have taken

Videos: Exhibits just the videos you have recorded

To view any individual photo or video, tap its thumbnail. Photo thumbnails appear as a picture square, while video thumbnails appear as squares with a single frame of the recording representing the video. A small camera icon with the length of the video in minutes and seconds overlays a video thumbnail's image.

Tap the blue camera button at the bottom of the screen to return to your camera.

> **NOTE:** When accessing the Camera from the lock screen, you'll only be able to view Camera Roll items taken from the lock screen. Other items in your Camera Roll remain hidden for privacy purposes when you access your camera from the lock screen.

Viewing Individual Photos

When in your Camera Roll, you will see thumbnails of the photos it contains (see Figure 13–8). To view a photo full-screen, tap the photo once. As you can see from Figure 13–9, you can view the photo in portrait or landscape mode.

Figure 13–9. *Viewing a photo in landscape and portrait modes*

Once you display a photo full-screen, you have several ways to interact with it:

- Pinch to zoom into and out of the photo.

- Double-tap to zoom into the photo. Double-tap again to zoom out.

- When your image is displayed at the normal zoomed-out size, drag to the left or right to move to the previous or next image in the album. When zoomed into an image, dragging the photo pans across it.

While viewing individual photos, flip your iPod touch onto its side to have your photo reorient itself. If the photo was taken in landscape orientation, it fits itself to the wider view. Tap any image once to bring up the image overlay, as shown in Figure 13–9. The image overlay features a menu bar at the top and bottom of the screen.

The image overlay menu bar at the top of the screen displays the number of the selected image out of the total number of items in the Camera Roll and the back button, labeled Camera Roll, to return to the album. Tap the Edit button to access your photo editing tools (see Chapter 5).

At the bottom of the screen you'll see the Camera button that returns you to your camera, the Share button (it looks like an arrow breaking free from a small box) and also a play button. The play button allows you to start a slide show, and tapping the trashcan icon displays a deletion confirmation menu. Tap the red Delete Photo button to delete the selected photo.

Playing a Slide Show

Playing slide shows on your iPod touch is as easy as tapping a single button, namely, the play button that resides at the bottom center of the screen. When you tap it, the Slideshow Options screen appears (Figure 13–10).

Figure 13–10. *The Camera Roll slide show settings*

Transition: By default, the slide show transition is Dissolve, but here you can also choose from Cube, Ripple, Wipe Across, or Wipe Down. The advantage of transitions is that they keep things lively. The disadvantage is that they get old really, really fast. For this reason, you probably want to skip nondissolve transitions in long slide shows.

Play Music: When set to ON, you can select music from the music library on your iPod that plays in the background of the slide show.

Music: Tap to select the song you'd like to play during your slide show.

Start Slideshow: Tap this button to begin your slide show. To stop a slide show, tap the screen.

Sharing Your Photos

You have a number of ways to share the photos you have in your Camera Roll. If these options seem familiar to you, it's because they're identical to the photo-sharing options I went over in my description of the Photos app in Chapter 5.

To access all the ways you can share your photos, bring up a photo full-screen, and tap the Share button, which looks like an arrow breaking free from a small box (see Figure 13–9). You are presented with a pop-up menu of sharing options (see Figure 13–11).

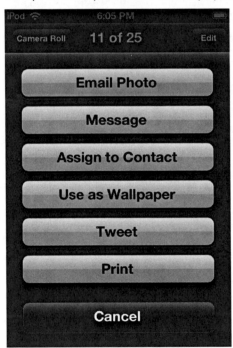

Figure 13–11. *The sharing photos menu*

Email Photo: Tap this to see an e-mail compose window appear on the screen. You'll notice that the photo has been copied into the body of the e-mail already. Enter the recipient's e-mail, a subject, and some body text, and then tap Send—your photo is on its way!

Alternatively, you can e-mail up to five photos at a time from within the Camera Roll. I discuss this option later in the chapter.

Message: This allows you to attach your photo to an iMessage (see Chapter 14). A new iMessage compose window will appear where you can write a message along with the atached photo.

Assign to Contact: This option allows you to assign a photo to an address book contact. Tap Assign to Contact, and then select the contact's address book entry from the pop-up menu. Move and scale the thumbnail of the photo that appears, and then tap the Set Photo button.

The next time you view the contact in the iPod touch's Contacts app, the image you selected for them will appear next to their name. This image will sync with their contact information in Address Book and Entourage on a Mac and Outlook on a Windows computer.

Use as Wallpaper: Tap this button to use the selected image as wallpaper on your iPod touch. Move and scale the image, and then tap Set. From the pop-up menu, you'll be able to select whether you want to use the image for the iPod touch's lock screen, the home screen, or both. This isn't the only way to set your iPod touch's wallpaper options. I'll talk about the other way in Chapter 15.

Tweet: Tapping Tweet opens a Twitter upload screen. This allows you to Tweet your picture directly to your Twitter account. You can also add a short message to the photo and your current location

Print: Tapping this prints your selected photo to an AirPrint wireless printer.

Viewing Videos

To view any video you have recorded, tap its thumbnail in the Camera Roll. The video will appear with a big play button in the center. Tap any area of the screen once to bring up the on-screen video controls (Figure 13–12).

Figure 13–12. *Displaying video from the Camera Roll. Tap once to bring up the on-screen menus.*

Once you display a video full-screen, you have several ways to interact with it:

▨ Tap the video once to play it. Tap again to pause it.

- Scrub through the video by tapping and holding the silver drag bar in the scrubber bar. The scrub bar shows you segments of the video represented by thumbnails for those segments.

- Hold your finger on the scrub bar for a few seconds, and you'll see the scrub bar stretch out. This gives you finer control over finding a specific spot in the video.

The video overlay menu bar at the top of the screen shows you the number of the selected video out of the total number of items in the Camera Roll and shows you the back button, labeled Camera Roll, to return to the main Camera Roll.

At the bottom of the screen you can tap the blue Camera button to exit the Camera Roll and return to the Camera app. Also you'll find the Share and Play buttons. The Play button enables you to start playing the video. Tapping the trash can icon brings up a deletion confirmation dialog. Tap the red Delete Video button to delete the selected video.

Editing Your Video

Apple has included limited video-editing functionality in the Camera app. Video editing isn't exactly the right word, though. *Trimming* is more accurate because you can shorten, or *trim*, the video at the front and end of the clip.

To trim a video, bring up the video menu overlays (see Figure 13–12). Next, grab the beginning of the scrub bar, and pull it to the right. This activates trim mode (Figure 13–13).

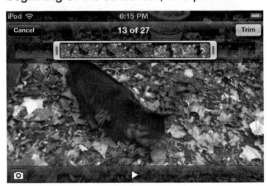

Figure 13–13. *Video trim mode*

In trim mode, you can drag the ends of the scrub bar, now outlined in yellow, toward the center. Dragging the ends shortens the clip at the beginning and the end.

Trimming is a great feature that allows you to highlight just the really good portions of your video clips. When you've adjusted your trim commands, tap the yellow Trim button to bring up a Trim dialog (Figure 13–14).

Figure 13–14. *The Trim pop-up menu lets you trim the original or save the trim as a new clip.*

This dialog provides three options:

Trim Original: This actually changes the original video recording. It permanently deletes the sections of video you have trimmed out.

Save as New Clip: This leaves your original video intact and creates a completely new video file of just the trim you specified.

Cancel: This closes the menu and returns to the clip with your trim points still set.

Remember that if you choose to keep the original clip, storage space on your iPod can quickly fill up. A one-minute clip filled up 120MB of space on my iPod.

Sharing Your Video

While viewing any single video clip, you have several sharing options. To bring up the sharing menu, tap the Share button, which looks like an arrow breaking free from a small box (see Figure 13–12). You are presented with a dialog showing three sharing options (see Figure 13–15).

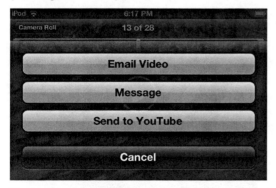

Figure 13–15. *The video sharing options*

Email Video: Selecting this command compresses the video clip as a QuickTime movie file. A new e-mail message window appears with the movie clip attached to the body of the message.

Depending on the length of the video clip, you may see an error message that says "Video is Too Long." If you see this, you are asked if you want to select a smaller clip from the video to e-mail. Tap OK to enter Trim mode and cut down the length of the clip.

What's interesting about trim mode is that the yellow trim selection bar is fixed to 54 seconds. You can shorten it or drag the 54-second trim selection bar around, but you can't increase the video length to more than 54 seconds. As of now, 54 seconds seems to be the longest clip length for e-mailing. Apple might change this with a future software update.

Once you have trimmed your video, tap the yellow Email button above the scrub bar. A blank e-mail with the video in the body of the message should appear.

Message: This allows you to attach your video to an iMessage (see Chapter 14). A new iMessage compose window will appear where you can write a message along with the atached video.

Send to YouTube: Selecting this option will allow you to upload your video to YouTube right from your iPod. On the screen that appears (Figure 13–16), enter a name and description for your video, select to upload it in standard- or high-definition, add tags, and finally select a YouTube category and then tap Publish. You must have a YouTube account to upload videos to YouTube.

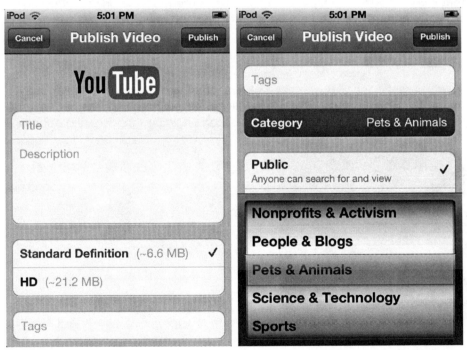

Figure 13–16. *Publishing a video to YouTube*

Sharing Multiple Pictures and Videos from the Camera Roll

As I mentioned earlier, you don't have to share your photos or videos one at a time; you can share multiple photos and videos by using the share and copy options on the Camera Roll screen:

Play a slide show: Press the play arrowhead at the bottom of the screen. Your photos and videos are displayed in a slide show (Figure 13–8).

E-mail, copy, or delete your photos and videos: While in the Camera Roll, tap the Share button in the lower-left corner. You'll see the All/Photos/Video sort menu at the top of the screen renamed to Select Items (Figure 13–17).

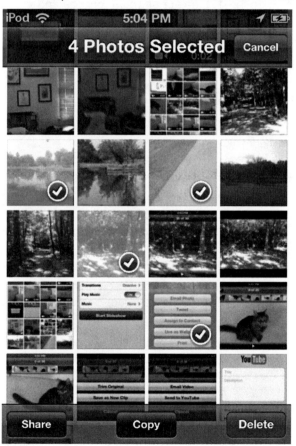

Figure 13–17. *The Select Items screen*

To e-mail: Tap up to five photos. A check mark appear on the photos once you have done so. Next, tap the Share button at the bottom of the screen. A pop-up menu appears with an Email button; tap it, and a new message compose window appears with the images pasted into the body of the e-mail.

You can only e-mail one video at a time, provided it is less than 54 seconds long.

To Print: Tap up to five photos. A check mark appears on the photos once you have done so. Next, tap the Share button at the bottom of the screen. A pop-up menu appears with a Print button; tap it to print the photos to an AirPrint wireless printer.

To copy: Tap up to five items, which can be a combination of photographs and videos. A check mark appears on each selected photo or video (see Figure 13–17). After you have selected all your photos, tap the Copy button in the lower-right corner of the screen. This saves the images and videos to your clipboard to paste into other things (like an e-mail or document) later.

To delete: From the Select Items screen (Figure 13–17), select as many photos and videos as you want, and then press the red delete button in the lower-right corner. A Delete Selected Items pop-up warning appears. Tap it to delete the items, or tap Cancel to cancel the delete.

Uploading Images to Your Computer

Although it's nice to have the options to e-mail and tweet our photos and upload our videos to YouTube, many of you will be primarily viewing your images on your computers. It's easy to get your pictures and videos off your iPod touch and onto your computer. Just plug your iPod into your computer via the USB-to-dock cable.

If you are on a Windows computer, your photo software such as Picasa or Adobe Photoshop Albums should recognize the iPod touch as just another camera and import the photos and videos as the application normally would. If you are on a Mac and iPhoto is open, iPhoto detects that your iPod is connected and asks whether you want to import the videos and photos from the iPod touch's Camera Roll.

Alternately, a feature of Apple's new iCloud service is called Photo Stream. If you have a free iCloud account, the 1,000 most recent photos and videos you take on your iPod touch will automatically be pushed to your other iOS devices and Macs and PCs.

Photo Stream relies on a Wi-Fi connection, but once you have that, the second you take a photo on your iPod touch, it will also appear in your iPhoto library on your Macs, your Pictures libraries on your PCs, and in the Photos app of every iOS device you own. Photo Stream is a pretty cool way to share all your pictures with all your devices simultaneously.

Summary

The front and rear cameras add some nice features to the iPod touch. The HD video-recording capabilities are amazing, but the still photography leaves something to be desired. Here are a few key tips for you to carry away with you:

▓ If you're going on vacation, leave your bulky HD video camera at home. Your iPod touch lets you record great-quality video at 720p. Just be sure to bring a laptop along so you can dump your video off onto its hard drive and make room for more video on your iPod touch.

▓ Do *not* leave your regular digital still camera at home if you are going on vacation. Yes, you can take still photos with the iPod touch, but it's more for social use, such as taking quick snaps of friends or self-portraits. If you want to catch that beautiful sunset over the ocean, do it on a point-and-shoot camera.

▓ Need a new profile picture for Facebook? The front camera on the iPod touch makes it easy to take self-shots.

▓ You can zoom while in still camera mode, but there is no zoom option while recording video.

▓ One minute of 720p video takes up about 120MB. Keep this in mind if you are going to be recording a lot of video because you'll need a lot of free space on your iPod.

▓ Apple has imposed a seemingly arbitrary limit on e-mailing videos. A video clip must be 54 seconds or less in length in order for you to e-mail it. If it's 55 seconds or longer, you'll be asked to trim the clip before you e-mail it.

▓ If you are taking pictures or recording video within range of a Wi-Fi network, the iPod's Camera app tags your photos and videos with geodata. Applications such as Apple's iPhoto can then display your photos on a map.

▓ With iCloud's Photo Stream feature, the photos you take with your iPod touch are automatically pushed to your other Macs, PCs, and iOS devices the moment you take them, provided your iPod touch has a Wi-Fi connection.

Chapter 14

Staying in Touch with FaceTime and iMessage

In the previous chapter, I introduced you to the iPod's front and rear cameras. Although those cameras are for taking pictures and recording video, they have another useful purpose. Perhaps the coolest new feature introduced to the iPod touch is FaceTime. FaceTime is a technology that brings easy and intuitive video calling to the masses. But video chatting isn't the only way you can stay in touch. In iOS 5, Apple introduced iMessage, which allows you to send free text messages to any other person with an iOS device.

In this chapter, you'll learn what the future feels like. I'll show you how to set up a FaceTime account, how to use the front and rear cameras for video calling, and how to explore the settings in the FaceTime app. I'll also show you how to send text messages through the iMessage app. Let's get started.

Getting Started with FaceTime

With the FaceTime app on the iPod touch, you can video call anyone with an iPhone 4 (or newer), an iPad 2 (or newer), a fourth-generation iPod touch (or newer), or a Mac running OS X 10.6 or newer.

Apple wants to make FaceTime the de facto standard for video calling, and in order to do so, the company has made the FaceTime technology an open standard. That means other phone manufacturers can build the technology into their phones, so one day, ideally, you'll be able to make a FaceTime video call on your iPod to someone with an Android phone.

Besides your iPod touch, you'll need to have a Wi-Fi Internet connection and an Apple ID to use FaceTime. The person who you are calling must also have a Wi-Fi connection, even if you are calling them on an iPhone 4. At this time, iPhone 4 owners can only use FaceTime over Wi-Fi, not over their service provider's 3G network. The service providers most likely put this limitation in place, since streaming live video over a 3G network takes a lot of bandwidth—something that is very costly for customers and service providers alike. It's would also be very taxing on the network itself if hundreds or thousands of iPod touch and iPhone users all tried to make FaceTime calls at the same time from the same location.

Signing In

To begin using FaceTime, tap the FaceTime icon on your home screen. The icon has the image of a video camera stamped on a metal background (Figure 14–1). If this is the very first time you've launched the app, you'll be presented with the FaceTime Get Started screen (Figure 14–2).

Figure 14–1. *The FaceTime icon*

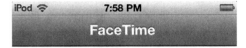

Figure 14–2. *The FaceTime Get Started screen*

I love this screen a lot because Apple practically brags how cool FaceTime is. Apple writes: "People have been dreaming about video calling for decades. Now it's a reality." We get it, Apple. FaceTime is very cool. But as anyone can tell you (or perhaps, tell

Apple), video calling is nothing new. People have been able to video chat via webcams on their computers for more than a decade now. What makes FaceTime so awesome is its mobility and ease of use.

If you click the "Learn more about FaceTime" link, Safari launches, and you are taken to Apple's iPod touch FaceTime web page.

Once you are ready to sign in, tap the Get Started button. The sign-in screen (Figure 14–3) appears; this is where you can sign in with your existing Apple ID or create a new account.

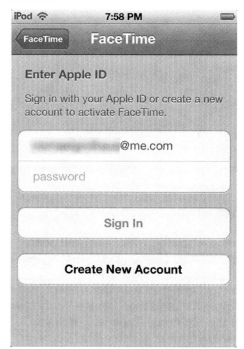

Figure 14–3. *The FaceTime sign-in screen*

Signing In with Your Existing Apple ID

To sign in with your existing Apple ID, fill in the e-mail and password fields, and tap Sign In. You already have an Apple ID if you use the iTunes Store, the App Store, or the iBookstore. You also have an Apple ID if you have a MobileMe or iCloud account.

When you sign in for the first time, Apple notifies you that people will call you on FaceTime using your e-mail address (Figure 14–4). They ask you which e-mail address you would like to use. You can use the same e-mail address that is your Apple ID, or you can enter another e-mail address.

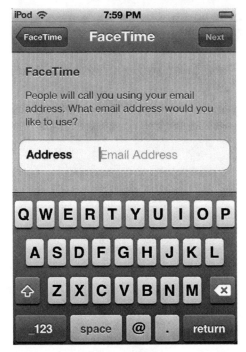

Figure 14–4. *Choosing which e-mail address you want to act as your FaceTime "phone number" (left).*

Once you have selected the e-mail address you want associated with FaceTime calls, tap the Next button. A short verification screen appears so Apple can verify that your e-mail address is authentic. A Check Mail button is displayed; tapping it opens the selected e-mail account in the iPod's mail app. Look for an e-mail with the subject "Please verify the contact e-mail address for your Apple ID," and then tap the Verify Now link in the e-mail. A Safari window opens displaying the My Apple ID page. There you'll be asked to enter your Apple ID and password to verify your FaceTime e-mail address.

Once you are presented with the "Email address verified" web page, return to the FaceTime app. You'll automatically be presented with the standard FaceTime screen (Figure 14–5), which you'll see every time you launch the app from now on. On this screen is a list of your contacts. You'll learn more about the FaceTime home screen in a bit.

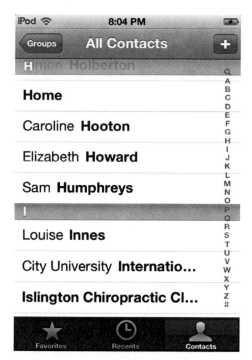

Figure 14–5. *The FaceTime app*

The first time you sign in, the process is arduous and time-consuming, but fear not! Once you have signed in, you won't have to do it again, even if you leave the app or shut down and restart your iPod.

Please be aware that this was the authorization procedure for FaceTime at the time the book was being written. Apple could always change its account creation and authorization process in the future.

Creating an Account

If you don't have some form of Apple ID, you can create one by tapping the Create New Account button (Figure 14–3). The New Account screen slides up (Figure 14–6). On this screen, enter your first and last name, your e-mail address (which becomes your new Apple ID), and a password of at least eight characters. This password does not have to be the same as the password for your e-mail account.

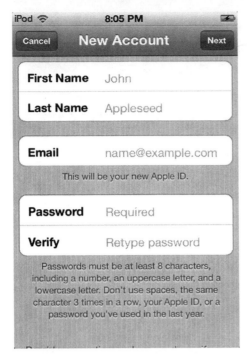

Figure 14–6. *The New Account screen*

On the New Account screen, you also need to choose a question and enter the answer. The question and answer are used in case you forget your Apple ID password. Finally, enter your month and day of birth and the country you reside in, and then decide whether you want to subscribe to the Apple e-mail list.

Once you have entered this information, tap the Next button. You are returned to the Sign In screen with your Apple ID and password already entered, and the sign-in commences. A short verification screen appears as Apple verifies that your e-mail address is authentic. A Check Mail button then appears; tapping it opens the selected e-mail account in the iPod's mail app. Look for an e-mail with the subject "Please verify the contact email address for your Apple ID," and then tap the Verify Now link in the e-mail. A Safari window opens and displays the My Apple ID page. There you need to enter your Apple ID and password to verify your FaceTime e-mail address.

Once you are presented with the "Email address verified" web page, return to the FaceTime app. You'll automatically be presented with the standard FaceTime screen (Figure 14–5), which you'll see every time you launch the app from now on.

Navigating Your FaceTime Contacts

When you launch the FaceTime app, you are presented with your contacts screen (Figure 14–5). The contacts screen is divided into three sections, all of which are accessible by tapping the buttons in the contact bar at the bottom of the screen.

Favorites: This screen allows you to add your favorite contacts to it. It's handy as a shortcut to the people you call the most.

Recents: This screen lists the recent FaceTime calls you've made or received.

Contacts: This screen lists all the contacts in your address book.

Let's look closer at each of these contact sections.

Favorites

The Favorites screen (Figure 14–7) lets you create and maintain a list of your favorite contacts. Favorite contacts generally encompass anyone you call the most, such as family, friends, and important work contacts. This screen acts as a shortcut to their FaceTime e-mail addresses or phone numbers.

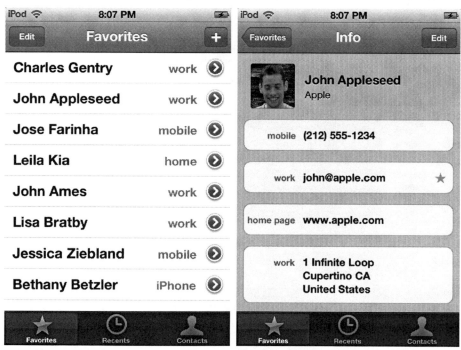

Figure 14–7. *The Favorites screen (left). Selecting the e-mail or phone number of a Favorites contact (right).*

Adding a contact to Favorites: Tap the + button in the upper-right corner, and then select a contact from the address book list that appears on screen.

Choosing the contact's FaceTime info: From your selected contact's information screen, tap the FaceTime e-mail address or phone number for the contact. If your contact is using an iPod touch, you must choose their associated FaceTime e-mail. If you contact is using an iPhone 4, you must choose their iPhone 4 phone number. Once you have chosen your contact's FaceTime info, a blue star (Figure 14–7) appears by their FaceTime e-mail or number.

Calling a Favorite: Once you have set up your favorites, simply tap their name in the Favorites list, and a FaceTime call will be initiated.

Tap the blue-and-white arrow next to a favorite's name to view or edit their contact information.

Recents

The Recents screen (Figure 14–8) displays a list of recently made or received FaceTime calls. This list can be sorted into two categories via the tabs at the top of the screen:

All: Shows you all the FaceTime calls you have made, received, or missed. Missed calls show up in red. The time of the call is shown to the right of the name of the person called. You can tap the blue-and-white arrow next to a favorite's name to view or edit their contact information.

Missed: Shows only the FaceTime calls you have missed.

To clear your Recents list, tap the Edit button in the upper-right corner of the screen.

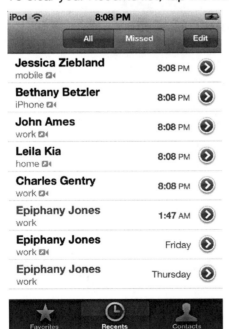

Figure 14–8. *The Recents list*

Contacts

The contacts screen features your entire address book (Figure 14–9). You can navigate it by all the contacts or by selecting just a group of contacts.

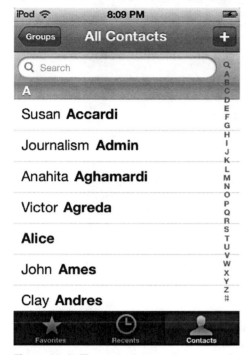

Figure 14–9. *The contacts screen*

When you find the contact you want to call, tap the name, and a contact information card ID displayed. Flick down the screen until you see their FaceTime e-mail or FaceTime phone number. Tap the correct one, and your FaceTime call begins.

Making a FaceTime Call

To make a FaceTime call, select a contact from your Favorites, Recents, or Contacts list. As I stated earlier, if you are selecting a contact from your Favorites or Recents list, tapping their name initiates the FaceTime call (Figure 14–10). To start a call using your Contacts list, tap the contact's name, then tap their FaceTime phone number or e-mail address. To cancel a call before the person has picked up, tap the red END button.

> **NOTE:** You can change your incoming FaceTime ringtone by navigating to the Settings app and then choosing **Sounds ➤ Ringtone**.

Figure 14–10. *Initiating a FaceTime call (left) and receiving a FaceTime call (right)*

When you receive a FaceTime call, a message appears on-screen telling you that a friend would like to share a little FaceTime with you (Figure 14–10). The front camera automatically activates so you can see if you look presentable. To accept the call, tap the green Accept button. To reject the call, tap the red Decline button.

Figure 14–11 demonstrates what a FaceTime call looks like. The image of the person you are talking to takes up a majority of the screen, while your image appears in a rectangle in a corner of the screen. Below the images is the FaceTime control bar, which gives you several options.

Figure 14–11. *A FaceTime video call.*

Mute: Tap the microphone icon to switch between muting and unmuting a call. While the call is muted, you can still hear the person you are calling, but they cannot hear you. While a call is muted, the other person can still see you, so be careful what you do!

Switching cameras: Tap the Switch Camera icon in the bottom right of the screen to switch between the front and rear cameras. The icon looks like a traditional still camera with swirling arrows on either side. Switching cameras changes what the person you are talking to is able to see. When the camera is switched, your friend sees whatever the rear camera on the iPod touch is pointed at.

Switching cameras during a call is an awesome feature. It allows your friend to see what you are looking at, like your newborn crawling on all fours, for example.

Ending the call: To end a FaceTime call, tap the End button.

> **NOTE:** You know that the iPod touch has two cameras, but did you know the front one has been specifically designed for FaceTime? Apple made sure it has just the right focal length and field of view to focus on your face at arm's length.

Other FaceTime Calling Options

FaceTime gives you several advanced calling options that help with its usability:

Change orientation: You can rotate your iPod into landscape mode, and the image your caller sees changes to match. Landscape mode is useful during FaceTime calls if you want to show your caller a wide shot of something using the rear camera, like a beautiful sunset from your backyard.

> **TIP:** To avoid unwanted orientation changes as you move the camera around, lock your iPod touch in portrait orientation by pressing the Home button twice and flicking right until you see the portrait lock button.

Moving picture-in-picture: That little square in the corner that shows you what your caller is seeing can be moved around. Tap and hold the square and drag it to any of the four corners of the screen. This is useful if the square is blocking something on the screen that you want to see.

Multitasking during a FaceTime call: You can use any app on your iPod touch while on a FaceTime call. To do so, while in a FaceTime call, press your iPod's Home button once to be taken to the home screen. You can then launch any app you want. To return to your FaceTime call, tap the glowing green "Touch to resume FaceTime" bar at the top of the screen (Figure 14–12).

Figure 14–12. *You can use other apps while on a FaceTime call. Touch the green bar at the top of the screen to return to the FaceTime call when you're done.*

The multitasking feature is particularly nice when you are on a FaceTime call. It allows you to check the Yelp app for restaurants while you're making dinner plans with your FaceTime caller, for example.

While you are multitasking, you can still talk to your FaceTime caller, but neither of you can see the other.

FaceTime Settings

FaceTime has several settings. You can find them in the Settings app under FaceTime (Figure 14–13).

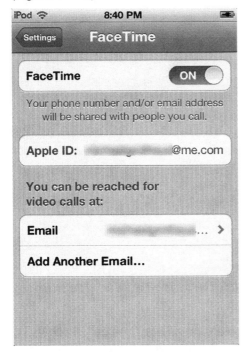

Figure 14–13. *FaceTime settings*

Turn FaceTime on or off: Tap the FaceTime switch to ON or OFF. While off, you cannot make or receive FaceTime calls.

Change your FaceTime geographic location: Tap your Account e-mail. From the pop-up menu, tap Change Location. Choose your location's new region from the list of regions.

View your FaceTime account settings: Tap the e-mail address associated with your FaceTime account. From the pop-up menu, tap View Account. The account settings screen from Figure 14–6 shows up on-screen. Tap any field to change your account settings, such as your name or security question.

Sign out of FaceTime: Tap your Account e-mail. From the pop-up menu, tap Sign Out. This immediately signs you out of FaceTime without any more warnings. To sign back in, reenter your Apple ID password on the Sign In screen.

Remove a FaceTime e-mail address: You can unlink your FaceTime e-mail address by tapping it and then tapping the Remove This Email button.

Adding more e-mail addresses: FaceTime allows you to associate more than one e-mail address with your FaceTime account. This is handy if you use more than a single e-mail address; one for friends and one for work colleagues, for example. If multiple e-mails are associated with your FaceTime account, people can initiate a FaceTime video call with you using any of your e-mails.

To add additional e-mails, tap the Add Another Email button, and then enter your other e-mail address. Repeat this step for each e-mail address you have. With each e-mail added, you'll need to check that account for the FaceTime verification message from Apple and click the link in that message before the address can be added to your FaceTime account.

Getting Started with iMessage

Now with iOS 5 you can send free text messages to anyone with an iPod touch, iPhone, or iPad running iOS 5 or newer. Apple calls this feature iMessage. If you've ever sent an SMS or MMS text message from an iPhone before, you know exactly how to use iMessages because both traditional texting and iMessages are done through the exact same app: Messages (Figure 14–14).

Figure 14–14. *Use the Messages app to send iMessages.*

When you launch the Messages app, you'll be presented with a list of any previous iMessage conversations (Figure 14–15). The most recent message received moves that conversation to the top of the screen.

Figure 14–15. *All your iMessages in one place*

Reading Conversations

To read any past conversation, tap it in the Messages list shown in Figure 14–15. The conversation window appears (Figure 14–16). As you can see, conversations consist of individual iMessages with the same person. Your messages appear on the right of the screen, and your friend's messages appear on the left.

Figure 14–16. *Reading conversations*

From an iMessage conversation screen, you can simply tap the reply field at the bottom of the screen and enter your reply. Tap send to send it. I'll describe how to create an iMessage from scratch in a bit.

Deleting and Forwarding Individual iMessages

From an iMessage conversation window you can also delete or forward individual iMessages. Tap the Edit button at the top of a conversation window (Figure 14–16). Dots appear next to each iMessage along with a red Delete button and a blue Forward button at the bottom of the screen (Figure 14–17).

Figure 14–17. *Deleting and forwarding conversations*

To delete one or more iMessages, tap each message so a red dot appears next to it, and then tap Delete. WARNING: the messages are deleted instantly.

To forward one or more iMessages, tap each message so a red dot appears next to it, and then tap Forward. You'll be taken to a new iMessage screen that allows you to forward the selected iMessage to one or more people.

> **NOTE:** When you are in an active conversation and someone is typing a reply, you'll see a grayed-out chat bubble with three dots in it. That way you know that the person on the other end is in the middle of replying to you.

Deleting Entire Conversations

Besides displaying all your previous iMessage conversations, the main iMessages screen (Figure 14–15) is where you can also delete entire conversations. Tap the Edit button, and then tap the red-and-white minus sign that appears next to the conversation you want to delete. Tap the red Delete button to confirm the deletion.

Sending a New iMessage

On the main iMessage screen (Figure 14–15), tap the new iMessage button that's in the top-right corner. It looks like a pencil over a piece of paper. The new message screen appears (Figure 14–18).

Figure 14–18. *Creating a new iMessage. A blank message, left, and sending a group message, right.*

At the top of the screen, start typing the name of the message recipient. The Messages app automatically fills in their information from your contacts. You can also tap the blue + button to display a list of all your contacts. As you can see in Figure 14–18, you can send iMessages to a group of people.

Tap the text field above the keyboard and start entering your text (Figure 14–19). When you are done, tap the Send button, and your message is on its way!

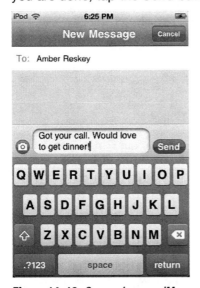

Figure 14–19. *Composing your iMessage*

Attaching a Photo, Video, or Contact to an iMessage

With iMessages, you can send, photos, videos, and contacts to friends with or without an accompanying text message. Adding any of these attachments is done with a few taps. To add an attachment to an iMessage, tap the camera icon next to the text entry field (Figure 14–19). The attachment dialog box appears (Figure 14–20).

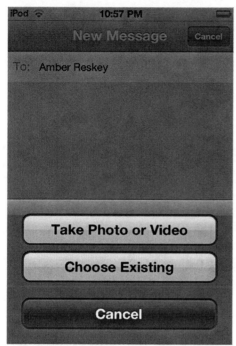

Figure 14–20. *Attaching a photo or video to your iMessage*

Choose Take Photo or Video to record a new video or take a new picture with your camera, or select Choose Existing and grab a photo or video from the photo albums or Camera Roll on your iPod touch. After you have selected your attachment, it appears as a thumbnail in the text entry field (Figure 14–21). Tap the Send button to send the message.

Figure 14–21. *An attached photo in an iMessage*

iMessage Settings

iMessages have some settings that you can use to further increase their functionality. They can be found in the Settings app under Messages (Figure 14–22).

Figure 14–22. *The Messages settings are where you configure read receipts, enable iMessages, and more.*

iMessage: You can turn iMessages on or off. Toggle the switch to OFF to disable iMessages. Doing so prevents messages from being sent from or received on your iPod touch.

Send Read Receipts: When this is set to ON, others are notified when you have read a message they've sent.

Receive at: iMessages work by using your iPhone phone number or an e-mail address. iMessages also allows you to associate more than one e-mail address with your iMessage account. This is handy if you use more than a single e-mail account, one for friends and one for work colleagues, for example. If multiple e-mails are associated with your iMessage account, people can initiate a iMessage chat with you using any of your e-mail addresses.

To add additional e-mail addresses, tap *Receive At*, tap the Add Another Email button, and then enter your other e-mail address. Repeat this step for each e-mail address you want to add. You'll need to check each e-mail account added for a iMessage verification message from Apple and then click the link in that message before the e-mail address can be added to your iMessage account.

Show subject field: When this is set to ON, you have the option of adding a subject field to your iMessages. This is handy if you are sending iMessages in a more formal manner, say to professional contacts.

Summary

FaceTime is an awesome feature, and its popularity is sure to grow as more devices become FaceTime-compatible. iMessages brings free texting and chatting to any device running iOS 5 or newer. In this chapter, you learned how to set up your FaceTime account to send and receive video calls, and also how to send and receive messages using iMessages. Here are a few more tips for using FaceTime and iMessages:

- If you are planning to make a lot of FaceTime calls at home or in the office, you may want to invest in an iPod dock so you don't have to keep holding your iPod at arm's length. A dock helps you eliminate those horrible up-the-nose and double-chin points of view that happen when holding the iPod at arm's length.

- Use FaceTime from the sky! If you're on a plane that offers Wi-Fi service, you can use FaceTime to talk to your friends and family back on the ground!

- Don't forget to use the rear camera to show your caller what you are looking at. You don't have to turn your iPod touch around to show them!

- FaceTime is an amazing feature for those who can't speak. The screen resolution is crisp enough where sign language can easily be read.

- Watch out for bright backgrounds. If light is glaring in through the window behind you, it's likely to cause your viewer to see you in silhouette. To fix this, move your iPod's camera just a tiny way away from the light source, and your face should show up clearly.

- Using iMessages is a great way to keep in touch with friends who live far away. It's like instant messaging but is always on. Individual messages are delivered for free as texts to your friends no matter whether they are on an iPod touch, iPad, or iPhone. The only requirement is a Wi-Fi connection (or 3G if your contacts are using an iPhone).

Chapter 15

Customizing Your iPod touch

The iPod touch has myriad settings allowing you to customize how the device works and looks. You can adjust all of these settings in the Settings app on the home screen of your iPod touch. The iPod's Settings application offers many ways to enhance your iPod experience, in addition to those options tied to a particular application. These general settings control everything from screen brightness to sound effects to keyboard tricks. I've explored various options in the Settings app throughout this book. This chapter covers the remainder of these extra settings and discusses how you can use them in your day-to-day routine. I'll start this chapter by showing you the top five settings people use the most.

Tap the Settings app icon shown in Figure 15–1, and you'll be presented with the Settings screen, a list of preferences for the iPod touch and other applications that are installed on it (see Figure 15–2). To select an app's settings, tap the name of the app.

Figure 15–1. *The Settings app icon*

Figure 15–2. *The Settings screen*

Any settings discussed previously in the book are not mentioned in this chapter. Some settings have been described before because it makes more sense to change those settings when you are using a specific iPod.

Six Customizations You'll Want to Use Settings For

The Settings app lets you really customize your iPod touch to its fullest. However, most people won't be messing around with all the advanced settings. Before I launch into explaining all of the general settings, let's go through the top six settings people use the most.

Airplane Mode

This one is for all your frequent fliers and business travelers. Airplane Mode puts your iPod into a preconfiguration that allows you to use it on a plane without the flight attendant telling you to turn your device off. To enable Airplane Mode, tap the switch to ON (Figure 15–3). You'll notice that an orange airplane icon appears in the upper-left menu bar where the word *iPod* usually is.

Figure 15–3. *Airplane mode. Note the orange airplane icon in the top-left menu bar.*

When Airplane Mode is on, no Bluetooth, or Wi-Fi signal emanates from the device. In other words, Airplane Mode disables antennas that can interfere with flight instrumentation. When Airplane Mode is enabled, you are not able to use wireless Bluetooth headsets or access the Internet on your iPod. You can reenable Wi-Fi when the plane is in flight, even while using Airplane Mode. This allows you to purchase and use in-flight Wi-Fi and even have a FaceTime video chat with your friends and family back home if you own a fourth-generation iPod touch.

Note that during takeoff and landing, you are instructed to turn off all portable electronics, regardless of whether they are in Airplane Mode or not. To turn Airplane Mode off, tap the switch to OFF.

Twitter

In case you haven't heard, Twitter is the Internet phenom social network and micro-blogging service that allows users to instantly send messages to friends and followers in 140 characters or less. It seems like the whole world is tweeting these days, from your next-door neighbor to celebrities and politicians. As you've seen throughout this book, Twitter is highly integrated into iOS 5. You can tweet directly from Photos, Safari, YouTube, Camera, and Maps, plus many other third-party apps.

Before iOS5, you had to log into your Twitter account in every app that supported tweeting. With iOS 5, there's just a single login location for Twitter, and that means your Twitter account ID is integrated system-wide for easy tweeting.

To set up your Twitter account, go to Twitter in the Settings app. In the Twitter settings (Figure 15–4), enter your Twitter ID and password, and then tap Sign In. If you don't have a Twitter ID, you can tap the Create New Account button and set up a new Twitter account right in the Settings screen

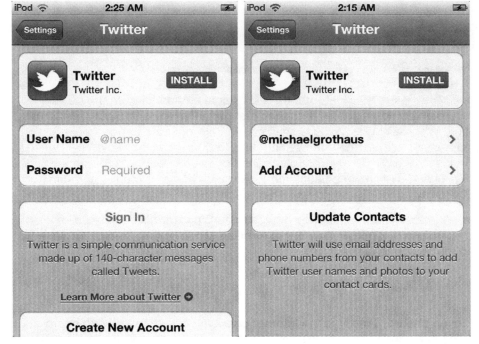

Figure 15–4. *Signing into Twitter*

Once you are signed into Twitter, you'll be able to tweet directly from iOS 5's built-in apps like Safari, Maps, YouTube, and more. Also, on the Twitter Settings screen you can tap the Install button to immediately download and install the official Twitter app, which lets you fully interact with Twitter.com and all your friends and followers.

In Twitter Settings, tap your account name for additional settings. These include the ability to let your friends find you on Twitter using your e-mail address and automatically tweeting your location when you post a tweet. Finally, you can tap Update Contacts to add Twitter usernames to the people in your Contacts lists.

Sounds

The Sounds settings enable you to select which ringer and alerts sound effects you hear while interacting with your iPod touch (Figure 15–5). These settings are useful when you are using your iPod in a public place like a library or a coffee shop.

Volume slider: This slider, at the top of the screen, allows you to turn your ringer volume up or down. The ringer volume refers to the ringtone you hear when someone initiates a FaceTime call with you.

Change with Buttons: When this is switched to ON, you can use the physical volume buttons on the side of your iPod to adjust the volume level of the ringer and alerts. When set to OFF, the volume of the ringer and alerts is separate from the volume of the other sounds (like music playback) on your iPod touch.

Ringtone: This allows you to choose your FaceTime ringtone from one of Apple's 28 built-in ringtones. If you've synced your own ringtones from iTunes (see Chapter 2), you can also select that ringtone here.

Alerts: By default the iPod plays a sound effect whenever you send or receive mail, have a calendar alert, lock your iPod (by pressing the button on the top of the iPod), press a key on the on-screen keyboard, and more. On the Sounds settings screen, you can choose to change any of these sound effects or even disable them entirely. Tap the sound effect you want to change and then select a replacement sound effect from the list of effects or choose None. Your boss won't know you're typing an e-mail to your girlfriend with hands under the table while in a meeting.

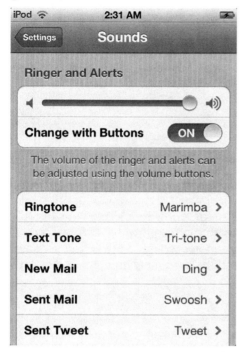

Figure 15–5. *Use Settings ➤ Sounds to choose how your iPod plays back system alert sounds like clicks.*

Brightness

Choose **Settings** ➤ **Brightness** (see Figure 15–6) to control your iPod's screen intensity. The slider at the top of the Settings screen lets you manually set exactly how bright your screen is, from very dim (on the left) to very bright (on the right).

A lot of people who jog at night will benefit from turning down the brightness on their iPod touch. Why? Your eyes adjust to the darkness, and when you bring up your iPod to change a song and the screen turns on, it can temporarily blind you if it's set too bright. I've had friends trip and fall while jogging at night because of the sudden blinding light from their iPod touch screen.

Figure 15–6. *The Settings ➤ Brightness control allows you to set the overall screen intensity for your iPod touch.*

The Auto-Brightness option, beneath the brightness slider, controls another light-level feature. It determines whether your iPod samples the ambient light when it wakes up as you slide to unlock. When enabled, it adjusts the screen according to the light it senses in the room. I personally find the Auto-Brightness settings extremely irritating and always leave this option disabled.

Wallpaper

Setting your iPod's wallpaper makes your iPod unique. Who else is going to have a photo of your two-year-old smearing cake batter on her face?

The Settings ➤ Wallpaper screen allows you to set your system wallpaper from a library of commercial-grade photos that shipped with your iPod. You can also select wallpaper from any image, such as your personal photos, on your iPod touch. Select Wallpaper to see your current lock and Home screen wallpaper settings (Figure 15–7). To change either wallpaper, tap the Lock and Home screen image, and you'll be presented with a list of all the photos on your iPod. The Wallpaper collection is full of images that came with your iPod touch. Below it is a list of all of your photos.

> **NOTE:** Unlike the images in your Photos library, you cannot move and scale the iPod's library pictures. They are sized at 640-by-960 pixels, perfectly matched to your screen.

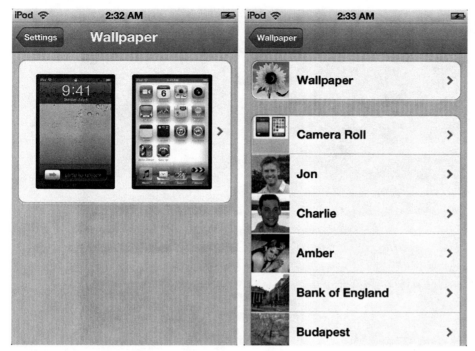

Figure 15–7. *Settings ➤ Wallpaper offers the ability to set wallpaper for the lock screen and the home screen on your iPod touch (left). Select from Apple-supplied wallpapers or use photos from your own collections (right).*

When you've found the image you want to use, you can move and scale it with your fingers and then tap the Set button (Figure 15–8). From the pop-up menu, choose to use that image as the lock screen wallpaper, as the home screen wallpaper, or as both wallpapers.

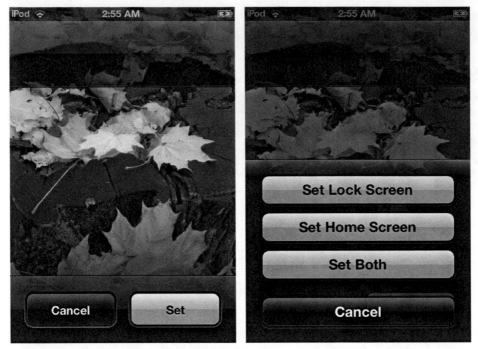

Figure 15–8. *Move and scale your image (left), and then choose to use it as wallpaper for the lock screen, home screen, or both.*

Location Services

On the iPod touch there are dozens of features that rely on knowing your current location. These include Maps, time zone settings, Weather, photo geolocation, and more. However, in today's privacy-sensitive world, people want to be able to control what apps or processes have access to their current location. That's where Location Services comes in (Figure 15–9).

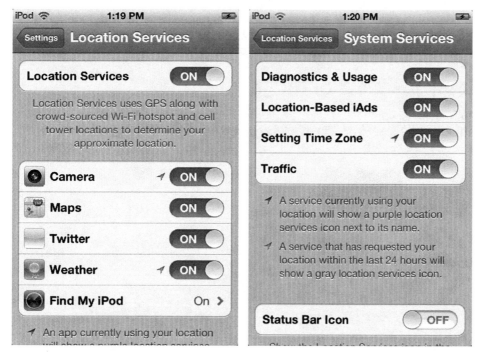

Figure 15–9. *Left, the Location Services settings can be used to disable all location services or just disable some apps from reading your current location. Right, the System Services screen gives you control over iOS 5 location services.*

To control location information on your iPod, navigate to **Settings ➤ Location Services**. If Location Services is set to ON, any apps that can automatically find your location (like the Maps app) are able to do so. Any app that has permission to read your current location shows up in the list. But before any app can access your current location, you must give it approval to do so. A pop-up notification automatically appears when an app requests your current location (see Figure 15–23).

Apps can use your location in any number of ways. The Facebook app, for example, can use your location to tell your friends where you are posting from. The Maps app uses your location in order to help identify where you are on the map.

Location services are very handy. However, today it's easy to get paranoid about people finding you based on your device's location. To turn all location services off, tap the Location Services switch to OFF (Figure 15–9). Alternatively, leave location services on, but disable location services on a per-app basis.

> **NOTE:** When an app has used your current location in the past 24 hours, you'll see a tiny gray arrowhead icon next to its name in the Location Services settings. When an app is using your current location now, the tiny arrow next to it on this screen is purple. Whenever an app is currently using your location, that tiny arrowhead also appears in the menu bar.

You can also control the amount of access other iOS services have to your location. On the Location Services screen, tap the System Services button, and then toggle on or off services such as location-based iAds, traffic, and diagnostics.

Other Good-to-Know Settings

Under Settings ➤ General, you'll find that the General settings (Figure 15–10) are the "meat" of settings that have to do with the iPod touch itself, like sharing, networking, and security.

Figure 15–10. *The General settings screen*

"About" Your iPod

Your iPod summarizes its capabilities and storage levels, listing the number of songs, videos, photos, and other important information on the Settings ➤ General ➤ About screen (see Figure 15–11). Here, you'll find basic details about the space available and remaining on your iPod, as well as your current Wi-Fi address.

Figure 15–11. *The Settings ➤ General ➤ About screen lists basic information about your iPod.*

At the top of the screen, tap Name to change your iPod's name. If you scroll all the way down to the bottom of the About screen, you'll see a link labeled Legal. Tap this to jump to an insanely long list of Apple legal notices. It's a boring document to read, but it's an amazingly good place to get some practice flicking your screen. You almost never run out of text to scroll through.

Software Update

New to iOS 5 is the ability to update the iOS software without having to plug your iPod into iTunes and download the software from there. These automatic updates are referred to as *over-the-air* (OTA) updates. Now any time a software update is available for iOS, a red badge appears on the corner of the Setting icon. You can also manually check for iOS software updates by navigating to **Settings ➤ General ➤ Software Update**. Any available IOS software updates are listed there.

Usage

Usage is another new Settings screen that allows you to see how much storage each app on your iPod is taking up. View your usage at **Settings ➤ General ➤ Usage** (Figure 15–12).

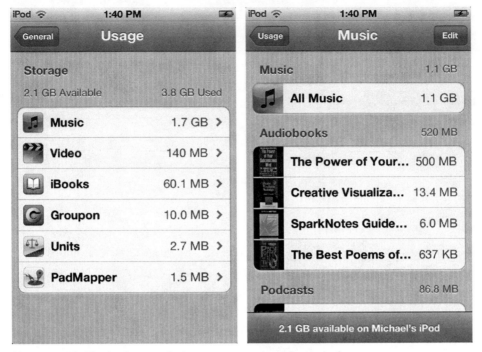

Figure 15–12. *Viewing how much storage space each app is consuming*

In Figure 15–12 you can see that the Music app is taking up the most storage space on my iPod. If I tap Music, I can see that all my songs take up a combined 1.1 GB of space, followed by Audiobooks taking up 520 MB, and Podcasts taking up 86.6 MB.

If you tap the Edit button on any app's usage screen, you can selectively delete any of the items to free up space. You can even delete entire apps (but not the ones that shipped on your iPod touch) to free all the space they take up.

Usage is handy if your iPod is almost full but you want to download a movie at the airport to watch on the plane. You can free up some songs or other content in apps to get enough space to download that movie.

iTunes Wi-Fi Sync

As I mentioned in Chapter 2, you can now sync your iPod touch wirelessly when it's in range of your computer and on the same Wi-Fi network. When you plug your iPod touch into a power source, it automatically syncs over the network. You can also manually initiate syncing from your iPod at any time by going to Settings ➤ General ➤ iTunes Wi-Fi Sync (Figure 15–13) and tapping the Sync Now button.

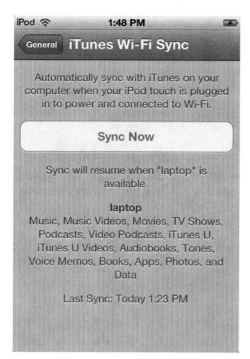

Figure 15–13. *Initiating a Wi-Fi sync from your iPod touch*

Network

The settings found on the **Settings ➤ General ➤ Network** screen duplicate the Wi-Fi settings covered in Chapter 4. They also include a switch to enable or disable virtual private network (VPN) connections and options to customize your VPN connection.

A VPN is usually used for secure communications over public Internet connections. When this option is enabled, you can configure your VPN account settings with the Network settings screen. Consult your IT department or network provider for details on how to set up your iPod for a VPN connection.

Bluetooth

The Bluetooth settings allow you to turn the iPod touch's Bluetooth signal on or off. This is also where you'll find a list of Bluetooth-compatible devices that your iPod is aware of. To pair a Bluetooth device, select it in the list, and then enter the pairing code. For keyboards, a random code is usually generated. For devices such as Bluetooth headsets, look for the code written on the headset. Note that some newer Bluetooth devices no longer use pairing codes and will show up in your pairing list automatically and ask whether you want to give the device access. To unpair a Bluetooth device, select it from the list, and choose Forget this Device.

If you aren't using any Bluetooth devices with your iPod touch, keep Bluetooth turned off to save battery life. Don't forget to switch it back on when you want to use Bluetooth headsets, use external keyboards, or play games between iPod devices.

Auto-Lock

Use the Settings ➤ General ➤ Auto-Lock screen (see Figure 15–14) to determine the time period after which your iPod automatically locks. Autolocking is an energy-saving feature. When locked, your screen turns off—although music playback continues—and you must swipe to unlock and return to any previous activities. Choose from 1, 2, 3, 4, or 5 minutes, or choose Never to leave your screen always on. This last option wears down your battery very quickly indeed.

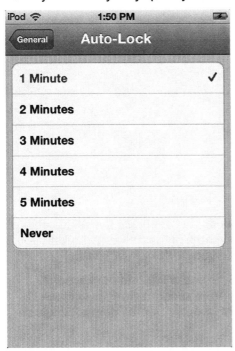

Figure 15–14. *Save your battery and save your screen by setting an autolock time in Settings ➤ General ➤ Auto-Lock.*

Restrictions

If you share your iPod touch among your family or buy one for your children, you may want to limit what they can do on it. The Restrictions settings (Figure 15–15) lets you restrict access to Safari, YouTube, the iTunes Store app, the ability to install apps, the Camera and FaceTime apps, and the ability for apps to use location services. In addition, you can also choose what content you want allowed on the iPod touch. Settings include restricting In-App purchases and limiting access to movies, music, TV shows, and apps that surpass your chosen ratings. Finally, you can also limit multiplayer gaming in Game Center.

> **TIP:** Enabling restrictions for YouTube or Facetime is a great way to "remove" factory installed apps from your iPod! They're still there, you just won't be able to see their icons on the Home screen!

Figure 15–15. *The Restrictions settings*

As you can see, Restrictions is all about protecting your children not only from age-inappropriate music and movies but also from potential outside threats such as strangers calling them on FaceTime or apps that post their current location online. When you enable restrictions, you'll be asked to enter a four-digit passcode. You (or your children) will need this passcode to change or disable any restriction you've set up. The only way your kids can get around these restrictions is if they completely reformat the iPod to factory conditions. However, if they do this, they lose all their music and movies on the iPod.

Date and Time

The settings found on the Settings ➤ General ➤ Date & Time screen (see Figure 15–16) allow you to specify how you want your system to handle time. Here, you can choose between a 12-hour (9:30 p.m.) and a 24-hour (21:30) clock, set your time zone, and override the system clock to set a new date and time.

Figure 15–16. *The Settings ➤ General ➤ Date & Time options allow you to set a separate time zone just for your iPod calendar events.*

Keyboard

You'll find five very clever and helpful typing settings on the Settings ➤ General ➤ Keyboard settings screen (see Figure 15–17).

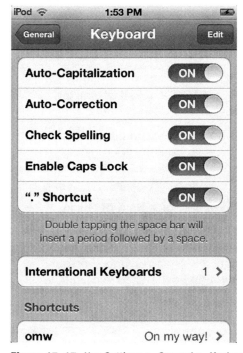

Figure 15–17. *Use Settings ➤ General ➤ Keyboard to set several handy typing shortcuts.*

Auto-Capitalization: When this feature is set to ON, the iPod is smart about guessing when you're at the start of new sentences. After detecting a period, question mark, or other sentence-ending punctuation, it automatically presses the Shift key for you.

Auto-Correction: When this feature is set to ON, the iPod will suggest words to you as you type. Switch it to OFF to get rid of those word pop-ups.

Check Spelling: When this is set to ON, the iPod spell-check features underlines misspelled words in red. Tap the underlined word to see spelling suggestions.

Enable Caps Lock: When selected, Enable Caps Lock treats all taps on the Shift key as the Caps Lock function—setting it either on or off. When it's disabled, you must press the Shift key before each capitalized letter. The Shift key switches itself back off after each use.

"." Shortcut: Enabling the period shortcut feature lets you add a period and then a space to the end of sentences by double-tapping the spacebar.

Also, as discussed in Chapter 3, this is the place where you can set text shortcuts that enable you to type using acronyms that expand to full phrases (in other words, typing **ttyl** will expand to "talk to you later").

The International Keyboards option on the Keyboard settings screen allows you to set the language for your keyboard. This setting is identical to the one found on the International settings screen we'll discuss now.

International

On the Settings ➤ General ➤ International screen (see Figure 15–18), you'll find all the settings you need if you want your iPod to operate in a different language.

Language: The primary system language determines how all your menus and buttons display. Whenever an iPod application supports multiple languages, your setting here tells that application which words and phrases to use, internationalizing that application appropriately.

Voice Control: Choose the language you'll be speaking your voice commands in.

Keyboards: The keyboard language sets the default keyboard layout for when you type. If you use a lot of foreign phrases, you may want to switch to an international keyboard for certain tasks. Be aware that the keyboard automatically changes when you set a system language. The rather mysterious number shown on the settings screen (1 in Figure 15–17) indicates the chosen keyboard.

Figure 15–18. *International settings let you set your system language, regional keyboard, and date/time formats.*

NOTE: You can also choose keyboards in **Settings ➤ General ➤ Keyboard ➤ International Keyboards**. The two options lead to identical settings screens.

Region Format: The region format switches the standards for how dates, times, and phone numbers display. December 5, 2009, for the U.S. region would display as 5 December 2009 for the U.K. region. Use this setting to augment your language settings with a country norm.

Calendar: This setting changes the calendar format according to which calendar you follow. Select from Gregorian, Japanese, Republic of China, or, coolly enough, Buddhist.

Accessibility

Apple wanted to make sure everyone could use the iPod touch as easily as possible. To that end, Apple built in accessibility features to help people with disabilities use the iPod touch. To see all the accessibility options, on the iPod touch go to **Settings ➤ General ➤ Accessibility** (see Figure 15–19). Let's go through these settings one by one.

Figure 15–19. *The Accessibility settings*

As you can see from Figure 15–19, Apple has divided its accessibility options into three main categories: Vision, Hearing, and Physical & Motor.

VoiceOver

With VoiceOver turned on, a user can simply touch the screen to hear a description of what is beneath his finger, and then double-tap to select the item. With VoiceOver enabled, the iPod touch speaks when the user has a new e-mail message and can even read the e-mail to the user.

It's important to remember that when VoiceOver is turned on, the iPod touch's Multi-Touch gestures change. As a matter of fact, when VoiceOver is enabled, pretty much all of the gestures we've taught you in this book are irrelevant. The Voice Over settings are also where you can pair your iPod touch to a Braille device.

VoiceOver Gestures

I list common VoiceOver gestures here, but be sure to carefully read Apple's VoiceOver article at http://support.apple.com/kb/HT3598 for complete VoiceOver gesture controls.

Tap: Speaks the selected item.

Double-tap: Activates the selected item.

Triple-tap: Acts as a double-tap normally would. Triple-tapping an item when VoiceOver is enabled effectively double-taps that item.

Flick right or left: Selects the next or previous item.

Two-finger tap: Stops speaking the current item.

Two-finger flick up: Reads all text or items from the top of the screen.

Two-finger flick down: Reads all text or items from the current position.

Three-finger flick up or down: Scrolls one page at a time.

Three-finger flick right or left: Goes to the next or previous page (such as the Home Screen pages, Weather pages, or Safari web pages).

Zoom

Zoom allows those who are vision-impaired to magnify their entire screen. This is different from the standard pinch-and-zoom features of the iPod touch's regular software. Accessibility Zoom magnifies everything on the screen, allowing the user to zoom into even the smallest of buttons. When this option is selected, the user can double-tap any part of the iPod touch's screen with three fingers to automatically zoom in 200 percent. When zoomed in, you must drag or flick the screen with three fingers. Also, when you go to a new screen, zooming will always return you to the top middle of the screen.

Large Text

Large Text allows those with vision impairments to enlarge the text in alerts, Contacts, Mail, and Notes. They can choose from 20-, 24-, 32-, 40-, 48-, or 56-point text (12-point text is the normal text you see on a web page).

White on Black

For some people with vision difficulties, inverting the color of a computer screen so it resembles a photographic negative allows them to read text better. Turning on White on Black does just this.

Speak Selection

With this option selected, any selected text (such as the text you select when copying and pasting) is spoken aloud.

Speak Auto-text

With this option selected, any autocorrection text (such as the spell-check pop-ups that appear when you are typing) is spoken aloud.

Mono Audio

With this selected, the stereo sounds of the left and right speakers or headphones are combined into a mono (single) signal. You can then choose which speaker, the left or the right, you want to hear the mono audio come from. This option lets users who have a hearing impairment in one ear hear the entire sound signal with the other ear.

Assistive Touch

Apple recognizes that for people who have limited motor skills, using a small multitouch screen like the one found on the iPod touch can be difficult. With this in mind, Apple created Assistive Touch. When Assistive Touch is enabled, a black-and-white dot is always displayed on the iPod touch's screen.

Tapping the dot displays an on-screen menu overlay (Figure 15–20) that allows users to tap icons that represent gestures. Instead of tapping or swiping with two fingers, Assistive Touch allows the user to simply tap a button that performs the gesture automatically.

Figure 15–20. *The Assistive Touch onscreen menu.*

Triple-Click Home

If you are sharing an iPod touch with someone with disabilities, selecting this option allows users, by triple-clicking the iPod touch's physical home button, to quickly toggle VoiceOver, Zoom, White on Black, or Assistive Touch on or off. You can also set it so triple-clicking the home button causes a pop-up to appear on-screen asking the user what accessibility feature they want to use (Figure 15–21).

Figure 15–21. *The Accessibility Options pop-up menu*

NOTE: With the exception of the triple-click home feature, all of these accessibility settings can also be configured from within the iPod touch iTunes Preferences window on the Summary tab (see Chapter 2). Click Configure Universal Access to choose your settings.

Reset

At times, you may need to reset certain iPod features via **Settings ➤ General ➤ Reset** (see Figure 15–22). Each of the following options offers a slightly different twist on restoring your iPod to factory conditions and provides a different degree of security.

Figure 15–22. *The Settings ➤ General ➤ Reset screen allows you to return your iPod to factory-fresh settings.*

Reset All Settings: This option returns all settings to those that are factory installed.

Erase All Content and Settings: This option deletes all content from your iPod—music, calendar events, videos, contacts, and so forth—and resets your settings at the same time.

Reset Network Settings: This option restores your Wi-Fi network settings to the defaults. This ensures that your iPod will not automatically connect to any "known", but dangerous, network you might have once encountered.

Reset Keyboard Dictionary: This option "forgets" all words you have typed into your iPod. The onboard keyboard dictionary is smart about learning the words and names that you type, but it also learns a lot of personal information (including passwords) at the same time. Tap this option to delete this dictionary from your system.

Reset Home Screen Layout: This resets your home screen icon arrangement to the default one that shipped on your iPod touch. Any third-party apps appear in alphabetical order starting on the second home screen page. Any Web Clips also appear in alphabetical order mixed in with the third-party apps. Finally, any folders you created are deleted, and their apps all appear on the home screens.

Reset Location Warnings: Any time an app (such as Facebook, Starbucks, Maps, and so on) wants to use your current location, it must first ask you for permission, as shown in Figure 15–23. Resetting the location warnings means every app on your iPod has to ask for your permission again before it can use your current location.

Figure 15–23. *The Current Location warning pop-up*

iCloud

As previously mentioned, iCloud is Apple's cloud-based services that offers users free e-mail, calendar, and contacts on the Web. iCloud also allows you to automatically sync documents between all your devices, like your Mac or PC, your iPad, and your iPod touch. iCloud works automatically and effortlessly in the background. For example, if you are editing a Pages document on your Mac, you can pick up your iPod touch and launch the Pages app, and the document you were editing on your Mac appears with all of your previous changes. You can start editing where you left off.

To enable iCloud on your iPod touch, go to **Settings ➤ iCloud** and enter your Apple ID and password. That's it. Now all your documents, e-mail, contacts, and calendars are synced wirelessly across all your iCloud-capable devices.

Third-Party App Settings

The remainder of the settings in the Settings app deal with third-party application settings. Any apps that adhere to Apple's developer policies keep their settings here (see Figure 15–24). Most apps do, but some don't. A lot of users think an app's settings should be contained in the app itself, and many developers end up doing just that. With that in mind, it's a good idea to check the Settings app to see whether you favorite apps have additional settings that aren't contained in the app. Also, note that virtually all games have their settings stored within the app, rather than under the iPod Settings app.

Figure 15–24. *The Settings app houses most third-party app settings as well.*

Voice Control

Not only can your iPod touch talk to you using VoiceOver technology, you can command your iPod touch using Voice Control. Right now, Voice Control is limited to music playback functions and telling you the time. It's a shame too, because Voice Control works quite well and, in addition to FaceTime, is one of the features that makes the latest iPod touch seem like a Communicator from *Star Trek*.

To use Voice Control, press and hold the Home button until you hear a beep and to see the Voice Control screen appear (Figure 15–25). On the screen you'll see Voice Control suggestions flow behind an audio waveform. You can use any of the following commands to interact with the music player on your iPod:

Control music playback: Say "Play" or "Play music."

Pause music: Say "Pause" or "Pause music."

Go to next song: Say "Next song."

Go to previous song: Say "Previous song."

Play an album, artist, or playlist: Say "Play," and then say "Album," "Artist," or "Playlist" and the name or the album, artist, or playlist.

Shuffle the current playlist: Say "Shuffle."

Find out more about the currently playing song: Say "What's playing?" or "What song is this?" or "Who sings this song?" or "Who is this song by?"

Use the Genius feature to play similar songs: Say "Genius," "Play more like this," or "Play more songs like this."

Find out the current time: Say "What time is it?" or "What is the time?"

Cancel Voice Control: Say "Cancel" or "Stop."

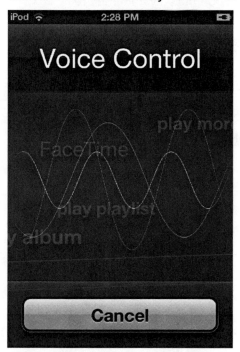

Figures 15–25. *The Voice Control screen*

Apple says to remember to speak clearly and pause slightly between words. Ironically, the most useful situation to use Voice Control in is while jogging—just the situation when you can't speak or pause normally without huffing and puffing.

Summary

The settings screens discussed in this chapter allow you to customize your iPod to your personal needs and conditions. Here are a few thoughts to take away with you from this overview:

- The Settings app also contains the settings screens for many third-party apps.

- If younger children have access to the iPod touch, you might want to seriously consider activating the Restrictions settings.

- Your Auto-Lock settings are a highly personal choice. Delay locking for long enough that you don't get frustrated with screen locks, but keep the autolock time short enough that you don't needlessly kill your battery.

- Don't sell or pass along your iPod without using the Reset settings to erase your personal data. You can also do a complete system restore via iTunes.

- Use the **General ➤ About** screen to quickly access your iPod's serial number. This is handy if you are talking to AppleCare over the phone.

- The iPod has myriad accessibility options for people who are hard of sight or hearing.

- VoiceOver is a cool technology that lets you speak commands to your iPod. Unfortunately, you're limited to speaking commands for music playback only.

Index

Z

CPSIA information can be obtained at www.ICGtesting.com
Printed in the USA
LVOW050255071211

258186LV00009B/1/P